My Life in Music

My Life in
MUSIC

By John Erskine

1 9 5 0

WILLIAM MORROW & COMPANY

New York

Printed in the United States of America
Published simultaneously in the Dominion of Canada
by Wm. Collins Sons & Co. Canada Ltd.

TO OUR FRIENDS
JOHN AND
AMY PERRY
✢✢✢✢✢✢✢✢✢✢✢✢✢✢✢✢✢✢

CONTENTS

✳✳✳

My Life in Music

CHAPTER ONE

❉❉❉

Music in My Boyhood

I

NO STORY of my life in music would be complete without mention of my father, James Morrison Erskine, the chief musician in our family. He had a magnificent, beautifully trained tenor voice, and being British he adored exercising it in choruses. He sang in the choir of St. Bartholomew's Church, located in those years at Madison Avenue and Forty-fourth Street, and he was a member of Dr. Leopold Damrosch's New York Oratorio Society. Choral groups were very popular in the 1880's. Father and some forty other young amateur musicians belonged to one which met at one another's homes.

When I was four I remember being put by my mother on a chair in the hall of our house in Harlem so that I might hear Father and his friends sing. Father, watching me proudly from the living room, insisted that every note registered. Mother thought sleep a more logical explanation of my hypnotized stare.

I have still an earlier memory of music. On a hot summer day in 1883 when I was little more than three, Mother and Aunt Nanna took me to Coney Island. We went by water.

As we climbed to the upper deck of the boat I could see the light dresses of women and children rippling in a welcome breeze and I could hear wonderful music. We traced the music to its source—two old Italians, one playing a harp, the other a violin. Today whenever I hear that wistful haunting combination of harp and violin I see the old iron steamboat and smell the sea air.

When Mother and Nanna told the rest of the family about my delight in the music on the Coney Island boat, Father struck some chords on the piano for me. As soon as I was able to sit on a piano stool without toppling off he taught me simple exercises and scales. I realize now what an active music life he must have led, for when he wasn't singing in a choral group he was discussing or trying out a new song with some of his many musical friends—among them Carl Walter, the young German who was substitute organist at St. Bartholomew's. Mr. Walter could run trills with both hands and evoke a beauty of tone which was more Russian than German. His appearance as well as his agile fingers fascinated me. He cut his brown hair in bangs and he wore flowered waistcoats. Being very young, I was impressed more by these details than the noble quality of his music. Neither he nor I knew then that he was to be a great musical influence in my boyhood.

In 1885 we moved to Weehawken, New Jersey, of all places, for two very good reasons: it was handy to the Erskine ribbon factory at Union Hill, and our family needed a larger house. Father built us an architectural mistake but we loved it, perhaps because there was ample room for everyone, including Mother's two sisters, Annabella and Margaret Hollingsworth—Nanna and Memmen to my sisters and me. At that time Father and Mother had three children: Anna, my senior by a year and ten months and known always to me as Sister; myself—called Bru by the girls; and Helen, or Das—short for Daisy. Lois, Rhoda, and Robert came later.

We lived in an atmosphere of music. Father's silk weavers

were Swiss, German, and French artisans skilled in their trade of ribbon-making on the intricate Jacquard looms. Holidays and week ends they paraded to spirited tunes, sang in enormous choruses, and serenaded us with lovely Old World carols. Sundays Father would hitch up Bess, the family horse, and drive us to Hoboken for service at Trinity Episcopal Church. Shortly before we moved to New Jersey Father resigned from St. Bartholomew's choir. Mother did not want him to give up his music—she need not have worried. He soon knew most of the musicians in Hoboken, including Frank Fruttchey, the gifted pianist, and Homer Bartlett, the composer. And in no time at all he was soloist at Trinity. Edwin Burhorn, the organist who accompanied him, proved to be a brother of the head bookkeeper at the Erskine mill. Their sister, Etta, our first governess, played the piano with style. It seemed quite natural that she should succeed Father as my music teacher. However, I made no real progress in music until he asked Frank Fruttchey to take me in hand.

As soon as the Episcopalians of Union Hill and Weehawken could raise the money they built their own house of worship—Grace Church in Union Hill. Father, who had assumed financial responsibility for all the music, invited Mr. Fruttchey to be organist and choirmaster. He was a born musician with a natural sense of pitch. Sunday mornings, on the way to church, he would confound us by tapping some metal sewer pipe or fire hydrant for the key in which to pitch the singing, then carry that tone in his memory until he could hum it for the choir.

Every Monday and Friday he came to our house to give me my music lesson. I can still see his tall gaunt figure suddenly popping into view as he turned off the Boulevard and into Pleasant Avenue. He approached at a brisk pace and carried a roll of music tucked under his right arm. My greeting was not enthusiastic. Mother said I spent more time looking at the clock than at the piano keys. But she did not relent. From my fifth year on I practiced in hours and half hours chimed off by the family clock. Today that clock graces the living room mantel of my New York apartment. When it chimes I hear Mother calling me to practice. I learned to play on the big square piano which had been given her as a girl in Lansingburg, New York. Sunday nights, from my childhood up, we gathered around the piano to sing hymns. Father played our accompaniments and joined in with his fine tenor. Mother and the girls filled in with sweet but untrained sopranos. Our aunts sat on the sidelines and applauded. Neither one could carry a tune. I don't know why, but we classed Mother with them, perhaps because their people—the Hollingsworths and the Scarboroughs—were notoriously unmusical. Even their uncle John Scarborough, Bishop of the Episcopal Diocese of Southern New Jersey, was no exception. He was all Yorkshire. Mother resembled him more than anyone else in her family, but she had a sense of adventure which was Irish. In that I am very like her.

One Sunday morning we were all kept in the house by colds. At her wits' end to entertain us, she sat down at the piano.

"Children," she announced, "I will play 'Silvery Waves' for you."

We couldn't have been more surprised if she had jumped off the moon, when she played the piece very well.

Her brother, our Uncle Wee-wee—William Hollingsworth—always acted as if he knew something about music, but whenever he talked he was sure to give himself away. One evening he happened to be sitting on our side porch when the Grace Church choir, thirty members in all, crowded into our living room for rehearsal. After the practice ended he came in for ice cream and cake.

"You worked very hard," he said, "but I must say you worked in vain. Why didn't you make more noise? Then you would have real church music."

II

All the Erskines were musical. My grandfather, John
Erskine, a Scots weaver, played the violin. He deserted the
Calvinist Church for the Anglican in Glasgow because the
music was more cheerful. But because he was a weaver the
snobbish Anglicans told him they had no room in their
church for him. He replied by emigrating to America—a
Methodist. He took with him his parents and his violin.
At twenty-six he owned his own lace- and silk-weaving factory
on Gansevoort Street in Greenwich Village. In 1856 he sold
this factory to the piano maker, Fisher and Company, and
built a second factory on West Thirty-fourth Street, where
he made wire for hoopskirts. Curiously enough, another piano
manufacturer, Steck and Company, bought this building,
and he moved a third time to a new building on West Forty-
fifth Street, where he specialized in ribbons and sashes.
Many years later the factory was shifted to New Jersey.

While he was still a young man he built a brownstone
front at 128 East Eightieth Street, and concentrated on a
very deep high-ceilinged kitchen with excellent acoustical
properties. Here, of an evening as his wife Orcilla prepared
supper, he played his violin.

In later years there stood in the back parlor a two-manual
organ which I played vigorously almost before my feet could
reach the pedals. In a corner bookcase of that same room
rested Uncle Arthur's flute. He had placed it there before
going to Philadelphia on a business trip. A few days after
he left, Grandma got up in the middle of the night and began
to dress herself. Grandfather, half-asleep, demanded to know
what in Heaven's name she was doing.

She said, "I must go to Philadelphia at once."

Grandfather was so emphatic in his criticism of her "crazy
dream" that she started to undress. As she was climbing back
into bed the front doorbell rang. A telegram from Philadel-

phia brought word that Uncle Arthur had been stricken with typhoid and was calling for her. He died soon after she reached him.

She loved to recall the days when Uncle Arthur was living and all of her family made music together; Aunt Lizzie at the piano, my father at the organ, my grandfather with his violin, Uncle Will with his cello, Aunt Orcilla and Uncle Charlie with their singing, and Uncle Arthur with his flute.

When I was nine years old Grandfather died. Unable to find either a streetcar or a cab, he had walked from his factory on West Forty-fifth Street to his home on East Eightieth Street, in the blizzard of 1888. Pneumonia, brought on by exhaustion and exposure, killed him. He left his violin to me and his silk mill to Father.

In the summer of 1892 Father went to France on business. While he was gone our family suffered its first deep sorrow— Lois died. Even as a child, when under any emotional strain, I found music a release. After the tragedy of Lois' sudden death I would slip off to practice the organ at Grace Church. I was old for my twelve years. It seemed more natural for me to be sitting at the piano or organ than playing games with boys of my own age. At the organ I usually improvised. In so doing music came to me for the familiar words of "Abide with Me."

I scored it that night at home. Uncle Charlie Erskine suggested having it printed and arranged so that the Grace Church choir should sing it as a surprise for Father.

Mother was also planning a surprise—the gift of a new piano. When she told Mr. Fruttchey, he held up his hands in horror. "But your husband is the head of the family. You should consult him first."

Instead she consulted Uncle Wee-wee. He called in Carl Walter and the reluctant Mr. Fruttchey. There were numerous visits to the Steinway showrooms on Fourteenth Street, and finally a handsome grand piano was delivered to the house. We could hardly wait for Father's return.

The Erskines as a family were emotional. In that I am all Erskine. I cry easily. Aunt 'Cilla and Uncle Will would burst into tears when deeply moved. Instead of crying, Father made faces and looked as mad as could be. The double surprise of the new piano and my first musical composition made him screw his face into a series of frowns and grimaces that would have frightened anyone who didn't know him for the gentle sweet soul that he was.

Frank Fruttchey remained at Grace Church long enough to lead the choir in the singing of my hymn. The following Sunday he left to become organist at Old Trinity Church in New York City. I begged to be allowed to play the organ in his stead. Mother used to say I had Father's height and her temperament. We could both talk. Neither one of us was ever at a loss for words. I reminded her that I would be thirteen the next week. She thought the idea of a boy my age being a church organist the most ridiculous thing she had ever heard of, and she said so very emphatically. But as Sunday approached and Grace Church still had no organist she relented. My choir robes and my height—I was almost six feet tall—helped me to appear older than I was.

Once I was an organist, my approach to music became doubly serious. I studied the symphonies of Beethoven, the oratorios of Handel, and the church music of Bach. Father, immensely pleased, said I deserved a better teacher. Frank Fruttchey had excited me about music, but he did not teach me to play it well. Whatever he played was brilliantly executed, but it sounded like Fruttchey and not Chopin, or Mozart, or whatever else he happened to be playing.

On a spring day in 1893 I got off the Lexington Avenue car at Sixty-second Street and rang the doorbell of Number 795, a high-stooped brownstone front. A kindly faced man with brown hair cut in bangs straight across his forehead opened the door. I had come to take my first piano lesson from Father's old friend, Carl Walter.

After he heard me play he said to Father, "You told me you were sending me a boy; you have sent me a musician!"

He was not always so complimentary. Among his other pupils was a Havemeyer. At the end of the sixth lesson he called on the little girl's mother.

"I came to tell you," he said, "what a remarkable child you have."

Mrs. Havemeyer flushed with pride. "Do you really think she has talent, Mr. Walter?"

"Not the slightest. She is remarkable for her lack of musical sensitivity. I have never met another human being like her. The kindest thing you can possibly do is stop her lessons immediately."

Frankness of this sort left him with few pupils, but he made a living and he was happy. I don't think I have ever met a more honest and sincere man.

Recently, in looking over old music, I came upon a mazurka of his. Beveridge Webster, the pianist, happened to call the next afternoon. I asked him to play it. Delighted though I was to hear its trills and runs, I had to admit they were strongly reminiscent of Gottschalk. Carl always felt that people underestimated Gottschalk. One of the first pieces he taught me was Gottschalk's "Apatheose." Ernest Hutcheson laughs at me for enjoying it. I don't care. Patterns in music, like everything else, go in cycles. Some day we will have a Gottschalk revival, and Carl Walter, hearing it from another world, will be happy.

One autumn morning, five years after I had begun to study with him, he abruptly remarked at the end of my lesson that I must not come again.

I was heartbroken. What had I done?

"You have learned everything I can teach you," he said. "Now you must go to Europe and study under the great masters. Let your parents send you abroad at once. If you continue, you will be a great musician."

I hurried home to tell Mother and Father.

Mother said, "If you should go, you should go." Her tone of voice told me more than her words that she did not want me to be a musician. I did not go. Perhaps the decision was wise, perhaps not. I think I would have been a composer.

CHAPTER TWO

❈❈❈

Edward MacDowell

I

THE STRONGEST musical influence that touched me in my youth had been the influence of Edward MacDowell. He taught at Columbia during my undergraduate days and for a short time while I was a graduate student. He remains a unique and cherished memory.

He always seemed to me an out-of-doors man, full of energy and health, and when he strode across the campus in his tweed suit, with his cane hooked over his right arm, even the least musical passer-by looked at him twice.

But his students remembered afterwards indications of the nervous collapse which brought him to his end almost before his remarkable genius was fully developed. When I first met Ernest Hutcheson and told him that I had studied with MacDowell, he told me the tragic story of Heymann, MacDowell's teacher at the Frankfurt Conservatory, and the curious fate of pupil and teacher in falling victim to the same mysterious disease. He recalled that, when he first heard MacDowell play in America, he recognized at once the peculiar and exquisite playing of Carl Heymann, but, he added, he also recognized the defect of Heymann's playing which perhaps had some reference to the mysterious nervous disease. Heymann, he told me, had a nervous way of playing, a marked tendency to exaggerate speed and to distort the tempos. This was MacDowell's own characteristic fault. I never in my life heard such speed as he could produce in difficult passages.

When MacDowell went to the Frankfurt Conservatory, of which Joachim Raff was the head, the most brilliant teacher of the piano was Heymann, noted throughout Germany for his beautiful playing of an extraordinary intelligence and originality. He played music to bring out the poetry in it. He always avoided, even in Bach, any interpretation which could suggest a five-finger exercise. When MacDowell first heard him play, he decided at once that this was the teacher he had been looking for, and to Heymann he became the favorite and ideal pupil.

After enormous success in concert tours through Europe, he fell victim to the nervous disease not unlike that which overtook MacDowell later. When Heymann, on account of his disease, was forced to give up all teaching, he nominated MacDowell as his successor in his Frankfurt professorship. But the faculty, with the exception of Joachim Raff, decided that MacDowell was not the right man, giving as the reason for their opinion that he was too young. The probable reason was that he was too much like Heymann. He had mastered the same type of poetic piano playing which of course was a rebuke to the ordinary performers of the dry-as-dust type.

II

MacDowell had as assistants at Columbia Leonard Beecher MacWood, who looked after the elementary classes, and the late Gustav Hinrichs, an admirable and experienced musician who trained the College orchestra, conducted the music at University ceremonies, and organized a chorus at

Barnard. MacDowell had leave of absence in the middle of each winter for concert tours. His schedule, on paper, was rather light, but he was very busy with his composing, he practiced enough to keep in concert form, he was conductor of the Mendelssohn Glee Club, and he was full of ideas for music at Columbia.

For one slight illustration in passing—at our commencements the candidates for the various degrees used to go in a body to the platform in the gymnasium, receive their degrees from Seth Low, the president, and then walk back to their seats. Mr. Hinrichs and the band filled in while the candidates went up and came down. MacDowell, seeing an opportunity, composed for these brief processions a set of fanfares, extremely dramatic, almost startling. I was present at their first and only performance. They dwarfed other items in the ceremony, and the Faculty and Trustees, as I recall, looked startled at so much trumpeting as though Gabriel were putting on a rehearsal.

When the flagpole at the right of the library steps was dedicated, MacDowell called for volunteers to sing "The Star-Spangled Banner" and he himself conducted a rehearsal. I can see him now, listening with an anxious face to the performance. A few days later he issued another call for a permanent chorus, not a glee club of the kind then popular, but a male choir which should give three or four concerts a year of the best music. The response was large, and after he had weeded out by gentle discouragement the least effective voices he began to drill us. I boomed happily through rehearsals. The Grace Church choir and family hymn singing had strengthened my bass.

As the time neared for his concert tour, MacDowell suggested that we choose one of our number to carry on rehearsals. On his return, after further polishing, we would give our first concert. The chorus elected me, perhaps because my bass could be easily heard, and we worked hard. Late in January MacDowell met us again, fresh from his successful trip, apparently in the best of spirits. He sat himself in an armchair at one end of the glee club room and told me to run through the program. After three or four numbers, however, he got up from his chair, walked to a window and looked out, obviously unhappy. I went over to see what was the matter. "It's my mistake," he said. "We'll disband at once."

"Good heavens, Mr. MacDowell, what have we done?"

"Nothing. Nothing. I was thinking of my youth—of young voices, lyrical, floating. This doesn't sound that way. Quite impossible! We'll disband."

I pleaded with him. "We know some of the places are rough, but if you'll tell us what you want . . ."

He shook his head and walked out of the room, leaving me to break the incomprehensible news. For the pleasure of recalling friends of my youth who have gone far, I name here some of the singers in the chorus he ordered disbanded. Frank Hackett, now headmaster of the Riverdale Country School, Theophilus Parsons, the painter, and his brother, Geoffrey Parsons, chief editorial writer for the *Herald Tribune*, were among the boys singing first bass. One of the tenors was Roelif H. Brooks, now the dignified rector of St. Thomas Church.

MacDowell never met the chorus again. Perhaps it was my temporary leadership that ruined the enterprise. I suggest the idea myself in order to get ahead of you. But the singers, some of them at least like Maurice Krickl and George Matthew, were very good indeed. Many had choir positions in New York, and a few of them were soloists.

III

I once asked MacDowell if he would ever write an opera.

He said, "No. Never. I always feel foolish whenever I try to write an opera. Just imagine my wife singing to me when she wants to get some groceries, 'Alexander, I am going to buy a can of beans and five cents worth of onions.' How, in

God's name, could I write music for that? I couldn't keep a straight face if I tried."

My last intimate contact with him occurred in the spring of my senior year when my class, in the Columbia tradition, produced *The Governor's Vrouw*, an operetta after—much after—Gilbert and Sullivan. Sydnor Harrison, later a novelist and author of *Queed*, wrote the book. Melville Cane collaborated on the book and wrote the lyrics. Melville is my life-long friend. He happens to be a famous lawyer, but to me he will always remain a poet. His verse frequently appears in the *New Yorker*. He has written several books of poems and been awarded the Columbia medal for excellence in law and poetry. In college he was rather a wistful, reticent boy who remained apart from the others.

One evening when we were working on *The Governor's Vrouw* I met him running up the stairs of the rehearsal hall two steps at a time. We could hear the chorus singing "To Stand by Thee, Columbia," the song for which he had written the words and I had composed the music. His face revealed his pleasure.

"I've never seen you look so happy, Melville," I remarked.

He nodded. "I know. For the first time I feel I belong here."

Remembering this I was doubly glad when "To Stand by Thee, Columbia" was reprinted in the school songbook.

For *The Governor's Vrouw* I composed and scored all the music, and the University orchestra furnished the accompaniment. As a matter of pride I didn't ask MacDowell's help in the scoring, but of course I was eager to know what he thought of it. In the cast were a number of really first-rate singers, some of them members of the too quickly abandoned chorus and of MacDowell's University classes. George Matthew, gymnast as well as tenor, took the role of the heroine and turned one of my songs into a serious hit, in spite of the décolleté gown he wore and the biceps he couldn't disguise. We performed a week in the Carnegie

Lyceum, the little underground theater at the corner of the building at Seventh Avenue and Fifty-seventh Street. The Lyceum was then entered from the street, but it has long been out of use for public performances. The small stage is still used, I believe, by the dramatic school in the Carnegie quarters of which MacDowell held his first classes. After the Carnegie week we gave a final performance at the Brooklyn Academy of Music.

I had furnished the opera with a pretentious overture of which, I must confess, no one but myself saw the need. The overture began with a slow sustained passage in which I required the horns to play very soft and very high. They played, of course, not soft but out of tune. Every performance opened with this dismal sourness. MacDowell came one evening with MacWood, and my impression is that he enjoyed the opening horrors better than anything else in the opera. When he met me on the campus next day his smile was extensive.

"Do you know what you ought to do with those horns?" he said. "Isn't there a stove somewhere backstage? Rest them on the stove for ten minutes before you begin. They need warming up."

Other composition students of his did him more credit. During my later college days the music department gave fortnightly or monthly performances of student work, programs which averaged high in quality. At one corner in the small Barnard theater I heard three songs by Angela Diller sung by a young lyric tenor whom I had met in MacDowell's classes. The songs were beautiful. The tenor's name then was Hugh Martin. After some years of study abroad the lyric voice came to the Metropolitan Opera House in a heroic transformation, and Hugh had become Riccardo.

IV

Shortly before or after this student recital, some kind words of MacDowell's put an end to any musical career for me. He told me he was glad I was going in for music, and, stimulated by what I thought was a compliment, I asked if he thought I had any special talent.

"No," he said, "nothing special, but enough to make a good craftsman if you work hard. Would a law student ask whether his teacher thought he'd make a Supreme Court judge? A good, honest, hard-working lawyer has a creditable place in society. Without a host of such lawyers the profession wouldn't progress. Until we have thousands of excellent craftsmen in music, there'll be no foundation for great talents when they come."

These were the last words MacDowell ever spoke to me. I interpreted this wisdom in my own way. He spoke of foundations, but it seemed to me he meant paving stones, one of which I preferred not to be.

At commencement I was awarded the Proudfit Fellowship in Letters. Now I could go on to the Graduate School. Fate, or so I thought, had destined me to be a scholar, perhaps in time a teacher, and maybe—some day—a writer.

The summer of my graduation I went to the Thousand Islands on a vacation and took Sister along. I mention the trip only because we made the acquaintance of three lively and interesting young girls—Minnie, Ida, and Stella Harris. Their father was an English sea captain. From him they inherited a love for travel and the money to indulge that love. Minnie had a superb voice.

In the autumn of 1900 Father sold his Union Hill factory and Weehawken house. We moved to a New York apartment at 340 West Eighty-fifth Street. Our new friends, the Harris sisters, lived just around the corner at 500 West End Avenue.

Father was still singing magnificently. He and Minnie joined in duets to my accompaniments. I set to music for him Rossetti's "My Love Has Come"—his favorite poem. He sang it constantly. Every week end we would have an impromptu concert in which Ida and Stella Harris also gave us fine singing. In such a manner, even though I pursued the academic life, I found myself being exposed to more music than ever. Before I knew it, I was adding Schubert, Schumann, and Mozart songs to my repertoire and, in the process, practicing the piano several hours a day. But this was only for relaxation.

I had made up my mind to be a teacher.

CHAPTER THREE

✠✠✠

Amherst

I

I WENT from my four years in the Graduate School at Columbia University to be an instructor in English at Amherst College. On a salary of $1,000 I found I could save money! Living in those days did not come high.

Having been told that Mrs. Baxter Marsh lodged bachelor instructors, I rang her doorbell first. She showed her rooms graciously enough and appeared happy when I decided upon the second floor front at fifteen dollars a month, but her face lengthened after she heard that I played the piano. I gathered she thought all music sinful. Later I concluded that this state of mind was probably brought on by the playing of my next-door neighbor, Ernest Wilkins, the assistant instructor in Romance Languages. It was not so much the quality of his playing as the lack of quality in his piano, a rented upright.

Despite this absence of tune in his piano, Ernest loved music. Through him I soon came to know well other musicians in the college: William Newlin, the instructor in mathematics; John Franklin Genung, head of the English department; and William Bigelow, professor of music. Whenever Bigelow put on a big choral performance, Wilkins and Newlin helped increase the volume by singing in the chorus. At college concerts Genung, a squarely built man with a luxurious beard, played the viola in the orchestra. He was the most gentle, kindly soul in all Amherst.

Shortly after I arrived, the professor of German, a man named Franklin, died. Genung, anxious to give him a good send-off, took charge of the music at his funeral. After deciding upon a cathedral choir, he sent out a call for experienced musicians. Ernest Wilkins, Professor Bigelow, and Harold Loomis Cleasby of the German department immediately responded. Genung asked me if I would make the fourth. Of course I was secretly pleased. Mother used to say I was a born ham, from childhood up always ready to perform—even at a funeral.

We had a marvelous time at the rehearsal. Nungie's laugh and twinkling eye got us through in great style. I sang bass to Bigelow's tenor. At the services we did even better. I could see from Genung's expression that he was very happy over the results. In front of the church, as we waited for the casket to be lifted into the hearse, he suddenly boomed out in his deep voice, "Boys, we must do this more often."

He had entirely forgotten why we were there.

He loved Amherst. Stephen Marsh, who knew him well, once remarked to him, "Nungie, it seems to me that the two greatest small colleges are Williams and Amherst."

Genung quickly replied, "You are wrong there, Stephen. The greatest college is Amherst."

II

My chance meetings with William Bigelow formed the basis of a friendship which ended only when he died in 1941.

With characteristic New England realism his friends had nicknamed him Biggie because he weighed over 200 pounds. He was my good companion all the years I taught at Amherst.

We settled many a music problem Saturday nights at Rose Warren's Inn over sirloin steak, fried onions, and beer. When he married Jane, these good talks and good meals were continued in his own home.

He had been born in Amherst and studied for the operatic stage in Germany. Instead of continuing his singing career he taught music at Amherst. He was better than his job. He never should have taken it. Amherst people liked him, but they never praised him. Yet the undergraduates had a training in music which few get today. In one respect his extremely fine concerts at Amherst given by the student chorus, which was usually augmented by a large contingent of women from the village or from the neighboring girls' colleges, added greatly to my musical progress.

The music critic of the *Springfield Republican* made it his habit to attend these Amherst concerts and to write his criticism of the performances almost on the spot, or in the train on his way back to Springfield. On one occasion when the music critic could not attend the performance he suggested to Mr. Bigelow that I should write the review for him. This experiment in music criticism proved so interesting that for the remainder of my stay at Amherst I wrote all the reviews of Mr. Bigelow's concerts as they appeared in the *Springfield Republican*.

I mention this fact only because it was my first introduction to an aspect of music in which I had had no experience. The accompaniment of Mr. Bigelow's concerts was furnished by a local orchestra made up of students and townspeople. This strictly local orchestra performed at all the rehearsals, and I had an unusual opportunity to study the orchestration of great choral works and oratorios. For the public performance, the climax of all the rehearsals, Mr. Bigelow imported the first desks of the Boston Symphony. The magnificent playing of these artists, superimposed upon what I had been listening to in rehearsals, furnished me with some valuable information

about the difference, or some of the differences at least, between amateur musicians, however enthusiastic, and professionals.

III

Many celebrated artists played at these college concerts. I
met Olga Samaroff and Josef Hofmann for the first time in
Amherst. I remember being impressed by Olga's absolute
poise. After she had played a difficult program, we went backstage to congratulate her. She came running down the stairs
humming some tune.

"How can you sing so lightheartedly after that tremendous
program?" demanded Biggie.

She laughed. "Why not. It went well, didn't it?"

Hofmann had an amazing repertoire. Before his recital he
sent up a choice of five programs. Biggie asked my advice on
the choice of pieces. I suggested Schumann's *Fantasie*, all of
the Chopin *Preludes* in a suite, and the *Appassionata*.

When the performance was over Hofmann walked with
Biggie and myself to the home of the president, George
Harris, where a party was being held in his honor.

As we crossed the campus he turned to Biggie. "I am perplexed. What kind of people live in this town who want a program like the one I gave this evening? Nothing but curiosity
made me play it."

The influence of music continued. My interest in it drew
me into choir work at the Episcopal church of the town, another Grace Church! There was a good but small two-manual
organ and a choir of predominantly women's voices, all fair
but none trained.

Early in 1907 the organist, a young woman to whom the
church paid $150 a year, married and moved away. So did her
brother, who pumped the organ. Dwight Billings, a leading
Amherst citizen, offered to pay for an apparatus which would
pump the organ by water. I came up with a counter offer to

drill the choir for nothing provided that Mr. Billings supply the pump, and the church give me the organist's salary of $150 a year with which to replenish its music, there being no choir library.

I suddenly found myself organist and choirmaster of Grace Church—a post I held for the balance of my stay in Amherst.

In 1909 Columbia University called me home as Associate Professor of English. It wasn't easy to say good-by to Amherst. The town and college gave me a round of parties. At my final vesper service the choir sang their best—Stainer's Magnificat and Nunc Dimittis in B flat, Martin's two great hymns, "Hail, Gladdening Light!" and "Holiest, Breathe an Evening Blessing."

Today on the dining-room table of our New York apartment stands a handsome silver dish. On the inside is inscribed,

Presented to
John Erskine
By Grace Church Parish
Amherst, Massachusetts
As a token of affection and gratitude
23rd June 1909

Forty years later I went back to Grace Church for the dedication of its new organ, far larger than the one on which I had played. To me the tone was no sweeter, but there was more volume.

During that last visit, the marvelous landscape of Amherst again took possession of me. I wondered why I had ever left it.

CHAPTER FOUR

✠✠

The Influence of Music

I

WHILE we were living in Weehawken, Father used to take us to St. Agnes Chapel on West Ninety-second Street in New York to hear the excellent music, and after we moved to the city St. Agnes became our church.

When I returned to Columbia in 1909 I found Father busy superintending the St. Agnes Sunday School with all of his early enthusiasm for making every department in a church function successfully. I volunteered to play the organ for his classes, for it seemed to me that he was getting old. I wanted to be with him all that I could.

Helen was now in Barnard and Bob at Columbia. To make it easier for them Father and Mother had taken an apartment at 606 West 113th Street. As usual there was a great deal of music in our home. Bob had developed a splendid baritone and was singing in the Columbia Glee Club. Rhoda played the piano magnificently. If she had kept her health I believe she would have been a far better pianist than I. Her music possessed an intimate personal quality which seemed to express her thoughts.

In addition to singing in the Glee Club, Bob played the organ at St. Peter's Church in Chelsea. When he had other engagements I gladly substituted for him. Otherwise I usually attended vesper service at St. Luke's Chapel on Hudson Street. In this case, the attraction was Pauline Ives. We had met several years before when her family attended St. Agnes Chapel. Now St. Luke's was her church. We were married there on June 9, 1910. Until then my life had centered around books and music. I hoped to continue it so.

We returned from our honeymoon to an apartment at 415 West 115th Street, close by the University. My belongings consisted chiefly of books. They soon filled the shelves of my study. But I had no piano!

Eventually I bought a secondhand Steinway grand and anticipated many happy hours of playing it. Gradually Pauline made it very plain that she was not fond of music. If I played at all it was with the sense that my "noise" distressed her. It reached the point where I would wait until she went out before touching the keyboard.

On March 5, 1911, I forgot my fear of disturbing her. Our son Graham was born at five that Sunday afternoon. The nurse put him into his bassinet and carried it into the living room. I asked her to place the baby close by the piano. I had been praying that my son would like music. I sat down at the piano and played very softly. When the little tike looked up and seemed to understand, I cried.

In 1949, a few weeks after Graham's elder son, John Peter Erskine, was born, I went to Reno to make his acquaintance. I sat in the living room holding him while Graham and Hazel, my daughter-in-law, took turns playing a Bach Chorale and some Handel records. My grandson listened intently for a few minutes, then dropped off to sleep in my arms, happy in the knowledge that he had the good luck to draw parents who enjoyed beautiful music.

II

In those early years at Columbia I gave myself to literature, first as teacher, more and more as author. For twenty years piano playing was neglected while I wrote books and lectured on good books. Though I don't call myself inconstant, these were the years when I thought I had said good-by to music.

Yet more than I realized, music followed me, even into the classroom. My approach to literature I supposed was orthodox, but critics friendly and otherwise soon told me it was not. Intending no innovation, I was teaching literature as music had been taught to me, on the principle that any art is learned by practice, and that the practice is based on the tried experience of the craft and on study of its masterpieces. I assumed that students of literature wished to write and that it was my business to show them how. Had I never studied music I might have been content to draw a salary for repeating to my classes the opinions of professors more famous than I about authors more famous than they. If at examination time the students still remembered my secondhand utterances, I might have rewarded their courtesy or their good luck with a high mark, which reward added to other marks similarly acquired might have qualified their brows for the academic laurel. From this respectable exchange of compliments my acquaintance with music diverted me. A music teacher gives no marks. He prepares you for performance; how good you are, the audience decides.

In one other respect the influence of music continued. My conscience was troubled when the class went to sleep or otherwise were less than attentive. Every late arrival in a lecture period seemed to criticize the lecture, and I blamed myself, not the student. The artist on the concert platform should, of course, be more than an entertainer; he is there to interpret, to make great music come to life, but nothing has come to life if the audience goes to sleep. A teacher puts on a performance before an audience, and fairness to those who have paid admission, to say nothing of loyalty to his subject matter, might well suggest the obligation to be interesting. A teacher should prepare for his next class as a virtuoso prepares for his recital. To know the material is not enough; the presentation must be planned, the contrasts of tempo and the bravura passages. This is academic heresy, of course, but in art it is honest doctrine, and my music training forbade and still forbids me to see merit in the leaking-faucet style of utterance which undermines the distinction between a classroom and a dormitory.

There have been arguments, I know, on the other side. I have heard from more than one colleague the theory that moral discipline is most conveniently furnished by lectures which are almost impossible to listen to. George Herbert, otherwise of happy memory, went out on a limb three centuries ago, rashly asserting there is no such thing as a bad sermon:

> *"The worst speak something of good; if all want sense,*
> *God takes a text and preacheth patience."*

But dullness remains dullness. I wouldn't advise hanging up Herbert's verses for a motto in classrooms or concert halls or even over pupils.

Though my study of music influenced my teaching, it did not in those years make any parallel contribution to my writing. In the classroom I was aware of an audience and of the obligation to seize and hold their attention, but in my books, whether prose or verse, I had the bad habit of addressing principally myself. My writing was a form of meditation, a thinking out loud. I saw the fault but not the cure for it.

III

In spite of my concentration on the scholastic life, I occasionally gave myself up to music, practicing for hours at a time. But any permanent alliance with it was again laid aside, and being as I thought still free I wrote an essay which I called "The Moral Obligation To Be Intelligent." It appeared in the *Hibbert Journal*. My writing career began with that essay though I did not realize it until the following year— 1914.

It was unusually hot in New York that summer. I packed my family up and moved them to a cottage at Manasquan, New Jersey, overlooking the Atlantic Ocean. Here Graham might play to his heart's content in the white sands of the beach.

Soon after our return to the city in September I received a letter from Frederick S. Hoppin, the president of Duffield and Company. He had just read my essay printed almost a year before in the *Hibbert Journal*. Would I care to discuss its publication as a book, providing I had other essays to give it the proper length?

Under the title of *The Moral Obligation To Be Intelligent*, that book appeared in 1915. It was successful enough to bring offers from other publishers for more books along the same lines. I was tremendously stimulated and began not only to write essays but to compose music. I set Longfellow's poem, "Stars of the Summer Night," to music for the Columbia Glee Club. I remember feeling very pleased that Father liked it well enough to sing it again and again.

Pauline and I now had my family for neighbors. My parents, my sisters, my brother, and my Aunt Memmen lived in the apartment adjoining ours. My beloved Aunt Nanna had died several years before. The next death to hit us was Father's.

· The day he was buried Pauline gave birth to our daughter, Anna. Mother took charge of the baby's coming, and in the doing assuaged her own grief. Anna has her vigorous mind and sense of humor—she is all Scarborough in that—and while she enjoys music, she is not particularly musical herself. Her interest lay, even as a small child, in another direction—the theater. When she was nine we went to Europe during my

Sabbatical year. We spent part of the winter in Paris. One afternoon some friends who were calling happened to mention a current matinee idol—Robert Bruniere.

"I'd like to meet him," someone remarked.

"I've met him," said Anna. "See. He gave me his autograph."

To our utter amazement she held up a notebook with his signature written boldly across it. The previous day she had coaxed her French nurse to take her backstage at the theater where Bruniere happened to be playing. That love for the theater persisted. She is now Mrs. Russel Crouse. In the living room of her home stands the twin to the Steinway grand in my apartment, my gift to her when she was still in her teens. I hoped that her children might find it useful. They do. Already Timothy, her elder child, now almost four, is practicing on it the finger exercises I taught his mother.

CHAPTER FIVE

✠✠

Ernest Hutcheson

I

IN THE summer of 1916 I went to Chautauqua, New York, to give some courses in literature in the summer schools there, then directed by Percy H. Boynton, professor of English in the University of Chicago. Mr. Boynton was a warm friend of mine, all the closer in friendship because he was an Amherst graduate. For several years he had invited me to give some courses in his summer session, but in 1916 the invitation carried a warning that this would be the last year he could give me this invitation which, up to then, I had been unable to accept.

It was not convenient for me to leave my little family and make the visit to Westfield, New York. For the second year I had rented a small home at New Canaan, Connecticut, and I wanted to enjoy it, but since Percy was asking me for the last time I agreed to teach two courses for the first half of the Chautauqua session, that is, for three weeks.

I did not realize until I began writing this chapter that a whole generation has grown up which never heard the word Chautauqua, and much less know its meaning: an educational assembly combining lectures and entertainment held out of doors.

The idea originated with two distinguished Methodists, Bishop John Heyl Vincent and Lewis Miller. They called a general assembly of Sunday-school teachers in 1874 and named as the place of meeting a grove on Lake Chautauqua in western New York. There were classes in literature, talks on politics, and recitals of really good music. Teachers came and brought their families. The Assembly proved such a success that it was not only repeated each year after that but copied all over the United States.

Physically the pattern has remained the same; compact rows of little white frame houses clustered around a big wooden auditorium, with green trees and open fields for a backdrop. Famous men and women from the world over have advanced stimulating ideas from the platforms of our Chautauquas. At New York's Chautauqua I met many distinguished people, among others Thomas Edison. His wife was a daughter of Lewis Miller.

The English courses given here were excellent, but not to be compared with the courses in music. The new director of the music department was Ernest Hutcheson. I had never met Mr. Hutcheson, though I was familiar with his piano playing, and I had long heard of his skill as a teacher of his instrument. He had made a notable reputation at the Peabody Conservatory, and each summer he brought to Chautauqua as assistants a group of unusual teachers whom he trained at the Baltimore school.

His predecessor at Chautauqua had been William Hale Sherwood (1856-1911) who had studied in Berlin and later with Liszt, had given successful concerts in America at the New England Conservatory in Boston, and had established the Sherwood Piano School in Chicago.

When Ernest Hutcheson began his career in Chautauqua, his assistants were Miss Eliza Woods, Austin Conradi, and Arthur Wilson. Conradi is still teaching at Peabody, where he has established an excellent reputation by his teaching and his own accomplished playing. Miss Woods has only recently retired from active teaching. In World War I, Wilson, a young man of great charm and unusual talent, served in the aviation and lost his life in that service.

Mr. Hutcheson and his family took their meals at a table maintained by Miss Jessie Grassie, well known to all the piano students who went in those days to Chautauqua. Percy Boynton suggested to Ernest Hutcheson that I probably would like to join the circle. The invitation came at once, and my acquaintance with Ernest Hutcheson and his remark-able wife began in the spirited conversations at the Grassie lunch table.

II

Ernest Hutcheson already had the reputation which he always has deserved and maintained among musicians as a man of extraordinary culture, well read and widely traveled. He was even more remarkable for his character than for his accomplishments. I once heard his wife, Irmgart, say that she never knew any human being who had so strong an ethical sense. This praise, however high, did Ernest less than full justice. Musicians, like other artists, are sometimes disappointing in their response to moral obligations. In the course of time I saw Ernest Hutcheson invite to his home rival piano teachers simply because he was proud of his pupils and wanted them to have the advantage of knowing personally, and performing for, all distinguished players.

Afterwards Mr. Hutcheson would keep his temper even if the guest of the evening introduced the young pianist to the public as his own pupil. I never saw Mr. Hutcheson cherish a grudge against a colleague who had played him false. The only reference I ever heard him make to this despicable weakness of certain other piano teachers was the remark that artists, quite as much as doctors and judges, ought to feel the importance of raising the ethical standards of their profession. Of course the musical profession was never deceived by any attempt to steal away a promising pupil. The first-rate teacher is rare, and the profession in general is not deceived by the emergence of a single prodigy.

Those who know Mr. Hutcheson well have frequent occasion to remark on his immense debt to his guardian and first teacher, the Reverend George William Torrance, Mus. D., University of Dublin. Mr. Torrance, educated as an English clergyman, was by temperament and gifts dedicated to music, and when Ernest Hutcheson at the age of five or six was discovered to have a remarkable sense of absolute pitch, his relatives and friends naturally felt that his neighbor, the distinguished clergyman Dr. Torrance, should hear his prowess at the piano. Mr. Hutcheson tells delightfully what happened to his youthful conceit and willfulness, characteristics he must have outgrown at an extremely early age. Somewhat over-conscious of his own importance, he became at first unwilling to play for Dr. Torrance, though he had no other errand in calling on him. Dr. Torrance, recognizing extremely youthful conceit, did not urge him to play until at last the boy decided it was time to show himself off. But then, to his astonishment, he could not sound a note on the keyboard. Dr. Torrance, as he later discovered, had decided not to hear him, and by holding the action rigid he silenced Ernest for the afternoon. I have heard Mr. Hutcheson say this was the most salutary lesson he ever received in manners and thoughtfulness.

It was Dr. Torrance who sent Ernest to the Leipzig Conservatory, where he himself had earlier studied with Moschales.

III

The three weeks of my first visit to Chautauqua made me familiar with Mr. Hutcheson's character and with his musicianship. When I left the summer school I expected to see him again in a few weeks, but instead I went to the war in France.

The founding of the American University at Beaune provided me with many of the most cherished memories of my life. In the organization of the University, music had only a slight place. The army sent us numerous students who had already studied the subject and who knew how to play some instrument, in most cases the piano. But at the end of World War I the piano makers of Europe had all become manufacturers of munitions. Our professor of music, Franklin Whitman Robinson, searched a large part of France and even a larger part of Germany without finding a single piano in condition good enough to be worth purchasing.

At the camp of the American University at Beaune the study and investigation of the subject of music had to be limited to the performances of military bands.

Dr. Walter Damrosch had already established at Chaumont, at General Pershing's request, a training school for military bands and their leaders. Since the University of Beaune was thought of later, it would have been a foolish waste of effort to establish there another training school for bandmasters. The only time in my life that music was for me an entirely quiescent subject was during the brief months at Beaune.

IV

In the autumn of 1919 I encountered Ernest and Irmgart Hutcheson on the top of a Fifth Avenue bus. They were in a particularly happy mood, enjoying a joke which he had just heard somewhere and was relating to her. Perhaps his high spirits were caused by the series of historical concerts which he was just then giving in Carnegie Hall. I heard all the series and determined that I must study with him.

This early series began with the clavier composers of the

sixteenth and seventeenth centuries, followed by the romantic composers, Schubert, Mendelssohn, Schumann, Chopin, Brahms, and Liszt, and finally a generous selection from modern composers.

When Mr. Hutcheson recently published his fine book, *The Literature of the Piano*, I was interested to see how large a part the framework of his early recital series in Carnegie Hall played in the organization of the more highly developed account of piano literature which embodied many opinions and changes of opinion which he could hardly have held twenty or thirty years ago.

Toward the end of the recitals, in fact as a sort of preface to the final one, he told the audience—chiefly piano students —his reasons for giving the series and the kind of use he thought students might put it to. The speech was illuminating and provocative. He said afterwards that he made it at the suggestion of his wife, who feared that the recitals without any explanatory account would miss their desired effect. Whether the little speech was absolutely necessary, I can't say. For me the recitals were more than successful in explaining themselves, but ever since that experience I have looked forward to the too rare occasions when I have heard Ernest Hutcheson talk publicly about his beloved art.

The best of his speeches in my opinion I heard him make one summer at Chautauqua, when he told us with a personal intimacy which is rare with him what he found in music to make him give his whole life to it. He said he was like the lame man in the New Testament who crouched at the Gate called Beautiful begging alms. As Peter approached to enter the Temple the beggar halted him.

Peter shook his head, "Silver and gold have I none. But I say to thee, arise and walk."

"The man went off leaping with joy," said Ernest. "And that is what music has done for me. I stood at the Gate called Beautiful asking for alms, and I received a miracle."

I have heard no more eloquent account of the art which from earliest boyhood has been his master passion.

I knew I must play again. While I lectured or conducted a class, the question remained in the back of my head waiting to pounce on me—if I wanted to play, what excuse had I for not playing? Was I afraid? Why postpone an ideal?

CHAPTER SIX

✢✢✢

The Farmhouse in Wilton

I

WHEN I came home from France in the late summer of 1919, the country was facing the usual postwar housing problems. My family were living in the New Canaan house on which I had taken a long lease before going to France. Originally I had expected to use this residence as a summer home and I had played with the idea of buying it when I returned, but real estate prices had gone up fantastically and, warned by the difficulty of finding at any price a city home near the University, I bought a small farmhouse on Nod Hill, in Wilton. With the house went an abandoned farm of more acreage than I needed or wanted, but at least I had here a summer home for my children and, as it turned out, the nucleus of a rather large place which could have been an all-year-round residence. The view from Nod Hill was magnificent, extending to the Sound. On clear days we could see the far-off steamboats and sailing craft. The sloping landscape which spread toward the Sound was in the autumn a checker-board of color and in the spring a riot of green. I had little money when I bought the place, but the price was low and a mortgage helped me out. With a small borrowed sum I installed enough essential plumbing to make the house habitable; in fact, I thought I was embarking on an extremely modest venture. The taxes on the place were less than fifty dollars a year. I flattered myself that they would not go up. The farmhouse on Nod Hill would always be the kind of country retreat a college professor could afford.

In the autumn of 1919 I rented an apartment at 39 Claremont Avenue. Mother and my sisters continued to live on West 115th Street. Bob had married Margaret Wiese in the early part of the war and was making his home in Scarsdale.

Wherever I went I heard music. My sister Rhoda was busy practicing. Bob and his wife Marg both played, and on the floor below us at 39 Claremont, Professor Walter Henry Hall, choirmaster and organist at Columbia, practiced.

I became possessed with a yearning to play the piano again, really to play it. It wasn't what I'd call an inner impulse; it seemed to come from outside of me, and I fought against it as obviously absurd. I had a profession and plenty to do; why clutter up my busy days with piano practice, especially when nothing would come of it? Technique acquired in childhood can to a certain extent be recovered, but there's no substitute for years of experience, and I had lost a quarter century, more or less. I didn't wish to abandon teaching and writing; long ago I had decided against music, and there would be no point in retracing my steps now. Yet the yearning grew. I must play again.

With some of the money earned from my lectures I bought a Steinway grand—one of the best B models I have ever touched. To the annoyance of Pauline I began to practice. Some of my friends heard me. They couldn't help it. Two of them invited me to join them in playing chamber music. They were Robert Schuyler, professor of history, who had played a violin at the performances of *The Governor's Vrouw*, and Harold Sproul, graduate student in English. We specialized in trios of Brahms and Beethoven. Eventually we were supplemented by Burnet S. Tuthill, a Columbia graduate and clarinet player; Frederick Charles Hicks, Law librarian, a flute player; and Herbert Dittler, a member of the Music Department who was a violinist.

In the beginning we attempted, rather unsuccessfully, to keep our performances to ourselves. Gradually we began to perform for curious friends.

II

Then in April, 1923, I asked my friend Ernest Hutcheson to take me in hand, if he believed I could be reassembled from my dilapidated condition. Having heard me play, he advised a summer diet of Czerny and Bach, and turned me loose with his blessing until autumn.

But at that rate I should never have caught up with myself, and music knew better than I how short the time was. On the campus a few days later Walter Henry Hall asked if I'd play a concerto, the Schumann for example, at one of the orchestral concerts during the summer session. Professor Hall, as I knew, believed in miracles and his optimism frequently got him into jams where he needed them, but I said I'd play. I had to say so! Something terrible would happen if I attempted the difficult piece, but something much worse if I didn't. From early June to August I practiced six or seven hours a day, cursed by my family for the pitiless noise or bombarded with petitions not to make a complete ass of myself. I can recognize now a certain reasonableness in these protests, but I was not then open to reason; I was obeying orders.

Obeying, you understand, under compulsion. On the day of the concert I would gladly have sold out for three cents. I wondered whether my friends would remember me more kindly if I played the concerto or if I committed suicide—not after the performance, of course, but before. Yet I knew I must go through with it, and when the fatal moment came I managed to scrape together the necessary courage. My playing couldn't have been worse, but knowing how bad it was I resolved to make it at least exciting. I went after that audience, and you may take my word for it that no one fell asleep. As for the applause at the end, never before or since have I heard such a thunderous expression of relief.

Ernest Hutcheson knew nothing of this performance till it was over. I didn't want him to call out the police. When I wrote him the news he replied that the Schumann was indeed a beautiful composition and he thought he could teach me how to play it.

III

In the autumn of 1924 I enrolled as one of Mr. Hutcheson's regular students, going to his apartment at 2 West Eighty-eighth Street for my lessons, and once a week on Wednesday evenings taking my turn in playing before the other members of his large class. Usually some distinguished pianist would be present to hear Ernest's pupils. His presence created a special terror for the performers. That was why Mr. Hutcheson had invited him. But the distinguished pianist made a far less formidable audience than the other pupils, who always knew every note in the music you were to play and who always made you despair of equaling the amazing technique or the poetic interpretations of the very young. Here also, as at Chautauqua, there were some visitors who came with an ignoble motive, to steal away, perhaps, one of Ernest's most worthwhile pupils. Perhaps I ought to make it clear without delay that none of the visitors tried to steal me away.

My lessons were stimulating from an intellectual as well as practical viewpoint.

At the end of the evening Mr. and Mrs. Hutcheson encouraged both pupils and visitors to linger for good talk about music or some other art. Since Mr. Hutcheson was well read and had a prodigious memory, he and I usually got into a discussion of some book, old or new. In my lesson periods I learned quickly to recognize his pre-eminence as a teacher. I dare say he was from some points of view as good a teacher as I ever met in any subject. His special skill was in developing the pupil's personality and in avoiding any encouragement to imitation or insincerity. He wanted the pupils, whatever they played, to express themselves and at the same time to show that they understood what the composer was saying.

The pupil sat at one piano, Mr. Hutcheson beside him at another, but the second piano was not used in order to tell the pupil what he should try to express. Mr. Hutcheson would not touch his piano until his pupil had played the piece to the end. He would then suggest that what the pupil had been trying to say could be made clearer by a different approach. With a surprising clearness he would suggest the different approach, still without specific illustration at the keyboard. The object of the discussions was to arouse the pupil's imagination and to stimulate self-criticism. When the pupil began to understand what he himself wanted to say in the performance of a given piece, Mr. Hutcheson would often remark that the purpose now began to be clear, but it could be achieved by much simpler methods.

At this point he would permit himself to illustrate on the keyboard. At the very end of the lesson his most characteristic comment might be something like this:

"I would not play that passage the way you do, but I think your way of playing it is right for you, and I advise you not to change the interpretation."

The chances would be that your curiosity was at once aroused to hear how he would play the passage, and if you asked him to do so he would demonstrate the contrast and explain the two interpretations, always managing somehow to rouse your appreciation not only of your own interpretation but of his.

IV

When I accepted the reckless invitation of Professor Hall to perform the Schumann concerto with the University's Summer School orchestra, Ernest was sorry for Schumann.

But if I hadn't taken that big chance I should never have written *The Private Life of Helen of Troy*, or my other novels. The courage which the Schumann performance called out stayed with me, and after that playing I discovered that at last I could write directly to the reader. Whether the *Helen* book would please anybody or whether I had revealed myself as God's triumph in idiots I didn't know, but my mind was easy as I corrected the last proofs and sat back to see what would happen. Never again would I hesitate to be myself, no matter what that sincerity would lead to. On every page I had talked to the reader as to a trusted friend. The *Private Life* and everything I've written since is for the ear rather than for the eye. My books would have luck if they were read aloud.

Other books equally profitable followed *The Private Life of Helen of Troy*. Having in my hands an unexpected amount of cash, I enlarged and rebuilt the old farmhouse and joined two neighbors, Mr. Charles F. Street and Colonel Frederick Pope, in constructing a dam so that the small river and the springs on the property of all of us became an extensive lake. In other words, I made an estate out of what should have remained a modest home on an old New England farm. It was folly, but I enjoyed doing it, and I did it for my children and especially for my first wife, Pauline Ives, who had discovered the farmhouse and had always loved the location and the view. I gave her the whole property, and for a number of years I continued to hope that she and the children might be finding enjoyment in it long after I was in my grave. But the approach of World War II ran up wages for labor and living costs, both my children were grown up and had careers of their own which would take them away from Nod Hill, and my son would be called to the Army when our country entered the war. Another family with young children to provide for wanted to buy the place, and we all agreed that for us a chapter was closed and we should let it go.

V

If I did not foresee how the Nod Hill farmhouse would develop as our fortunes changed, I foresaw still less that residence in Wilton would lead me straight back to my youthful interest in music. When I bought the farmhouse I was acquainted with none of the residents. I did not know that Miss Lillian Littlehales, the cellist, and Miss Gladys North, the violinist, spent their summers in the southern part of the village; and that near them lived another fine violinist, Miss Mary Dows Herter, later Mrs. William Warder Norton. I did not know that Marie Rosanoff, the cellist, would be spending her summers with her husband, Lieff Rosanoff, near her friend Miss Littlehales, or that Sascha Jacobsen, the leader of the Musical Art Quartet in which Marie Rosanoff was the cellist, would soon buy a farm only slightly north of us and would of course convert the barn into a music room.

Without the slightest intention, I was moving into a community of musicians and music lovers, and in a very few years I should be caught in a stream of influences which would take me out of Columbia University and into the Juilliard School of Music.

Miss Littlehales and Miss North had been among the original members of the Olive Mead String Quartet, which had been organized in 1904. This quartet toured the United States until 1915. Miss Littlehales gave the impression of being austere and forbidding, quite the opposite of her music. She came to Wilton in 1929, the year in which she wrote the biography of Pablo Casals, the great Spanish cellist. On July 31, 1949, Miss Littlehales died in Mexico City, where she is buried.

The original Olive Mead Quartet was formed by Miss Littlehales and Miss North in addition to Olive Mead herself and Miss Elizabeth Houghton. Later Vera Fonaroff took Miss Houghton's place. I did not meet Miss Fonaroff at Wilton, but later on I knew her quite well as a violin teacher at the Institute of Musical Art, the school organized by Frank Damrosch and amalgamated with the Juilliard School of Music under my presidency, as I shall describe in a later portion of this book.

The Olive Mead Quartet made for itself a splendid reputation, but the Musical Art Quartet, under the direction of Sascha Jacobsen with the collaboration of Marie Rosanoff, became in my time what would be fair to describe as one of the most remarkable, certainly the best known, of string quartets. Marie was large, wholesome, and of heroic build. She is the one cellist I have ever seen who satisfied both the eye and the ear when she played. In 1944 Sascha Jacobsen moved to California and the happy association of this group of players was broken.

In my Wilton years the friendship of Miss Littlehales and Miss North and the constant association with Marie Rosanoff and Sascha Jacobsen was for me a strong and lasting influence on my musical life.

In the Wilton farmhouse I had a very inferior upright piano, but I was soon practicing on it energetically. I didn't blame Pauline for wanting to lynch me. The piano was simply God-awful.

Miss Littlehales, meeting me in the village one day, wondered if I would care to make music with her. When I put in an appearance at her cottage, she cautiously explored my musical capacity by asking me to play for her something approximately as difficult as a chorale or hymn tune. Having passed my examination satisfactorily, I was promoted to some music more difficult, and for a short while I had the pleasure of playing now and then with Miss Littlehales, who was a splendid artist. She had a great deal to say—in words and music.

VI

I can't recall now by what steps I formed the habit of playing with Marie Rosanoff and Sascha Jacobsen, but we were invited by the good neighbors who had charge of the Wilton Public Library to give a concert for the library benefit. During all my stay in Wilton this concert was an annual event. After I built my study with its large music room, Sascha, Marie, and I performed what was for me an extraordinary amount of chamber music, chiefly Brahms, but a good deal of Schubert also, and some unforgettable Tschaikowsky. At the end of the evening we would have drinks, sit around the fire, and talk music.

Meanwhile, through the Library concerts and through the ordinary life of the place, we had learned to know well and to love with the warmest affection many of our neighbors. I remember especially the Middlebrook family, particularly Miss Sarah Middlebrook, her friends and neighbors Mr. and Mrs. George Thompson, my old college classmate Charles Ogden, a cousin of the Middlebrooks, Mr. and Mrs. Frederick Gotthold, their son Arthur and his charming wife Florence, and many others.

Mrs. Frederick Gotthold was an accomplished painter and one of the most enthusiastic gardeners I have known. She excelled in her flower paintings, and it may be that she raised flowers primarily in order to paint them.

Mr. and Mrs. Warren Lynch, in their large and attractive place, kept open house for us all, particularly, as I remember, for the children, of whom they were very fond. With the Lynches lived Mr. and Mrs. Isaac Spinney. The Lynches and Spinneys were supporters of the Library concerts and of all our other musical enterprises. I don't remember that they were particularly musical, but their public spirit was remarkable.

The same could be said of Mr. and Mrs. Tom Hall, who came to Wilton after our first summer there and who brought into our quiet life a note of remarkable vivacity. He was an artist who wrote and an author who painted. He had money. Rosemary Hall and Baird Hall, who wrote amusing stories, were the young people of the family. With their cousin Nancy Baird, they were favorites in every party. With these I remember also as loyal supporters of the Library concerts Mr. and Mrs. George Weston, Mr. and Mrs. Edgar O'Hayer, Colonel Baird, Mrs. Shape, and Mrs. Fred Thompson, whose specialty was horses. She taught all our children to ride, and organized the junior riding club. Dr. Strong, the venerable rector of the little Episcopal Church, a most popular member of the community, was her father.

Dr. Strong's spirit was youthful and his eyesight was still keen, but his hearing was not. One bright summer day he presented himself ahead of time at a dinner party. The maid said the hostess would be there in a minute, and would he kindly make himself at home in the library, the first turn to the left.

With the best of will he stepped down the hall, turned to the right, and opened the door into the guest suite. He failed to catch the sound of a nearby shower bath, but he could hardly overlook the attractive matron who stood before him, in slippers, stockings, and brassière, about to put on her evening gown. At her scream a young woman, her daughter, emerged from the shower, wet and shining. The minister backed out.

The hostess, coming in from the garden, found him in the library staring firmly into space. At dinner he had the matron for partner, and the daughter faced him across the board. He may have said his prayers, but he contributed nothing to the conversation and he kept his eyes on his plate.

Our nearest neighbor in Wilton was Sam Lockwood, the well-to-do farmer who lived opposite us across the road, and two remarkable brothers, Fritz and Charles Meyers, builders, who made music with the hammer and saw. They eventually put up all the improvements and additions to the original house, aided by George Gilbert, expert carpenter and gardener, who for many years looked after our Nod Hill home and who, I hope, still cares for it. All three came to our concerts. So did Sam Lockwood. He stands out in my memory as New Englandish but rather good fun.

The number of artists in Wilton, chiefly painters but also some sculptors, was quite large. From the nearby colony of Silvermine, between Wilton and New Canaan, my wartime friend Daniel Putnam Brinley, the mural painter, came with his charming wife to all our Wilton parties. He was as tall as Dunsany. She recited Chaucer to music. Mrs. Frederick Gotthold and E. J. Thompson, the marine artist, educated us all in the enjoyment of good painting. A fine seascape of Mr. Thompson's hangs over my living-room mantelpiece today.

The Gottholds had a delightful place just south of the old farmhouse in which my family lived. Mr. Frederick Gotthold was a retired merchant—tall, thin, and thoughtful, with a suave and princely manner. Whether or not he loved music and paintings I did not at the time stop to inquire, but he was surrounded, we might say, by nothing else, and he had the gift of seeming to take delight in whatever life offered.

When he died several years later, his wife asked me to read his burial service, which I did. Leonora Speyer was there with Edgar, her husband. I had met Leonora at the Poetry Society when I was president. Edgar I did not know

As they walked out after the funeral he said to her, "Leonora, engage that man now to read my burial service."

Mrs. Gotthold, like her singularly dignified and courteous husband, seemed a belated representative of old-school manners and taste. Whether he or she would have enjoyed modern music at the Library concerts I doubt, but the neighbors in general appreciated the classics, which were what we tried to give them.

Mrs. Gotthold had converted the large barn behind the house into an impressive studio where many of the neighbors called almost daily to see what she had been painting. I frequently told her she would be a better flower painter if she were not an accomplished gardener and a well-trained botanist. Her pictures in their early state seemed more beautiful to me than when she had worked over them and perfected the botanical details. More than once I urged her, most impertinently, I fear, to let herself go and put on canvas some of her characteristic love of life. One morning when I visited her studio a new picture was leaning against the wall, a nude, remarkable for its vitality. Without stopping to find out who had painted the picture, I congratulated my friend on having struck the right note at last. Several of her friends were in the studio at the moment, and she had placed the nude where I was sure to see it and make exactly the comment which did spring to my lips. The picture was the work of an American artist with whom she had studied years before, Benjamin R. Fits. It was a preliminary study for a picture which is now in the Metropolitan Museum, "The Reflection." Later Mrs. Gotthold gave me the lovely thing, and I cherish it in my home to this day. Fits must have had Mrs. Gotthold's own disposition to work too long on his things. The sketch of the nude is far freer and more dynamic than the labored and academic picture which the Museum acquired.

Toward the end of her life Mrs. Gotthold had occasion to spend some months in Italy, and while on this visit she made a number of crayon landscapes full of imagination, as her carefully wrought flower pictures often were not. The last talk I ever had with this good friend was on her return from Italy, when she was showing me the crayon sketches.

For our home on Nod Hill she had painted us a screen with four panels, each showing the kind of flowers produced by that landscape in one of the four seasons. When my first wife eventually sold the Wilton place, she gave the screen to the Wilton Flower Club, to which she and Mrs. Gotthold had been devoted.

VII

In more than one way my years at Wilton gave an opportunity to renew my fondness for music. Trinity, the little Episcopal church, contained a small pipe organ. George Boyd, who had married into the Middlebrook family, was like me an enthusiastic amateur organist. His business was real estate, his passion music. He was a little man with carefully trimmed hair on the longish side, as an organist should wear it. We took turns during the summer playing the organ for Dr. Strong's choir. I can't remember now why or on what occasion I was drawn into this exercise, which produced no musical results of importance and probably did not stimulate the little congregation in their worship or prayers. The choir was abominable. They had a good time, but none could sing. There was nothing in Wilton comparable to the opportunity I had found in Amherst when I took charge of the music at Grace Church.

After the success of *Helen of Troy, Galahad,* and *Adam and Eve,* as I have already said, I rebuilt the old farmhouse. The architect or, as it turned out, the architects were both the sons of colleagues at Columbia. While the original farmhouse was still unimproved, I told Fritz Woodbridge, the son of my old friend Professor Frederick J. E. Woodbridge, that when I enlarged the house he, a student of architecture, would be the architect in charge. When at last I had the money I kept my word, as much as anything out of affection for Fritz's father. Meanwhile Fritz had made a partnership with Larry Moore, the son of the Professor of Latin at Columbia, Frank Gardner Moore.

We decided to keep the house somewhat in its original style, as the eighteenth-century farmer had built it out of wood from the grove of oaks which had crowned Nod Hill, but the revised building was only partly a wooden structure. For the most part it was built of stone, the stone being furnished by the boulders which we removed from the walls between the old pastures. Whether or not this was a correct architectural procedure I have never bothered to inquire. I liked the result in the completed building. I had reason to regret only my own lack of foresight in turning the rugged pastures into smooth lawns and squandering large sums of money to keep the lawns mowed. What I should have done was to plant, instead of grass, groves of pine. My neighbor, George Street, was wise enough to do this, and the hilltops which he owned were soon covered with magnificent trees. Everything flourished under him. He had a splendid estate and a genial wife. Colonel Pope, my neighbor to the south, was equally wise; he planted groves of fruit trees. In both cases they planned well for the future. Pope was in the munitions game. We always knew the next country that was going to break into war. It would be the last one Colonel Pope had visited.

VIII

When the old farmhouse was remodeled and greatly enlarged, there were still many boulders left over. Out of them I built a study, at first having in mind only a music room and a library, but the structure expanded itself until it became a complete house with kitchen and bedrooms. The large music room was a delight, not only to me but to my family, who were spared the noise of my practicing. I am glad to say the little building was the home and studio of Helen Hokinson until her death in 1949.

Daniel Putnam Brinley had built on the edge of a Silvermine meadow a diminutive château in pronounced Gothic style, with as much of his beloved Middle Ages in it as he could cram. He was the inspiration of many of our enterprises, encouraging all the musical events. His gifted wife, Gordon Brinley, revived the Middle Ages for us in her own way.

The main room of my new studio had a large fireplace, and

over the mantel Brinley painted for me one of his characteristic pictures in the tapestry idiom, portraying the landscape
in which the old farmhouse was set, with the study nearby,
and scattered carelessly and surprisingly in the Connecticut
setting Helen of Troy herself, with Paris and Menelaos, Galahad with Guinevere and Launcelot, Adam and Eve with a
strikingly bold and naked Lilith. It was a lovely decoration,
and years afterwards when we sold the place I gave the picture to the Wilton Library, partly because it would there be
seen by many of our old friends and their children, and partly
because I wished to leave a memorial of the Library concerts.

After the studio was built, the concerts were rehearsed
under that picture, and we had some special concerts, as on
the week end when Efrem Zimbalist and Alma Gluck visited
us. Alma Gluck was lots of fun—a human, gay soul who loved
good times. She was a wonderful cook. The week end she
visited us she baked a cake so delicious that we ate all of it at
one sitting.

She had stopped singing when I knew her. Already the
cancer which eventually killed her was affecting her voice.
She never mentioned her tragic illness.

Zimbalist was playing less and less. This I regretted, for
he was a great violinist. Whether or not he ever plays again,
he remains a noble man. We had many good talks at the
Wilton Farm.

✠✠

The Juilliard School of Music

I

IN 1926 Ernest Hutcheson told me one day that there was to be a reorganization of the Juilliard Graduate School in which he was teaching, and he hoped that I would accept an invitation to be one of the new Board of Directors. The invitation had not yet arrived, and I knew very little about the Juilliard, though everyone interested in music and living in New York understood pretty well that Augustus Juilliard had left a large bequest for the benefit of music, and as yet little had been done with it. The severest critics of the Juilliard Foundation blamed the trustees, appointed by Mr. Juilliard's will, and Dr. Eugene A. Noble, whom they had appointed Secretary of the Foundation. Perhaps the trustees had hoped to set up an organization as simple as that of the Carnegie Foundation, which had money to give away and a properly designated official to receive requests for donations.

In the course of time Dr. Noble assembled a group of remarkable teachers, and students to be taught by them. Otherwise little of Mr. Juilliard's money was spent. I gradually learned the reasons for this condition. In justice to Dr. Noble I gladly testify that the delay was caused by the difficulty in carrying out some of the terms of Mr. Juilliard's will. Mr. Juilliard wanted to provide for the education of promising young musicians. He wanted also to make his benefaction serviceable in some way to the Metropolitan, of which he was particularly fond.

But the Metropolitan Opera in the years immediately after Mr. Juilliard's death was not in need of money, or at least Gatti-Casazza did not think it was. Mr. Juilliard himself, before he made his will, is said to have asked Mr. Gatti whether the Opera needed any aid. Mr. Gatti replied that the Opera needed nothing except, perhaps, an additional warehouse to store the scenery. The scenery of the Metropolitan was already out of date and shabby. If Mr. Gatti had asked for new scenery, perhaps he might have got it, but there is no record of Mr. Juilliard's wish to store or otherwise to accumulate or perpetuate the old stuff. The trustees of the will explored through Dr. Noble the possibility of some collaboration with the Metropolitan, but Mr. Gatti, knowing that Mr. Juilliard was dead, did not encourage this approach. Since the Metropolitan Opera seemed to be at the moment unwilling to welcome any collaboration from the trustees of Mr. Juilliard's will, Dr. Noble began to set up a music school for the training of talent.

Dr. Frank Damrosch had established twenty years before the excellent Institute of Musical Art, quite the best music school in the city. Paul Cravath and Paul Warburg, both members of the Juilliard Board, felt it would be wiser to use Mr. Juilliard's money to develop the Institute of Musical Art than to set up a rival school. Dr. Noble made the proposal to Dr. Damrosch, who would have been glad of the additional endowment but who, like Mr. Gatti at the Metropolitan Opera, fought shy of any interference or supervision or control by the Juilliard trustees. It is easy to understand Dr. Damrosch's point of view; he told me himself about the proposal as he first heard it from Dr. Noble, and explained his reasons for wishing to have nothing to do with the Juilliard money. He had built up a remarkable school, thanks to the generous gift of Mr. James Loeb and others of the Loeb family. He had his own Board of Directors which could hardly be improved—Paul Cravath, Paul Warburg, John L. Wilkie, Harold Bauer, and others.

Although Frank was less distinguished as a practicing musician than his brother, Walter Damrosch, he was a born educator. His experience as director of public-school music in Denver and in New York City, his acquaintance with the methods of the best music schools abroad and with the best educators, made him feel justly enough that his school should not be tampered with by men, however admirable in their intention, who knew far less about music education than he did. The executors of Mr. Juilliard's will were bankers and lawyers. Dr. Noble, their representative, was a retired minister.

Much of the strength of Dr. Frank in his own school came from the loyal support he had always from his devoted wife. She conveyed to the students and the faculty her own sense of the importance of Dr. Damrosch's work in education. Indirectly and unobtrusively she spread his influence among them.

In the course of time the change in financial conditions made the trustees of the Metropolitan Opera, if not Mr. Gatti himself, wish that Mr. Juilliard's aid had been welcomed in time. The trustees of the Institute of Musical Art, far-sighted bankers and men of affairs, saw that the future of the Institute might be difficult if the world was to face hard times. Some of Dr. Damrosch's trustees, principally perhaps Mr. Paul Cravath, approached the Juilliard Board with the suggestion that the original offer might be renewed, even though the Juilliard trustees had already established their so-called Graduate School and through Dr. Noble had assembled a quite extraordinary faculty. If the Institute of Musical Art had permitted the Juilliard trustees to take it over, the Graduate School would not have been established, but when the Institute trustees raised the question again, even though late, the Juilliard trustees agreed to an amalgamation of the two schools and reorganization under an amended charter.

The original Juilliard trustees, their successors, and associates would constitute the Juilliard Foundation. The original trustees of the Foundation as named in its charter were (to quote therefrom) "Frederick A. Juilliard, George W. Davison (president of the then Central Union Trust Company), and Charles H. Sabin (president of the Guaranty Trust Company), together with such persons as they may associate with themselves and their successors."

A secondary group of nine directors would have charge of the Juilliard School, henceforth to consist of the Graduate School and the Institute of Musical Art, which were to be fused into a single unit as quickly as possible under a single president. The nine directors of the School were to represent the Foundation, the Institute, and the general musical public in equal proportions.

Then Mr. Hutcheson told me that he had heard I was to be invited to come on this new Board. I was to be, of course, one of the representatives of music lovers in general. Without delay I received the invitation from Dr. Noble, and promptly accepted.

II

On Tuesday, November 23, 1926, the directors of the Juilliard School met for the first time at the residence of John L. Wilkie, in a charming early New York house at 16 West Twelfth Street. When I received Mr. Wilkie's invitation for that evening, I had never seen him, nor did I know the others of the proposed Board. Mr. Hutcheson, who suggested me to Dr. Noble, was not in the group, though later he became, of course, a member of the Board when he succeeded me to the presidency in 1937.

The other eight directors were already there when I went to Mr. Wilkie's house, and I was deeply impressed by a short, black-haired gentleman, decidedly bald, who stood in front of the fireplace and fixed on me his piercing eyes. Mr. Wilkie promptly introduced him to me. He was Paul Warburg, like Mr. Wilkie an important member of the trustees who had served Dr. Frank Damrosch in the Institute of Musical Art. Whether by intention or by accident, Paul Warburg and I were seated next to each other at the dinner table, and before the meal was over and we had settled down to the business of the evening we knew each other quite well. That group of men and their successors had a talent for friendship and for collaboration in cultural enterprises, but I remember Paul Warburg with special affection and admiration. Until the end of his too short life I turned to him for guidance in all the difficult tasks which were soon to be mine. He understood Dr. Frank Damrosch and the history of the Institute of Musical Art; he understood also his fellow trustees of the old Institute Board, and he knew in advance all the difficulties of consolidating the Institute with the school which Dr. Noble had assembled, then known as the Juilliard Graduate School. I believe he even understood what Dr. Noble had so far been trying to accomplish.

On that November evening at Mr. Wilkie's house I made the acquaintance of John Morris Perry, a friend of Mr. Juilliard's and the lawyer of his estate. Mr. Perry probably knew far more than anyone else in the room about Mr. Juilliard's original intentions and the history of the handsome legacy. The first trustees and their associates named in the charter did try to organize their trust through Dr. Noble, whom they had made secretary of the Foundation. We, the new Board of Directors, were on trial.

As I remember the evening, John Perry was rather silent, but I noticed the extraordinary respect for his opinion which Paul Warburg entertained. In all the years I have spent with the Juilliard School and the Juilliard Foundation, my confidence in Mr. Perry and my personal affection for him have grown steadily. He remains the soul of Juilliard's benefaction.

When the Juilliard Graduate School was organized as an

educational institution, it was necessary to have a charter. There were general laws covering the organization of all schools and educational groups, and individual charters were frowned upon by the authorities. Aware of this and fearing that there might be difficulty in obtaining a separate charter, Mr. Perry made inquiries among Albany friends. They admitted it would be difficult for Juilliard to obtain a charter. However, because of the exceptional merit of the idea back of the school, a proposed charter was eventually passed by both houses of the Legislature.

When the final granting of the charter reached the desk of Al Smith, then Governor of the state of New York, Mr. Perry paid him a visit. Present at the meeting was Judge Parsons, the Governor's legal adviser.

Picking up the Juilliard documents the Governor shoved his derby hat back on his head, shifted his big black cigar, and said to Parsons, "How about this, Judge?"

Parsons examined the documents. "This is asking a special charter for a matter that is already covered by the general laws, Governor."

Al Smith said, "Let me see those papers, Judge."

After studying them he turned to Mr. Perry. "Who was this fellow Juilliard?"

"He was a woolen merchant," said Mr. Perry.

"Where was his place of business?"

"On Worth Street."

The Governor flipped back the papers. "Give me my pen. My uncle was a truckman for that man Juilliard. He always said there was not a squarer guy in the business."

After the bill was signed Mr. Perry asked the Governor if he might have the pen he had used. Al Smith gave it to him. It is now a treasured possession of the Juilliard School.

After Paul Warburg's death Mr. Perry, Allen Wardwell, and I were thrown together more and more in various causes, not only in Juilliard affairs but on the Board of the Metropolitan Opera. The first Board of the Juilliard School consisted of Paul Cravath, Paul Warburg, and John L. Wilkie, who had been associated with the Institute of Musical Art, James N. Jarvie (a close friend of Mr. Juilliard's), Dr. Noble, Mr. Perry, who had been associated with the Juilliard Foundation, Arthur M. Cox (a Columbia graduate well known in the musical world), Allen Wardwell, and myself—representing general musical interests.

All of us were present that first evening at Mr. Wilkie's. We began with the election of Allen Wardwell as Chairman of the Board, and of Wilkie as Secretary. The next business was the general exchange of information about Dr. Noble's Graduate School and possible ways of amalgamating it with the Institute of Musical Art. Dr. Damrosch would, of course, remain Dean of the Institute; that had been provided for in the agreement between the Juilliard trustees and the Institute. After some random discussion there seemed to be a general agreement that the two schools should be fused under a single president, who should choose a dean for the Juilliard Graduate School. There was agreement also that the new president should be a person of educational experience, whether or not he was a musician. All of the Board felt that the weakness of Mr. Juilliard's benefaction, or rather the failure to make the best use of it, lay in the fact that the so-called Graduate School had not yet become integrated with the educational system of the United States, whether in music or in any other subject. Mr. Juilliard's will, we agreed, would not be properly served unless the generous gift could exert a strong influence on the culture of the whole country.

At this stage in the discussion the other directors turned to me for suggestions as to the college or university presidents whom we should consider for this work. I suggested at once William Allen Neilson of Smith College. Dr. Neilson was not a musician, but he was a man of broad culture, of immense educational experience, and with rare genius for organization. The Board liked the suggestion and commissioned me to go at once to Northampton and deliver our invitation to Dr. Neilson.

At a later meeting of the Board I had to report that Neilson considered his educational career as too closely identified with Smith to be separated from the Northampton college so late in his life.

I then suggested President Thomas Stockham Baker of Carnegie Technological Institute, an accomplished musician who was well launched on his successful career as head of the Pittsburgh institution. I conveyed the invitation to Dr. Baker, who declined it, telling me frankly that the scientific work he had begun at the Carnegie Tech. attracted him more than what he called the possibly ungrateful task of starting the Juilliard School anew and in the right direction and of integrating it successfully with the Institute of Musical Art.

When I reported that he as well as Neilson had turned us down, my colleagues on the Board, who had been making some inquiries on their own account, asked me to be chairman of an executive committee to run the school for at least a year, the other members of the committee to be John Perry and Paul Warburg.

✠✠✠✠✠✠✠✠✠✠✠✠✠✠✠✠✠✠✠✠✠✠✠✠✠✠✠✠✠✠✠✠✠✠✠✠✠

CHAPTER EIGHT

Ernest Urchs

I

THE MOST interesting visitor at Mr. Hutcheson's Wednesday evenings was Mr. Ernest Urchs, who was long in charge of the concert and artists bureau of Steinway and Sons. He was a powerful character with much good humor and a natural disposition to speak his mind plainly. In the course of time he became one of my most valued friends, but I had never met him before the evening when he dropped in to listen to Ernest Hutcheson's class. Whether luckily or unluckily for me, I was to play for Ernest that evening the Coronation Concerto of Mozart. I suppose Mr. Urchs had heard really good pianists play all the famous pieces he was likely to hear in Ernest Hutcheson's class. My rendering of the first movement of the Mozart produced in him remarkable excitement, but certainly no approval. Before I had quite finished the movement and before Ernest had a chance to comment on it, Mr. Urchs sprang from the divan on which he had been resting, seized me by the shoulders, and expostulated:

"Man, don't you know Mozart is an extremely difficult composer, even for a professional pianist? He's nothing at all for an amateur to attempt! Limit yourself, I beg you, to some easier music!"

Ernest's students were amused at the onslaught I was enduring, and just to show I was a fairly good sport I laughed and made haste to agree with Mr. Urchs. When I had completed the second movement and the third, he was still fuming at my rashness in trying to play Mozart, and I was trying to explain that my teacher had wished Mozart on me.

Mr. and Mrs. Hutcheson held Mr. Urchs in good talk long after the other pupils had gone home. By that time Mrs. Hutcheson had evolved a breath-taking plan to raise money for the MacDowell Colony, which through Mrs. MacDowell's heroic activities was already well on its way to its great usefulness to talented Americans in all the arts. Why should not two or three amateurs, Mr. Urchs and I for example, give a recital, perhaps in Steinway Hall, the proceeds to go to the MacDowell Colony?

Before the evening was over, if I remember correctly, it was proposed that Olin Downes should be invited to join Mr. Urchs and me in the program, and that all the notable pianists who might happen to be in New York should be asked to write the criticisms for the various papers.

Other enthusiastic ladies were organized by Mrs. Hutcheson, and advertisements began to appear.

"Two concerts by Olin Downes, John Erskine, and Ernest Urchs. To be given on Friday afternoon, January 21, 1927, at three o'clock, and on Saturday evening, January 22, at 8:30, in Steinway Hall, 113 West Fifty-seventh Street. Tickets $5.00 apiece. The proceeds of these concerts will go to the MacDowell Colony, Peterborough, N. H. Please address requests for tickets to Mrs. Ernest Hutcheson, 2 West Eighty-eighth Street, New York City. Concert Management, George Engels."

II

In order that the performance might have as many chances to succeed as possible, Ernest Hutcheson gave over his music room at 2 West Eighty-eighth Street every Sunday morning to an impassioned rehearsal of the music, which involved many heated debates as to tempo and other fine points. Of course we all were eager to do well in the Bach Concerto, especially in the third movement, in which each piano takes its turn playing a not too easy cadenza. In the neighborhood of Steinway Hall we were soon known as the "Cadenza Kids," or perhaps Mr. Urchs monopolized the name, since it was his duty to meet every pianist who played the Steinway and to confer on business proper for that pianist.

In his office he produced the most extraordinary hospitality. He had a metal chest furnished with all kinds of liquors so that he could offer his great pianists their national drink or whatever they preferred. When the psychological moment arrived and the distinguished pianists needed entertainment, Mr. Urchs would signal to his business partners to hurry in from their offices and join the party. His enormous humidor, containing all sorts of cigars, was as formidable as his collection of liquors. His wife used to say that her husband, when he went on business trips, would drive her crazy with impatient telegrams, urging her to remember to keep the sponges damp in this corner or that of his precious collection.

Before the concert, once Mr. Urchs had dispensed hospitality, he seized the opportunity to play over his cadenza for Rachmaninoff, Paderewski, and any other great man who dropped into his office. It might be thought that this incessant performance for great technicians would undermine somewhat the self-confidence of the amateur, but that was not the result. Mr. Urchs was building up his nervous system for a supreme accomplishment, and I can think of no other man who approached his first appearance in public with so little nervousness.

III

The program was given in the evening as well as the afternoon on Friday in order to accommodate the quite remarkable audience, consisting chiefly of prominent professional musicians who wished to hear the performance and afterwards to see what the artist-critics did to us.

Josef Hofmann was the guest critic for the *New York Times*; George Gershwin for the *New York World*; Ernest Hutcheson for the *New York Herald Tribune*; Georges Barrère for the *Evening Telegram*; Ernest Schelling for the *New York Sun*; Josef Lhevinne for *Musical America*; Albert Spalding for the *Evening Post*; and Richard Singer for the *Staats-Zeitung*.

The concerts were soon referred to as the Urchs Concerts, I suppose because Mr. Urchs had a powerful personality which seemed to absorb the enterprise in himself. He had a passion for piano music, and strictly as an amateur he played well, but he liked to say that this concert was the first he had ever participated in, although he was now sixty-two years old.

The program included the Brahms-Haydn Variations, played by Olin and me, the Coronation Concerto, played by me to the piano accompaniment of my sister Rhoda, who was the best performer on the platform, and the Bach Triple Concerto in D minor, played by Olin, Mr. Urchs, and me, accompanied by a small string orchestra of the Institute of Musical Art conducted by Frank Damrosch.

The Coronation Concerto of Mozart was the concerto Mr. Urchs had rebuked me for playing in Ernest's class. My teacher had now trained me to play the lovely piece in a way even Mr. Urchs approved. The performance was made especially charming by the eager, sensitive accompaniment of my sister Rhoda.

I choose this place among my musical memories to speak

of what her sympathetic affection meant to me. Her talent
in music was rare. She was a pupil of Ernest Hutcheson's
before I was, and we shared the same admiration for him as
musician and man.

Only a short time after the Urchs concert she knew that
she was stricken with cancer. She was already teaching literature at the Juilliard School, and her last months were made
happier by her association with the teachers and pupils there.
She died in 1934.

IV

At the afternoon performance the Urchs cadenza came
off brilliantly. For the evening performance, however, fate
arranged an embarrassing trick to play on Mr. Urchs. He
asked Katherine Bacon, the well-known pianist, to turn pages
for him, especially in the third movement where his score had
to be turned in the very middle of the cadenza. Katherine
Bacon was as good a page-turner as any idealistic pianist
could desire, but woman fashion she carried her small handkerchief folded up in her left hand, and midway in the page-
turning the handkerchief slipped from her fingers and fell on
the keys, on the very keys on which Mr. Urchs wished to put
his fingers. The poor man didn't know the handkerchief was
there until it fell, and his surprise at seeing the little piece of
linen drop on his keys nearly paralyzed him. He had not the
presence of mind to brush the handkerchief away. He could
only stare at it in terror and stop playing. Frank Damrosch,
who didn't know the reason for the pause, brought his orchestra to a halt and waited for Mr. Urchs to begin again.
By the time locomotion was re-established, the evening was
completely spoiled for Mr. Urchs. He spoke of it for several
years. All of Miss Bacon's friends agreed that her prayers were
needed for the continuance of a brilliant career. We asked
whether Mr. Urchs would ever furnish another Steinway for
her to play on.

I enjoyed myself hugely at the Urchs concert. Whether

I realized it or not at the time, I was a performer. The more bids to play in public, the better I liked it.

In the summer of 1927 I played with the Chautauqua Symphony. When I returned to Wilton, Sascha Jacobsen invited me to play the Brahms A major Piano Quartet with the Musical Art Quartet at a benefit concert. That same autumn Mrs. Dwight Morrow invited me to speak at an Englewood, New Jersey, school. After the concert we went back to the Morrow home for refreshments. Someone brought up the subject of playing for friends.

I said, "When anyone asks you to play on the piano, tell them you will if it has clean keys."

Mrs. Morrow smiled. "Will you play for us?"

I asked her if the keys were clean. She ran her fingers over them. They were dusty. Laughing, she disappeared, returned with a cloth, wiped the keys, looked at me, and pointed to the piano stool.

I played.

❧❧

CHAPTER NINE

Walter Damrosch

I

IN THE course of time I received an invitation from Walter Damrosch to play the Schumann Concerto with the New York Symphony on the final tour which he made with that orchestra. The invitation came in the fall of 1927. I learned later that Ernest Hutcheson had roused Dr. Walter's curiosity to hear just how well or how badly I could play the famous piece.

I knew him but slightly. Our first meeting was at the Columbia University Club where I happened to be lunching with George Hellman. Damrosch was just back from France where, at General Pershing's invitation, he had established the AEF Bandmaster School at Chaumont. With characteristic enthusiasm he described the school to George and myself, explaining in detail how he had added wood winds to the brass and instituted an intensive course in music for the bandmasters. He referred particularly to Albert Stoessel —then only a name to me—and to Isidor Philipp, the French pianist. He said it was largely through Philipp's aid that he had been able to assemble his faculty at Chaumont.

As he talked I thought I had never met a handsomer man.

65

In addition to good looks he had the gift of making everyone feel at ease.

In December, 1926, I happened to meet him and his wife at a dinner Corinne Roosevelt Robinson gave. In those years the two families lived almost opposite each other on East Sixty-first Street, the Damrosches at 146, Mrs. Robinson at 147. She had all of her brother Theodore's charm. Her dinners were thought out to the last detail and she saw to it that every guest took part. On the particular evening that the Damrosches were there she had written a poem about each guest. In going through old scrapbooks I came upon the one for which Walter was the springboard. Here it is:

We talk of "Music of the spheres"
And how "the stars sang in their courses."
But Walter's music! One, who hears,
Shall sense the hooves of Neptune's horses,
As oceans of delicious sound
In palpitating waves abound.

Not "Walter von der Vogelweid"
Who sang the prize song of the ages
Can in our hearts so deep abide
Or leave such an imprint on Life's pages
As you, Oh! Dean of all the dears!
You are the "Music of the Spheres!"

II

When the invitation to play with the New York Symphony came from Walter Damrosch, Ernest told me to accept it and he went with me to the rehearsal to make sure I acquitted myself creditably. He coached me very conscientiously and the day I left telephoned to say my playing showed remarkable improvement.

I played the Concerto at Ann Arbor on February 1, 1928,

and I had the time of my life. I felt I could hardly hope to play to so large and so fine an audience again. I felt exactly the same way at Buffalo the following evening.

Mrs. Damrosch made the tour with the orchestra, and at the conclusion of these concerts guarded the door of the artists' room to prevent Dr. Walter's admirers from breaking in upon us before he and I had enjoyed a brief but refreshing and stimulating drink. This was during prohibition. She was a good sport. The fact that I cherish this memory in all its details will not, I hope, prejudice the revered figure of Walter Damrosch with any of his admirers. What they may have thought of me made no difference then, nor perhaps can do me much harm now.

The presence of Mrs. Damrosch on the brief visits of the New York Symphony to Buffalo and to Ann Arbor gave me my first opportunity to make the acquaintance of this charming woman, whose memory deserves to be cherished with gratitude by all New York musicians. She was devoted to the musical interests of her husband. Even my brief opportunity to observe her relations with the men of his orchestra showed me how large a part she had in his success. I soon learned that not only on these special occasions but throughout the year Walter and his music had always her loving attention. She represented an unusual tradition in American culture.

From her famous father, James G. Blaine, and from her brilliant mother she inherited an extraordinary equipment in social adroitness and wit. Walter Damrosch himself was the very soul of hospitality. He loved to have his friends around him, especially if they were members of his own profession, and still more when they were brilliant newcomers in the musical world whom he was introducing to friends who could best appreciate their gifts. Walter always regarded the members of his orchestra as his special musical family. He accepted the responsibility of looking after the personal happiness of all the first-rate musicians in New York so far as it was possible for one man to assume such a vast obligation.

III

On the first day of every year it was Dr. Walter's gracious custom to entertain at a lunch party in his home a large group of musicians, sometimes numbering a hundred or more. The first New Year's Day party of this kind which I attended was given in his spacious brownstone front on East Sixty-first Street. The guests were seated on campstools at small tables. The task of organizing and serving the refreshments was formidable. Mrs. Damrosch supervised the service assisted by her daughters, Polly Damrosch, afterwards Mrs. Sidney Howard, Gretchen Damrosch, afterwards Mrs. Thomas K. Finletter, and Anita Damrosch, afterwards Mrs. Robert Littell. The fourth daughter, Alice, was in Switzerland.

The Damrosch girls were assisted by Alma Gluck, then in the bloom of health and charm. All these ladies were wearing peasant costumes, suggesting Switzerland or Munich. The large house was ideal for such a party, and the ladies who assisted him in entertaining his guests themselves contributed unforgettable charm.

I have good reason to remember so many other happy gatherings at the homes which Walter and Margaret Damrosch later occupied—at 133 East Eightieth Street and at 168 East Seventy-first Street—that I should have difficulty in describing them in detail, but in 1937 I had the privilege of spending a peculiarly happy week at Blaine Cottage in Bar Harbor, the girlhood home of Margaret. Several members of the family were fellow guests. Polly Damrosch Howard came to Bar Harbor to act as chauffeur and otherwise to help entertain me. In the fine old house, rich in American memories, Walter was at his very best, full of brilliant conversation and tireless as always if he happened to be composing at the moment. He had converted the upper room of the old Blaine stables into a spacious workshop for his copyist.

When Walter's music did not monopolize his attention, he was landscaping the garden, and at all times he was full of ideas and busy talking. In the evenings friends came in for dinner, and musicians drove their cars many miles to take part in the fine concerts which Walter had organized.

Felix Salmond brought his cello for our entertainment, and older residents of Bar Harbor recalled for my pleasure the time when Mr. and Mrs. George Harris of Amherst College had spent their holidays at the famous Maine resort. The Blaine Cottage was a remarkable home, deeply marked by the strong characters which had lived there. When the house was destroyed by the disastrous Bar Harbor fire on October 24, 1947, it left a deep wound on Walter Damrosch and his wife from which neither entirely recovered. It may have hastened her death.

CHAPTER TEN

✦✦

Music Reciprocates

I

FROM February 6 to April 14, 1928, I talked my way across the country. The previous year I had signed a contract with Louis J. Alber, the lecture agent. I gave seven lectures a week, and at least once during each day, either at the lecture hall or in the home of the local chairman, I played the piano. A lecturer with parlor tricks was a novelty.

Music, unwilling that I should dodge the issue, was closing in on me. Eight months before I agreed to do this cross-country lecture marathon I had accepted the directorship on the Board of the Juilliard Graduate School of Music. Almost immediately my associates had made me chairman of the Administration Committee. I asked for a leave of absence and got it—both from Columbia and the Juilliard.

News of my association with the Juilliard had gone before me. In every town I was eagerly welcomed by music patrons anxious to promote local projects. My lecture tour was fast becoming a musical pilgrimage. When I returned to New York I found plenty of work awaiting me in my office at the Juilliard Graduate School.

At Columbia my office in Hamilton Hall was simple: plaster walls, plain book shelves, and the usual office furniture. At the Juilliard, faculty and students taught, sang, and played in a former Vanderbilt residence at 49 East Fifty-second Street. I drew an enormous oak-paneled room with a real gold-leaf ceiling. Margaret Miller, my secretary, had all the instincts of a first-class reporter. The day after I moved in I learned that we were occupying what had been Mrs. Vanderbilt's drawing room.

The entire house was on this same elaborate scale. There were something like fifty rooms, a magnificent grand stairway, and a ballroom which served admirably for a small concert hall. But from the very start I had an uneasy feeling that the house, although fireproof, might not be easy to get out of if there should be a fire. Also it was not practical for a music school. The teaching rooms were too small, the acoustics none too good, and the walls though thick were not soundproof. This does not mean that I did not enjoy my stay in it. I was having the time of my life those early months. My enthusiasm must have impressed the trustees.

In March of 1928 Allen Wardwell, chairman of our Board, asked me to take the presidency. I was tremendously attracted to the idea. I could see at once the educational possibilities. I knew the weakness of many of our public schools and universities in music. For one thing, there was a strong need for better musical equipment on the part of the teachers. It wasn't their fault. But nevertheless the situation existed. It could not be corrected until music was a recognized subject in general education. Here I might be of help, both to our schools and colleges and to the Juilliard. I did not know at the time that Paul Cravath, a member of our Board, had been exchanging letters with General Pershing about my work as director of the AEF University in Beaune. I learned later that I was chosen for my experience in education as well as my knowledge of music.

I accepted provided I might be given leave of absence to

take my son Graham to France for a year at the Sorbonne. That same day, June 23, 1928, I sent in my resignation to Columbia. Pauline, my wife, was not happy over this decision. She felt that I was tossing overboard the opportunity to be president of Columbia University. And—she would have to listen to more music than ever!

Of the many messages of congratulation I especially prized this letter:

My dear Professor Erskine:

I must tell you how glad I was to hear from Paul Warburg that you had consented to accept the presidency of the Juilliard School. As you can imagine, I had followed with eager interest all the developments that led to the adoption of the Institute of Musical Art, and was kept informed of the progress made in the often difficult negotiations.

Even though I knew nothing about your eminent qualifications for the office you have now accepted, your "Adam and Eve" would prove to me how deep is your insight into human nature.

James Loeb

March 20, 1928　　　　"Hochried," Murnau, Staffelsee

This was the man who founded the Loeb Classical Library. The Hellenic studies had been a basis for our friendship. He happened to be a benefactor of the Institute of Musical Art and a partner in the banking firm of Kuhn, Loeb and Company. He was also a scholar.

II

I spent that first year at the Juilliard making myself acquainted with the teachers in both branches of the school, and especially with Dr. Frank Damrosch, who collaborated generously in the proposed amalgamation, even though he made no secret of his disappointment that the Institute should not continue as a separate institution all his life. Admiring his ability as an educator and his personal good sportsmanship, I did my best to make his position in a difficult transition as happy as possible. I hope I gained his confidence, and I know our friendship continued unshadowed until his death in 1937.

In those first years this involved countless trips back and forth between the Juilliard on East Fifty-second Street and the Institute on 122nd Street and Claremont Avenue. Every time I made the trip I was reminded of the inconvenience of the Juilliard location.

The special problem which the trustees of the new Juilliard School hoped I could solve was the combining of the two schools, the fusing of the work of the brilliant faculty which Dr. Noble had assembled with the veteran organization over which Dr. Frank Damrosch had presided.

As an educator Dr. Noble's chief weakness was his failure to grasp the musical needs of the country and the sources from which would come our students. His strength was in his ability to recognize a fine teacher and his impulse to retain on his faculty as many fine teachers as possible. Without Mr. Juilliard's benefaction he could not have assembled the original faculty of the Juilliard School while it was located at 49 East Fifty-second Street.

In his piano department he had Olga Samaroff, Yolanda Irion—who remained only for a short time—Alexander Siloti, Carl Friedberg, Ernest Hutcheson, Mr. and Mrs. Josef Lhevinne, and for a brief while Ernest Schelling.

The voice department also glittered with great names: Marcella Sembrich and her pupil, Florence Kimball, Anna Schoen-René, Paul Reimers, and Francis Rogers.

In the violin department were Leopold Auer, Paul Kochanski, Hans Letz, and Louis Persinger. Rubin Goldmark taught composition and Felix Salmond the cello.

I doubt if Dr. Noble was an educator; he seemed to me rather a collector.

I stayed the week end at his magnificent summer home in Narragansett, Rhode Island. His collection of Bedlingtons—

Northumberland terriers—was the best in the country. He also collected Rolls-Royces and fine rugs and pictures. At the Juilliard he had collected teachers the same way, without much consideration of their fitness for their immediate purpose.

When he heard an eminent pianist, he tried to secure him for his faculty. The selection of the original faculty, therefore, was made by fate or luck rather than by Dr. Noble. There were soon far too many eminent pianists engaged to teach far too few talented pupils. The teachers themselves to some degree corrected this error, and the School had already shaken itself down almost to its permanent condition when I assumed the presidency.

I make no apologies to Dr. Noble's memory for these comments on him. The trustees who selected him as their secretary, since he had been connected with educational institutions in responsible positions, perhaps had a right to believe he understood the problems of education. He had been president of the Centenary Collegiate Institute in Hackettstown, New Jersey; then president of the Woman's College of Baltimore, now known as Goucher; and afterwards president of Dickinson College. He was ordained to the Methodist ministry and served as pastor in churches in Connecticut and Brooklyn. But his career had not been entirely comfortable for himself or for others. My own association with him was far from happy. He was to the best of his ability helpful and co-operative; I am sure of that. He was a man of many cultural interests and of considerable miscellaneous experiences in education, but the essence of education, the building up of a school to respond to the larger interests of society, was a secret which Heaven had concealed from him. I remember, however, with admiration the generous spirit of co-operation with which he retired into the background when the trustees, after their initial experiments, determined that I, rather than he, should be the first president of the School. The difficulty of the change was made somewhat, but not entirely, easy by electing

Dr. Noble one of the first trustees of the newly organized Board.

III

The first thing I did as president of the Juilliard School was to persuade Ernest Hutcheson to accept the post of dean. When I say persuade him, I am choosing my words carefully. He did not wish the position. His wife agreed with him that by temperament he was a teacher and an artist rather than an executive, and Dr. Noble expressed the same opinion at the meeting of the board when the appointment was discussed.

Ernest gave the impression of frailty which deceived those who didn't know him well. Actually he had an iron constitution. He was too superb a gentleman to be aggressive, but in his quiet manner there was a firmness that his pupils respected. Their affection for him showed in the fact that they all spoke of him as "Mr. Hutchie," in a tone of protective tenderness. He had the most honest mind of any man I've ever known. He was a great musician. I wanted him as my dean.

I raised the question during a visit I made to him at the summer school at Chautauqua, and I have not forgotten the worried look which came over his face as he considered the responsibilities of a kind of work which would be quite new for him. I suppose he realized that since he would be dean he would share with me the obligation to join what we used to call the Graduate School with the Institute. He would be brought into disagreement with his old friend Dr. Frank Damrosch on many points of policy, and though Mr. Juilliard's benefaction had been generous it was not large enough to provide easily for pensions for both teaching staffs. Talking over the problem, he and I agreed that if he accepted the invitation we must plan equally for the teachers of the Institute as well as for the remarkable staff of the Juilliard or Graduate School.

Let me remark in passing that the name Graduate School, invented by Dr. Noble, had neither for Ernest nor for me any clear meaning. "Graduate" implied not merely outstanding ability, but outstanding previous training. The implication of the term was that the teaching at the Juilliard or Graduate School was superior to that at the Institute. Generally speaking this was true, but Dr. Damrosch had engaged for his Institute faculty several teachers, notably Carl Friedberg, whom Dr. Noble had also engaged for the Juilliard faculty, and of course a first-rate teacher always attracts sooner or later first-rate pupils.

Musicians with any reputation as teachers have little difficulty in finding pupils; in fact, the applications are usually embarrassingly numerous, especially where the instruction is free. But real talent is rare. Some of the students at the Institute were not first-rate, but this was equally true of some students at the Graduate School. It would be primarily the duty of the dean to correct these contradictions and paradoxes.

Such problems were not attractive to Ernest Hutcheson, who would have preferred to spend the rest of his life, as he had spent the previous part of it, in studying the literature and the technique of the piano and in teaching well-chosen pupils.

In spite of all these arguments I remained firm in my determination to have Ernest for my dean. I have never changed my opinion on this point, and I think my decision to secure for the School the services of this great artist and gentleman was one of the wisest I ever made. Executive duties were not natural to Ernest, and some of the School problems cost him difficult hours, but his sense of honor compelled him to make even very difficult sacrifices to fulfill all his responsibilities.

Since the death of his wife Irmgart, I have at times thought that my appointment of him to the deanship and his acceptance of this post was far more difficult for her than for him. So long as he was simply one of the teachers on the Juilliard faculty she had acted as his secretary, making the calendar of his appointments with his pupils and becoming the guide, philosopher, and friend of all, from the youngest to the more mature who came to study with him. Her own musical talents were unusual, so much so that in their youth he had once proposed that he should remain only a teacher and she should become the artist-performer of the family. Later on, after he became dean, it was very difficult for her to stand aside and watch his management of the School, especially in details which she, with her gift for handling such problems, would have managed differently.

But in many respects the deanship did not change essentially the relation of both the Hutchesons to Ernest's pupils. He still held his classes in his home at least once a fortnight, and Irmgart entertained his pupils with undiminished hospitality.

IV

When Mr. Hutcheson had been engaged by Dr. Noble, one of his older pupils, Oscar Wagner, was engaged as his assistant, and when I asked Ernest to be dean of the Graduate School he stipulated that Mr. Wagner should continue as his assistant in both the teaching and executive parts of his work. Mr. Wagner had been a child prodigy of the Middle West and had come to Mr. Hutcheson's attention, I believe, through his precocious and beautiful playing. The climax of this part of his life was a tour he made in extreme youth to Australia as accompanist for Madame Marguerite d'Alvarez.

When I met Madame d'Alvarez years later she told me, perhaps by way of a joke, that she had selected Oscar as her accompanist partly because he danced so beautifully. "When you choose an accompanist for a lengthy tour," she laughed, "you might as well pick one who can fill in your leisure moments."

To speak of Oscar as Madame d'Alvarez did would imply, perhaps, that he was something of a playboy. Nothing could be further from the fact. He was devoted to his teacher, Ernest

Hutcheson, and made himself almost too much his faithful errand boy, servant, or slave. At the School we all depended upon him excessively. He was an excellent manager of important programs, musical or social, and anything he managed was executed with good taste and devotion. In time he became almost part of the Hutcheson family, spending his summers with Ernest at Chautauqua and carrying out commissions for him everywhere.

Some of us after a few years began to worry about his future, and one day when he and I happened to lunch together I asked him to tell me frankly what he wished his career to be. Unless he did far more piano playing, I doubted if he could build up or maintain whatever reputation he had as a pianist, or as a piano teacher. If, on the other hand, he was content to be simply Ernest's assistant in executive work, I wondered if he could look forward to any post satisfactory to himself at the remote date when Ernest would probably retire. I was not surprised, therefore, when at the close of Ernest's active presidency Oscar accepted an executive position with a California music school. For me the Juilliard, with his resignation in 1946, lost something which it has not yet recovered.

CHAPTER ELEVEN

✦✦

Concert Pitch

I

CONCERTED music in its earliest state was the music of individual voices singing together. The morning stars were the first concert. It may be presumed that the heavenly bodies, being selfless, find eternal satisfaction and sufficient excitement in brotherly harmony and counterpoint. But the human soul, in its fallen condition, likes solo work. I know I do.

The performance of the Schumann on the last tour of the New York Symphony caused the statement to be frequently made that I toured with the Symphony and New York Philharmonic and various other professional orchestras. This was not entirely true. Whenever I could I played with amateur orchestras. I considered it a possible service to music to give the encouragement of my own example to all amateurs, especially to the amateurs who give their time to orchestra rehearsals. I never for a moment was so conceited as to think myself a professional pianist.

My repertoire was small. I was asked to play the Schumann until the lovely work began to bore me. I particularly liked to play Mozart and César Franck. Perhaps I enjoyed best playing the second Concerto of MacDowell. I was using music to express my ideals. To say all that the human spirit yearns for, we need all the tongues. It would be a tragedy if any one of us cherished a worthy ideal which he lacked the proper language to express, and though we sometimes say that great artists express our souls for us, that is never exactly true. The higher mankind rises, the more obvious is the need of every individual to have the technique of as many arts as possible.

There is reason to doubt that we yet recognize this essential truth. It is not certain that our rapidly increasing practice of the arts springs from a wish to express our ideals. Perhaps we have got no further than the very elementary conception of culture which is concerned with the best that has already been said and thought in the world. We may not yet have recognized the need to express our own ideals or to say or think anything excellent ourselves. Until we become completely self-expressive, our culture will remain memorial and retrospective.

Thomas Jefferson believed that competent expression in the arts is necessary for any complete articulation of political or social or humane ideals.

More than a century ago he wrote to a friend in France revealing a vigorous faith in the value of the arts, especially of music. To quote from his letter, "If there is a gratification which I envy any people in the world, it is to your country its music. This is the favorite passion of my soul."

Among his domestic servants he retained a gardener, a weaver, a cabinetmaker, and a stonecutter, who doubled as musicians. He asked his friend if there might be found in France persons of these trades who could perform on "the French horn, clarinet, or hautboy, and bassoon, so that one might have a band of two French horns, two clarinets, two hautboys, and a bassoon, without enlarging their domestic expense."

Jefferson's idea of a domestic orchestra was natural at a time when European musicians were patronized as the private servants of kings and princes. We need not quarrel with the great democrat for failing to foresee the sturdier foundations on which music in this country would eventually rest. We need not quarrel with him, since so far as orchestras and opera companies are concerned we still depend to a large extent on private patronage and benefaction. But even in Jefferson's day and in his own experience there were beginnings of that amateur music-making which should characterize a democracy and which, in favorable circumstances, sets an example for the practice of the other arts. Almost every man in Virginia who as Jefferson would say "had an ear," and quite a number who had not, played the flute—Jefferson himself, for example, and Patrick Henry, and George Washington. The advantage of the flute was its high degree of portability. When a cultured gentleman rode out of an evening, he packed the sections of his dismembered flute in the long pockets of his coattails. The violin was almost as easy to carry around and it was an instrument of larger musical resource. Patrick Henry, who was perhaps the best violinist in Virginia during his lifetime, spent many an hour fiddling for the dances in his neighborhood. Benjamin Franklin preferred the harmonica.

II

In our country today the advance in all the arts is so great that we might easily indulge in a dangerous self-satisfaction. There is a growing and discriminating support for good music, a public taste which demands and receives from the radio, programs of the first quality, which demands and receives an increasing number of excellent opera performances, and which has caused to come into existence a large number of amateur symphony orchestras whose playing is admirable. But amateur orchestras rarely can pay the fee of a fine soloist, and I always played for nothing. Apparently the spectacle of a novelist at the piano risking his neck on a difficult piece of music had some drawing power with audiences. In quite a number of

places I was invited to repeat the concert the following afternoon or the following evening whenever the demand for
tickets outran the capacity of the hall.

If I lectured, the audience wanted music too. An invitation
to lecture at Yale was typical. William Lyon Phelps asked me
to talk to a group of women in New Haven on "Music in
America Today." Would I play something afterward?

I wrote back that I was ready to play till the cows came
home.

Each concert was a new and exciting experience. I remember with special pleasure the evening I played MacDowell's
Concerto in D Major with the Baltimore Symphony. When
the Mayor of the city came to thank me after the concert was
over, he placed in my hand an envelope containing a check,
which I immediately returned as a gift to the orchestra. The
local papers made rather more of this incident than of my playing, though they were polite enough about that too. A year
later when the Baltimore Orchestra was conducting a drive for
funds, I found in my mail a reminder that I had formerly been
a valued contributor to the fund, and I was invited to contribute again. I had the impulse, which I resisted, to say that
I never made a contribution unless I was permitted to play.

It wasn't all peaches and cream. The more adept I became,
the more the critics enjoyed taking potshots at me. Richard
Stokes, music critic of the New York Evening World, roasted
me frequently. My technique was far from perfect. I invariably played too fast and I was at times over-emotional.

On December 1, 1928, a little less than two weeks after the
Baltimore concert, I played the Brahms Piano Quintet with
the Musical Art Quartet at the John Golden Theatre. In the
quartet were my Wilton friends—Sascha Jacobsen, Marie
Rosanoff, Paul Bernard, and Louis Kaufman.

This concert was a far-off result of the evenings we had
played at the Wilton Library. The Musical Art Quartet drew
a large audience of their admirers. I felt that my part in the
evening was no particular addition. The acoustics of the small

theater embarrassed me; I had too little experience to judge them correctly. But no matter whether my piano performances were good or bad, I continued like a juggler to keep my three plates, teaching, writing, and music, in the air.

The *Evening Telegram* called me "An Admirable Crichton" and, delving in the yearbooks of Trinity Parish, discovered that I had once been a Sunday-school superintendent! It was true. I took Father's place at St. Agnes for a time.

When a man becomes a novelist he mirrors his own life to the world. Some of my colleagues, professional pianists, used to tease me with anecdotes about amateurs like myself. For example:

There was once a man who played the clarinet. He would play anywhere, any time, at the drop of a hat.

Performing at a benefit for the local hospital, he noticed an attentive stranger in the front row. The piece executed at the moment was "My Old Kentucky Home, with Variations." The listener's eyes moistened. The soloist turned on more expression. The man in the front row shed large tears.

At the close of the program the amateur sought him out.

"If I am not mistaken, you did me the honor to follow my playing closely."

"I did."

"You seemed moved by it."

"I was."

"Are you from Kentucky, by chance?"

"No," said the man, "I am a clarinet player."

III

Music in its greatest moments is a social art. At its second best it permits the individual to show off.

For several years I played with the Plainfield Symphony under the leadership of Louis Bostelmann, one of my colleagues at the Juilliard School. This amateur orchestra owed its existence chiefly to the inspiration of DeWitt Barlow, citizen extraordinary and indefatigable musician. He was active on the local school board, and later mayor of the township. The concerts of the Symphony were always held in the high-school auditorium. He himself played the flute, a pupil of Georges Barrère. His enthusiasm drew other citizens of Plainfield to study the same instrument. Since the Symphony then had more flutes than cellos, Mr. Barlow switched over to the cello section and in no time at all, as it seemed to me, he mastered another difficult instrument. He was a delightful man with remarkable curiosity about the scientific aspect of music. On more than one occasion he gave the students at the Juilliard provocative and useful lectures on acoustics. His business was dredging. On occasion his dredges had gone after pirate gold.

A far more prosaic but memorable recital for me was at the Church of St. James the Less, in Scarsdale, New York.

I clearly recall my program:

Variations in E major . . . . Handel
Five Tone Pictures . . . . . Grieg
Intermezzo in A major . . . . Brahms

I took part in this little concert because it was given under the auspices of the church choir. One of the singers was an old college classmate of mine, and the choirmaster was my brother Robert.

Like a race horse on a clear track I continued my wild dash. César Franck was a favorite with me. I promptly learned his *Variations Symphoniques* and played it at Chautauqua with Albert Stoessel conducting. The masterly way in which he guided me through that difficult piece made me his friend for life. He was a superb musician of broad experience and excellent taste, as Walter Damrosch had been quick to realize at Chaumont. When his AEF service ended, Damrosch invited him to become assistant conductor of the Oratorio Society. He was assisting artist with Enrico Caruso during the singer's last tour of this country.

Eventually Walter Damrosch retired as conductor of the Oratorio Society, Stoessel succeeded him, and soon afterwards became musical director of the Worcester Festival and of the summer concerts of Chautauqua.

I can see him now as he stood on the platform of the Chautauqua concert hall directing the course of my impetuous playing. He was tall—over six feet—broad-shouldered and easy in his movements. His features were regular. He wore his thick brown hair parted in the middle, and he never raised his voice or lost his temper, yet he conducted with fire and brilliance. His musicians adored him. Those musicians were famous in their own right. I remember particularly Georges Barrère, the great French flutist, being a member of Stoessel's Chautauqua orchestra.

Barrère was always eager to encourage a love of French composers. Just where he ranked César Franck I don't know, though it is easy to imagine that he preferred some other French composers. But as the orchestra walked out of the hall the afternoon I performed, he said to me quietly, "Thank you for selecting such beautiful music to play."

I had already been decorated by the French Government after World War I. Some months after the Chautauqua incident I received notice that I had been advanced in the Legion from *Chevalier* to *Officier*. One of my sponsors for this promotion was Georges Barrère. I always attribute something of the honor to César Franck.

IV

I had an interesting insight into the reactions of the families of amateur musicians when I played the MacDowell Concerto with the Milwaukee Philharmonic Orchestra.

The Milwaukee audience, as might be expected, was unusually musical. The orchestra, though amateur, was made up of genuine artists, and their relatives in the audience gave them enthusiastic support. So many tickets were sold for the evening and afternoon concerts originally planned that I was asked to add a third concert, which I did with the greatest pleasure.

During the numbers on the program which preceded and followed the MacDowell I slipped into the gallery and studied the audience. They unconsciously revealed the extent to which the music had become part of their lives. All of them seemed to be relatives of the players, and they must have heard a great deal of rehearsing at home. In one concert I had seated myself by accident among the friends and relatives of the first flute. For them the concert divided itself naturally into purple patches. Their interest in the performance quickened whenever the first flute—let us call him Bill—raised his instrument to his lips.

"There goes Bill!" exclaimed one of them, as though the flute player were stepping up to bat.

The violins and the clarinets did their part in dividing the concert into various kinds of enthusiasm, always for a relative and his particular instrument. I have imagined how a resident of Milwaukee, on a quiet evening, listened to the next concert as it was rehearsed piecemeal, instrument by instrument, in the various homes. I have never forgotten the highly social aspects of a community with music practiced by amateurs.

Music constantly brought me into contact with old pupils at Columbia. I frequently saw Samuel Chotzinoff of NBC, a student of mine. In Newark, when I played the César Franck *Variations Symphoniques*, Philip Gordon conducted. In his Columbia days he kept his music to himself. But after making for himself a responsible position in the Newark school system, he rapidly developed his abilities as an orchestra organizer, a composer, and a conductor. The concerts which I played with him and his student-orchestra were among the most enjoyable in which I took part.

Through Carl Friedberg I received an invitation to play the MacDowell Concerto with the orchestra of Wiesbaden. It was at the rehearsals of that orchestra that the young Mac-

Dowell had tried out the concerto as he composed it. I made the engagement with the greatest pleasure, but other duties prevented me from going abroad that summer, and the Baden-Baden concert remains a pleasant dream.

Altoona, Pennsylvania, is a bright spot in my memory because of Russell Gerhart. He conducted when I played the Mozart Concerto in D major.

I found him a unique figure in American music. He was born in Altoona, went to Europe to become a violin virtuoso, got back in time to serve in World War I. After the war, when his family and neighbors expected him to continue with his early ambition, he surprised them all by staying in Altoona and hanging out his shingle as a violin teacher. He had gone abroad to study only because there was no good violin teacher in his native town. Perhaps there were others like him. He guessed right. He soon had plenty of pupils. In a year or so he organized a concert for them, borrowing the high-school auditorium. There was no price for the tickets, but halfway through the performance a silver collection was taken up, all of which he presented to his pupil performers. Naturally he rapidly acquired more pupils. They studied hard since only the best were allowed to play. Gradually wood-wind and brass players showed up and volunteered for the concerts. He soon had a full orchestra, and he continued to take up a silver collection and divide it among the players.

Gerhart trained his best violinists to teach their instrument, and they became his assistants. For a long time he has taught only the top-flight talents, and since he is much sought after as a teacher his income from this source has been comfortable indeed. He owns his home, conducts the concerts, occasionally plays as soloist or appears as soloist with other orchestras. The Altoona Philharmonic is now a first-rate organization, able to engage the same soloists as the New York Philharmonic or the Chicago orchestra.

He has made his city music-wise, and has discovered a way to put a major orchestra on a sound economic basis. In this respect he is considerably ahead of the symphony organizations in any large city which I know.

V

Ernest Hutcheson asked me recently what I thought of music in America. The question was prompted by a remark of mine—I had played with something like two hundred different amateur orchestras in all parts of the United States.

I feel it should be a matter for reflection that our orchestras, whether professional or amateur, are occupied chiefly, almost exclusively, with masterpieces of another age or of other countries than ours. If we are not careful, the growing love of art in our country which leads young and old to practice music may end in the sterile condition of the old Chinese scholarship. So much has been accomplished by earlier and truly creative periods that, if we devote ourselves to memorizing and repeating the best that has already been thought and said and done, we shall have no time left to do our own living, or to express the ideals which spring from first-hand knowledge of life.

It may be I am dreaming too much of a millennium. There are things I would like to dream of about which I am not yet optimistic. For example, if conductors and concert artists would profit by my wise words, I think they would never make up a program without finding out about the good music their audience would like to hear. It may be that the great orchestras that come to our city do ask in advance what the children in the music schools and the high school are studying at the moment. I never heard of it, but it may be they do. It may be that the touring virtuoso or pianist asks, What are the children studying in the music course in your school? It wouldn't be so hard to put on the program one masterpiece they have just studied and send word to the children that now they have a chance to hear it. The reason I am not so optimistic is that it involves a thoroughly democratic point of view. For that point of view you must not only cease to ignore your audience but you must respect it, you must look up to it, you must really believe that when turned loose to express what it wants your audience will like just as good music as you like. That is what I believe. That is what old Europe did not believe. That is what we must believe—have faith in—before we will get back in our own way to a condition the arts once were in, when the artist thought of himself as rendering a public service, the most honorable in the world, for which he was to have an honorable and frank return. As when Blind Homer was careful to seize a position in the market place where the crowd was thickest, and the crowd immediately doubled or tripled because they had heard him before and he was about to sing again.

✠✠✠

CHAPTER TWELVE

School Centers

I

FORTUNATELY for my temperament the presidency of the Juilliard did not keep me stationary. In the last twenty-five years I have had the opportunity to see every state in the Union at least several times. All that traveling adds up to only a superficial acquaintance with the country. Yet there are large regions where the arts, it seems to me, are in a more flourishing condition than in New York. By that I mean the arts in those advanced places are springing out of the natural soil and occupying a natural place in the social life.

The young people who graduate from music schools have technique and proficiency. Nothing remains but to persuade people to listen to them. They must have something to say. At first what young artists produce is the expression of their youth. Later we begin to demand that they play and sing so that in their music we can listen to ourselves.

I urge familiarity with the masterpieces in all the arts—those engaged in one branch of art are likely to know too little about the others. Wherever I went on Juilliard business I hammered away at the quality of the teaching of music. It took effect.

In 1930 the President of the New Mexico College of Agriculture and Mechanical Arts asked me if the Juilliard School could and would supply him with a good violin teacher. At the moment he had two members on his faculty who were graduated from the Juilliard or the Institute of Musical Art, but he had no violin teacher. The inquiry suggested an idea which we soon put in force, not only in his school, but elsewhere in the United States. I wrote that we had a young and very gifted student, H. (Hine) Arthur Brown, a pupil of Paul Kochanski, to do the teaching he wished. We would gladly send Hine for three years, without any cost to the Agricultural College for the first year. If his teaching was satisfactory we would expect the Agricultural College to pay a part of his salary the second year, a larger part the third year, and after that to assume all of the salary. I added that we would pay Brown as a representative of the Juilliard at this center at the rate of $3,000 annually. We would also provide him with a small car so that he could get around in the neighborhood of the college, and we should expect him to give as many recitals as he found were desired; we didn't wish him to cease to be a performing artist.

Finally I added what I knew was a stiff condition. I said that Hine Brown had an unusual gift for conducting which ought to be developed, and I would send him to the college for service on its faculty if he could have an orchestra to conduct—an orchestra, no matter how modest. After a while the President of the College wrote to ask who would pay for the orchestra. I replied, the Agricultural College, of course. After another long silence the President surprised me by writing a cheerful inquiry whether I would be satisfied with an orchestra in Texas rather than in New Mexico. El Paso, just forty miles away, already had the rudiments of an orchestra which needed a conductor. He could arrange very easily with the backers of the orchestra in El Paso to incorporate their orchestra in the Juilliard plan.

I replied at once that so far as I could see El Paso was as good a place for an orchestra as New Mexico. The Juilliard School sent Hine Brown in 1930. In due time he gave his first concert in El Paso. The effect upon the music lovers in the landscape was, to me at least and perhaps to others, rather surprising. Many people drove in to hear the music, in some cases coming a long distance. They ate at the local restaurants or stopped at the local hotels, and the town discovered that music, even in that frontier district, might be a profitable business.

Very shortly El Paso took over the responsibility of Hine's salary, and he became employed, not by the Agricultural College, but by El Paso. His ardent admirer and backer was the leading newspaper publisher, Dorrance Roderick, who helped Brown organize the El Paso Symphony Orchestra. He has continued his work with increasing success, building up his orchestra, inaugurating choral concerts, bringing well-known soloists to El Paso, and inevitably enlarging his reputation as an indefatigable pioneer.

After three years in El Paso the Juilliard sent Hine to head the University of Louisville string and orchestra departments, and to conduct the Louisville Symphony, at the same time continuing as conductor of the El Paso Symphony Orchestra by commuting between the cities by air. Two years later the El Paso Symphony Association raised sufficient funds to assume Brown's salary, and he returned to that city as full-time conductor.

Hine's list of guest appearances include the Federal orchestras of Los Angeles, San Francisco, and Seattle; the Dallas summer season in 1933, and the Nashville Symphony. He now conducts the Tulsa Philharmonic Orchestra and the New Orleans Summer "Pops" Orchestra.

The Juilliard School has established more than twenty similar music centers throughout the United States. Two of them deserve special mention.

II

In 1929 the musical interests in Atlanta asked the School to send a representative to their city to organize what they reported as a waning popular enthusiasm for opera and symphonic music.

As usual we consulted Olga Samaroff, who knew the Atlanta district and something of its musical problem. She suggested that we send as our representative Miss Helen Riley, a young singer, whose general musical equipment and understanding of human problems Madame Samaroff greatly admired. It was arranged at once that Miss Riley should undertake the Atlanta work, and to start it off with something of a flourish I asked Madame Samaroff to go with me to Atlanta and introduce Miss Riley to the audiences before whom she would represent us. I took with us Sascha Jacobsen, the violinist, and Marie Rosanoff, the cellist, and on the inaugural evening we gave the invited audience a brief recital. Just why we did so, I do not now remember, but the Atlanta people were most cordial and seemed happy, and I returned to the School feeling that something important had been inaugurated.

At the next meeting of the School trustees I was asked by one of the Board what chance there was for the permanent success of these newly established centers. I remember now the frivolous reply I made which caused my colleagues to laugh, but which perhaps did not otherwise impress them. I said that Miss Riley was sure to succeed in Atlanta one way or another, and if the success was not immediate I would suggest that we send to Atlanta not a musical adviser but an oculist. As a matter of fact Helen Riley became Mrs. Howard C. Smith almost inside of the year.

In time she organized the Atlanta Symphony Guild which now sustains the City Symphony, and during the present sea-

son (1949-1950) she has been elected the Atlanta Woman of
the Year in the Arts. The citation which accompanied this
award pays tribute to her long and tireless work in carrying
music to the privileged and underprivileged alike.

III

Of all these representatives of the Juilliard, Jacques Jolas,
now head of the piano department of Cornell College, Mount
Vernon, Iowa, has proved the most useful as a teacher, as an
organizer of musical education, and as an inspiration to music
generally. He came to our attention at the School not as a student but as a possible addition to our piano faculty. He is a
well-trained pianist, and until he suffered an injury in his
right hand was an altogether brilliant one. But the School
already had plenty of piano teachers, and Madame Samaroff,
with her characteristic ability to recognize various kinds of
musical talent, suggested the moment she met him that the
proper career for Jacques Jolas lay in the field of teaching and
educational organization.

The School first sent him to Harrisburg to assist in the organization of an orchestra there. He then went to Louisville
at the request of the local authorities to reorganize and build
up a small musical conservatory. His final post as a Juilliard
representative was at Cornell College, which has taken him
on as a permanent member of its faculty. With immense
pluck and energy he has resumed his piano playing after a
serious illness, and now devotes much time to original composition. He has made himself known and widely recognized as
one of the dynamic forces in American music, both in the
United States and in Canada at the Banff School of Fine Arts.

Some of his winter pupils accompany him to the Canadian
resort, which is rapidly taking on the character of a summer
session.

The quality of Jolas' teaching seems to me unique; he does
not slight the technical aspects of piano playing, and his

pupils are excellent performers. But he cares most about the soul of music, and he develops in his pupils what I should call the inner life of music, the qualities of introspection and poetry.

At Cornell I have visited him and watched his work with his pupils and his influence on the whole school. He is the rarest kind of teacher: a poet, a philosopher, a spiritual leader. I am proud that in my administration the Juilliard School sent him out. No other teacher of my acquaintance is likely to contribute deeper or more precious things to musical education in the United States.

The Juilliard School also sent to Cornell College a Juilliard graduate who specialized in the teaching of voice, Mr. Francis German. He was the School's representative from 1931-1935, when Cornell College retained him as a member of its permanent faculty. Mr. German has maintained a fine record with his voice students, paralleling the progress of Mr. Jolas with his piano students.

The centers are not intended to be permanent in any one spot, at least not so far as the Juilliard benefaction is concerned. It is hoped that the presence of a competent musician in a community may develop the musical possibilities of the neighborhood to a point where the local musical program can keep itself going.

IV

I soon found that to maintain these centers involved frequent visits from myself or from members of the faculty. It was useful to have first-hand information about what was being done in our name. During a visit to any place I found myself usually invited to make addresses of one kind or another, or even to give a recital. The expense of these trips was considerable.

But the fact that practically all communities expected me to play the piano when I visited them compelled me to do a large amount of practicing which I had never thought of undertaking. When I accepted the Juilliard presidency, it was as an educator, not a musician. But I soon felt embarrassed not to play at least respectably. For a number of years my practicing amounted to two or three hours a day, even when I was not on tour, and for special performances more preparation was required. With an ever increasing amount of work to do this lengthy practice was almost impossible.

Then I remembered something Carl Walter once told me. He asked how much practicing I was doing for him.

"Oh, three or four hours a day."

"Do you practice in long stretches, an hour at a time?"

"I try to."

"Well, don't! When you grow up, time won't come in long stretches. Practice in minutes, whenever you can find them—five or ten before school, before lunch, between other tasks. Spread the practice through the day, and piano playing will become part of your life."

When he told me this I was about fourteen years old. So far as I can remember, I forgot his advice until much later, when I was teaching in college. I wanted to write, but recitations, theme reading, and committee meetings filled my days and evenings. During the first two years of teaching I wrote practically nothing, and my excuse was that I had no time. At the beginning of the third year, however, I recalled what Carl Walter had said.

I put an extra table in my study, where I could leave my manuscripts when I went out and find them undisturbed when I came in. Whenever I had five unoccupied minutes I sat down at that table and wrote a hundred words or more. At the end of the week I had a sizeable manuscript ready for revision.

Still later, when I was teaching at Columbia, I wrote novels by the same piecemeal method. Though my University schedule was heavy, in every day there were moments which could be caught. Now I could apply the same method once again to my piano playing, following literally Carl Walter's advice.

To my astonishment, I discovered that the small intervals of the day were enough for both the executive work, the writing, and the piano practice.

There is an important trick in this time-using formula; you must get into your work quickly. If you have but five minutes for writing, you can't afford to waste four chewing your pencil. Of course you will turn over in your mind what to write when you find another moment, and if you are looking forward to a bit of piano practice you will probably play the piece over in your head before you get to the piano. But even with this mental preparation there must be almost instantaneous concentrating. Fortunately it's easier than most of us think. This was the most helpful lesson I had from Carl Walter. I put it to test again and again.

If there was a local orchestra in the neighborhood of my visits, I was booked up. I liked attention. I'm frank to admit I enjoyed the spotlight. I was made particularly happy by what Mrs. William Brown Meloney wrote of me in the *Delineator*. "Erskine has proved Plutarch's philosophy that a man who can do one thing well can do many things well. He is an administrator, proving this when he ran the biggest college in the world, the University of the AEF. He is a dreamer; his poetry betrays him. He believes in youth; the students of Columbia University call him 'Roaring Jack' Erskine, and cut their classes to slip into his lectures. He might have made his fame as a musician. He is a composer, plays with distinction and can pack a hall any time the university announces one of his recitals."

I had sense enough to know this wouldn't last. A few of my friends did too.

Alfred Knopf said to me, "Some day they will put poison in your tea. You have too good a time."

❧❧

CHAPTER THIRTEEN

Artists in the Grand Style

I

TODAY, in the spread of what we hope may become a truly democratic spirit, some artists are afraid to be called aristocrats. Democracy is a generous social ideal, but in art it may carry with it the threat of commonness, of vulgarity—at times, of meanness. The democratic artist is too often content to express his fellow men as they are. The artist in the grand style, on the other hand, the aristocratic artist, dedicates himself as a kind of high priest to speak for human nature at its best. We call this kind of artist aristocratic because he lifts up his audience by the inspiration of beauty until they become aristocrats, at least for the moment.

Such an artist was Olga Samaroff Stokowski. No one knew and loved her art more than she did, but she never took a small view of it. She always saw human life in the large, and she saw music in its place in society. She never thought of music as a function of entertainment which began or ended in the concert hall. She never thought of it as concerning only the performer. Everyone should be a music lover, she thought, and if they were not there was something in them asleep which a great teacher could awaken. Music perhaps as the Greeks taught it, and as she loved to say in her more abstract and philosophical moments, which I admit were rare—she was too busy to indulge in abstractions—probably the Greeks were right that in music, if anywhere, man could find some key to the universe, some key to harmony, and rhythm, and melody. But she was quite sure that those who did not appreciate to the fullest this lovely art needed some miraculous aid, as though their eyes should be touched by the Divine hand and their eyes opened, or their ears touched so that they could hear.

She organized a brilliantly original method, The Layman's Music Courses, to teach the listener as well as the performer. She taught her pupils and taught her colleagues to appreciate more fully the social aspects of music. It seemed to me at times that she always had in mind what is to me one of the most superb, one of the most Divine ideas of the philosophy of Plato: That our knowledge of the finest things is another form of memory; that the soul in some previous existence had gone on the heavenly ride, following the chariots of the gods and catching sight of the Divine abstractions of strength, of honor, of love, of beauty; and in life, seeing something strong or something beautiful, we should feel a kind of homesickness, a slight pain, a longing which was the memory of earthly things in their pure state, and by loving the memory it would strengthen and create here perhaps something like the oneness we had seen develop.

When I first knew her at the Juilliard School, I think it is correct to say that she was not much interested in amateurs. Naturally, I was aware of that. She was a great professional. At that time I think she thought that a music school, to be great, should center its training on great professionals, great performers. I watched her change that point of view. It was very illuminating to see through the years how the scope of her concept of musical education grew and deepened. But the most remarkable thing to watch was that she lost nothing of her personal point of view, of her broadened ideas—not as some of us do by abandoning some earlier ideas, simply making a change—but that at the end of her life she excelled more than ever as a teacher of great pianists, of pupils that were a glory to them, and to herself, and to others. And she had added the interest of the layman, as she called the listener, in the problems of all kinds of music, in the possibilities of new kinds of composition and new kinds of harmony, and endlessly embroidered her life with the human race. She died suddenly in 1948, but I find myself still thinking of her in the present tense as the colleague and teacher of us all. She thought of her pupils as her colleagues. She counted on them never to give up anything good which time seemed eager to snatch away. She had loved the music of Europe. She had been feted in Vienna and Berlin and the other great cities. She was too magnificent a soul ever to be untrue to her memories, although times had changed and most of us thought of Europe with a certain sadness. She had known great people there and they were great always in her memory.

She counted on her pupils and she counts on them today, I am sure, to think of her as engaged as always in this pursuit of music and truth and human kindness which we knew as making her life. And she counts on her pupils as doing the same work after her.

It would not be entirely true to say that Leopold Stokowski owes his career to her. Yet, in a sense he does. She recognized his genius. She helped him at a time when he most needed help. On occasion it irked him. He once said, "I wish to God that Olga were not always so right."

She had a magnificence of character that amounted to saintliness. She was a friend of the wife who succeeded her. Her home was home to his children. It was she who suggested that we invite him to give a concert with the Juilliard orchestra.

We paid him $3,000 for conducting one performance, but he deserved every bit of it. He drilled the students for a week. I used to slip in the back of the auditorium a couple of times each day to see how things were going. He was very gentle with the students—like Olga, he had a very original attitude toward youth. She thought of youth as singing the tune of life known as the prelude to age.

He worked hard with our Juilliard boys and girls. The night of the concert, just before he raised his baton, I heard him say, "I want to tell you something. You're going to play the most beautiful concert that has ever been played." They did.

I watched Olga's face during the performance. It told me more than she had ever said, or not said, that she still loved him.

She and Irmgart Hutcheson were closest of friends, and together they organized the Schubert Memorial concerts, which attempted to provide new opportunities for young American artists to make their debut.

II

By fortunate accident, I believe, rather than by any thoroughly studied plan of Dr. Noble's, the piano teachers at the Juilliard Graduate School when I went to it represented various traditions and styles of teaching and playing. Ernest Hutcheson, completely English in temperament, preserved the best that Leipzig could teach in his time. Josef Lhevinne was the incarnation of the tone poetry in which Russian pianists excelled. Carl Friedberg, thoroughly original genius, was on the way to become a doctor of medicine before he transferred his allegiance to music. His attitude toward himself is that of a physician. His dinner parties are sybaritic feasts—the finest wines, the most epicurean food. Yet he himself is a vegetarian with a birdlike appetite. As the years pass he becomes increasingly frail, but he continues to show surprising energy in his teaching and playing. He had been a devoted admirer of Brahms, in the playing of whose music he still excels. He is the kindest of friends, and all of us have been indebted to advice generously given and which we should now refer to as psychology—advice as to how to control the nerves in musical performance, and how to build up a desirable effect upon the audience. Not least important among his kind services to his friends has been much good advice as to diet and health. He will remain to the end a passionate lover of music, but he will remain also at heart a physician, a healer.

Mr. and Mrs. Ernest Hutcheson and I lived for several years in the same house, 11 West Eighty-first Street. I had the penthouse, they a delightful old-fashioned high-ceilinged apartment on the second floor.

I protested, after accepting a couple of successive invitations to Sunday lunch, that I did not want to become a permanent boarder. But Irmgart overruled my objections. For the three years I was in the penthouse I lunched practically every Sunday with the Hutchesons. The guests were usually musicians: Alexander Siloti, Paderewski, the Josef Hofmanns, Jascha Heifetz and his first wife Florence Vidor, the Ossip Gabrilowitsches, Ernest and Lucy Schelling, Paul and Zosia Kochanski, Paul Reimers, Mr. and Mrs. Francis Rogers, Harold Samuels, Bruno Walter, Toscanini, Mme. Sembrich, Alma Gluck and Efrem Zimbalist, Mr. and Mrs. Albert Spalding, Rosina and Josef Lhevinne, Harold Bauer, the Walter Damrosches, the Felix Salmonds, Mr. and Mrs. Sergei Rachmaninoff, Leopold Stokowski, the Albert Stoessels, and Madame Anna Schoen-René who had known Ernest and Irmgart in Weimar. There were many others, of course, but these people remain clearly in my memory.

For one thing I was always struck by the fact that most of them had met years before in Europe. Ernest Hutcheson and Alexander Siloti had been under the same concert management in Russia.

Alexander Siloti was of course always a case apart among the Juilliard piano teachers, since he had been the favorite pupil of Liszt, and this fact always carried for Siloti peculiar implications. During the years when I knew him the tall kindly gentleman glided in casual conversation from one language to another, as though he found all the languages of Europe somewhat inadequate to convey his impulsive meanings. In his later years he gave most of his time to teaching, only on rare occasions returning to the concert platform, but invariably he explained to his colleagues that he would not have returned at all if Liszt had not appeared to him in a dream and scolded him for neglecting his art. This spooky information he conveyed to us with the utmost simplicity and sincerity. None of us doubted that Liszt had indeed in some mysterious way paid him a visit. The date of the concert would then be announced, the program would be a difficult one, requiring much practicing, and shortly before the announced performance Siloti would reassure all his friends by the further announcement that Liszt had told him only the night before that the practicing had been going well and the concert would be certainly a great success. Being then free of all doubt or worry, the old gentleman would mount the platform with superb confidence and would play like the demigod he was. Those latest recitals of his I rank among the privileges of my life to hear.

Siloti was not only a remarkable artist, he was a superb gentleman, a survival from the old imperial Russia. No one could catch him off guard, not even his most daring pupils, all of whom adored him but not all of whom treated him invariably with the courtly manners of imperial Russia.

One day when I was standing in the hall of the School building I overheard half a dozen of Siloti's pupils, girls and boys, arguing whether their teacher, as an old legend suggested, was merely Liszt's favorite pupil, or perhaps also his favorite child. At that moment the elevator came down with Siloti in it, and one of the boldest pupils, a girl if I remember correctly, suggested that they put the question to Siloti himself. I found it easy to hang around to see what would happen.

"Mr. Siloti, we have a serious question which you can answer better than anyone else. Was Liszt your father?"

Siloti was startled, but he smiled delightfully. "That question," he said, "once had a special meaning for me, and I did exactly what you are doing; I took the problem to the one person I knew who might give me the answer. I asked Liszt himself. He studied me for a moment. 'Well, let us see. What was your mother's name, Alexander? Where was she living when you were born, and where during the previous year?' I told him. He began counting thoughtfully on his fingers. Then suddenly he smiled and patted me on the back. 'My dear Alexander, to my great regret it is impossible.' "

Siloti was essentially a shy man. Paderewski, of course, was quite the opposite. He dominated any company. He had two loves, children and poker. Whenever he came to New York from Europe he brought countless presents to Mr. Urchs' children. We would come in to find him sitting on the floor trying out some toy with them. His gifts to the grown people were bottles of champagne—they came last.

He traveled like a prince, in a private car, with a group of friends—all poker players. The game never stopped. The private car would be parked on a siding, Paderewski would dash off for his concert, dash back, pick up his cards and continue the game. He looked like a superman. His mop of hair was red when I first saw him. Later it was white. I met him often at Ernest Schelling's apartment. Schelling had been a pupil of his. They were neighbors in Switzerland.

In 1934 there was a series of concerts at Madison Square Garden for the benefit of unemployed musicians. Paderewski and Rachmaninoff were on the program. Ernest Hutcheson and I both spoke. Paderewski played the first night. I was a little troubled. I wondered how even a great pianist could make himself heard in that enormous arena with so much steelwork and so many echoes. To my surprise even those in the farthest balcony heard every note. I asked Paderewski after the concert how he had made this possible.

"By playing every note very slowly," he said. "Only in that way can interference of this sort be overcome."

More than anyone else he represented the artist's approach to life. What inspired him was a positive and creative love. Music to him was one kind of music—the music of Bach, Beethoven, Liszt, Schubert, Mozart, and above all Chopin. He played them with a romantic worship which made his concerts a ritual. Paderewski always gave his own interpretation. After hearing him play Chopin at Madison Square Garden, I decided that if Chopin did not intend that it be played that way the error was Chopin's.

The next evening Rachmaninoff played at the correct tempo and only those in the front rows were able to hear him.

III

In the string faculty the outstanding teachers who joined the Juilliard were Paul Kochanski, Hans Letz, Felix Salmond, Edouard Dethier, and Louis Persinger, who was appointed in 1930 on the death of Leopold Auer. The last four still teach at the School with prestige undiminished. Letz was always a notable exponent of chamber music, and with Felix Salmond he still has charge of instruction in that special field, in addition to teaching violin playing. Salmond is the School's most notable teacher of the cello.

Paul Kochanski, whose early death in 1934 made the School feel its first serious loss, was one of the finest characters I have met anywhere in education. He was not only a master of his instrument, but an impassioned teacher of it for all competent pupils. Many of his pupils still talk of his generosity in giving them his time and advice. I personally am indebted to him for many hours of sonata playing, which made me in a sense his pupil. Whenever he came to my home or I went to his, he assumed without debate or discussion that we should at once practice Brahms or Beethoven or Mozart together, and as my competence was so inferior to his own he would give me the benefit of his knowledge and experience tactfully and without stint.

He was a delightful companion since, like Siloti, he was

supplied with inexhaustible humor, and like Siloti he served the School with a devotion that I began to think must be characteristic of Slavic people. Before his fatal illness struck him down, he was a remarkable wit and fun maker for all his friends. He did not equal Siloti in the occasional somewhat boisterous expressions of his high spirits, especially on the concert stage. The last concert which Siloti played happened to be at the Juilliard School, and I wondered why the student orchestra burst into laughter when the soloist left the platform. Feeling that they needed extremely severe discipline to correct their unseemly manners, I asked Oscar Wagner what on earth Mr. Siloti said or did just at that moment. Oscar broke the news to me that Mr. Siloti, who was extremely loose-jointed or even double-jointed, gave release to his own joy in having played well by scratching his ear with his right leg.

Kochanski, on the other hand, behaved with impeccable dignity in all public appearances, but in private he was well known for his amusing clowning. His colleagues at any informal gathering were likely to ask for his impersonation of orchestral players and the effect of their particular instrument on the characteristic expression on their faces. He would illustrate the difference between the player of the first violin and the player of the second, since the first violinist can look at the audience when he isn't glancing up at the conductor, and of course he cultivates the muscles on the back of the neck which are used in glancing down at his admirers. The flute player gradually has his face frozen into a different kind of surprise from the clarinet player, who flavors his astonishment with a mild expression of contempt.

As a teacher Paul Kochanski had the rarest of gifts, the ability to recognize in the young student talent or the lack of it. Of the candidates who presented themselves for entrance there sometimes were a few who to other teachers seemed not particularly gifted, but Kochanski was sure of their talent. His opinion was invariably justified in the outcome. By way of contrast, pupils of Kochanski's colleagues might seem beyond question talented, but if they failed to win his vote at entrance, in time his opinion usually was justified. I think he judged applicants less by their technical equipment at the moment than by deeper spiritual hints to which he was peculiarly sensitive—indications of their inner life and therefore of the directions in which they were likely to develop.

IV

In most music schools, so far as I have known them, the weakest spot is either the vocal or the composition department. The head of the vocal department at the Juilliard was Madame Marcella Sembrich, a great singer, a great human being, and a great voice teacher. While I was president of the Juilliard I was told on many occasions that she was not a good teacher of the voice, but invariably the information came from another voice teacher who had called on me for the strange purpose of applying for her job.

Apparently some vocal teachers are capable of extraordinary audacities, all of course in the disinterested cause of art. But I never agreed with the self-serving critics who thought that Madame Sembrich or any other accomplished singer who taught at the Juilliard was out of place there. With her were associated for many years Anna Schoen-René, Paul Reimers, and Francis Rogers. In Madame Sembrich's later years she had associated with her as assistant Florence Kimball (Mrs. Schuyler Smith), her own pupil, who still supplies much of the strength of the Juilliard vocal faculty. Like the great teacher she is, she wisely gives her attention to her pupils in special classes or purely social gatherings, which her pupils perhaps remember as the most precious part of their instruction. For years I have looked forward to the Christmas parties in which her girls have sung for her and her friends, and on occasion she has sung for them.

Her willingness to put her lovely voice as well as her teaching skill at the service of the School has impressed me more than once.

At the end of World War I, I went to a concert with René Galland, a member of the English faculty at Grenoble University. A soprano sang Chausson's lovely *Poème de l'Amour et de la Mer*. Not having heard this great music again, I said to Florence Kimball one day that I wished she would sing it. At the next concert at the School she and Albert Stoessel put it on the program, and her performance of the solo with the School orchestra remains a happy memory.

Madame Schoen-René excelled as a teacher of contraltos, baritones, and basses. Madame Sembrich did most for voices like her own. Miss Kimball, following her methods, during Edward Johnson's administration at the Metropolitan, supplied the Opera with many of the young sopranos who are now well known throughout the country.

When I first knew Paul Reimers, his health had begun to decline, and his reputation, once remarkably bright as a lieder singer, was wearing thin. I can recall only one public recital that he gave during my administration.

Francis Rogers also had already made his mark as a singer when I began to meet him daily at the School. He was, and still is, an artist of the highest ideals, and is rare among singers, who usually have too little time for reading in the history of their art.

Sembrich, Schoen-René, Reimers, Rogers and Kimball, the original vocal faculty, could hardly be matched for the inspiration as well as the skill they imparted to their students.

The Bohemians, New York's musicians' club, gave a dinner in honor of Madame Sembrich at the Hotel Commodore on December 18, 1927. The date was in commemoration of her debut, fifty years before on June 3, 1877, when she sang the leading soprano role of *I Puritane* at Phelarion, the summer resort of Athens. The toastmaster was Rubin Goldmark, president of the Club. On Madame Sembrich's right sat Otto H. Kahn, representing the Metropolitan Opera, where she sang regularly from its first year, 1886, until her retirement in 1909. In the anteroom before the guest of honor took her place at the table, Mr. Kahn tried hard to persuade her to cancel her resignation at the Metropolitan and to sing at least one more performance. I heard her amusing rebuff of what was a well-deserved tribute but which might not have served her great reputation if she had been less wise than she was.

"Mr. Kahn," she said, "I withdrew from the operatic stage when I thought it was time. Do you now wish me to make a public demonstration that even then I was right?"

CHAPTER FOURTEEN

++

Changes

I

THE ACADEMIC life is an ivory tower only if you insist on making it so. If you feel its walls are too confining, let it be your comfort to notice that it also has doors.

Because I was still hungry for music I played much. I had been so long in the classroom that it was strange to appear before an audience as a pianist. I was still nervous. That, I knew, could only be overcome in one way—by appearing before more audiences. I needed experience so I got it. Newspapers began to call me, "The amazing Professor Erskine." The *New York Times* described me as "a dignified and competent professor of English in Columbia University who has a way of startling the world by doing something different."

Time magazine, in reporting a recital at which I played, said "Astonishment was general."

Was this because at forty-six I had dared to live more fully?

We have exaggerated the importance of youth. We convince ourselves that youth is the time to learn, that education is completed somewhere around the twentieth year. To prop up this theory we say that youth is the time for daring,

youth has the spirit of initiative. This idea is fostered by the
young themselves. Along with this doctrine we hold that
youth is the time for branching out, but in middle age we
should settle down. After thirty or thirty-five we ought to
know just where we belong—our destined spot on the shelf
in the cabinet of fossils. We say that by the end of our youth
we ought to be grounded and rooted in our life work. Co-
lumbus, that is, should have remained a local pilot, Michel-
angelo never should have painted the Sistine chapel, and
Pasteur should have continued to manufacture wine and beer.

The truth is that only in middle age can we be daring, in
the good as well as the bad sense. Read your Ovid again,
your Cellini, or your Rousseau.

The moment you say, "If I only had my life to live over
again," you are ready not to die, but to live; you have your
chance at last.

II

Pauline spent most of 1928 and a portion of 1929 in France
with the children. When she returned to New York she took
an apartment at 39 East Ninety-third Street. Anna and
Graham were attending Horace Mann. Week ends and vaca-
tions they spent at Nod Hill in Wilton, now a country gentleman's estate. The royalties from my novel *Galahad* dug the
artesian well, the income from *Adam and Eve* made the remodeling of the barn possible. The Meyers brothers converted
it into an enormous playroom and laid a handsome oak floor
so that the children, as they grew older, might have a place
in which to give Saturday night dances. The barn was wired
for electricity. Graham and I made some unique side lights—
tin pie pans bent in half which served as reflectors. For refreshments there were soda pop, popcorn, and peanuts. A
victrola and later a radio furnished the music. Either Pauline
or some neighbor acted as chaperone. The dances became an
institution. Parents thanked us and we thanked ourselves. At
least we all knew where our children were on Saturday nights.

Pauline and the children each had cars. I also gave them saddle horses. I wasn't too keen about riding, but Pauline loved horses as I did music. It was only fair that she enjoy life her own way. The children rode well and they and she often won ribbons in the local horse shows.

I could never see any merit in purposeless riding. In the years when horses were a means of transportation, there was a real reason for using them. Perhaps that is something I've inherited from my practical Yorkshire mother.

In the autumn of 1929 I moved myself and my piano to the Berkshire Hotel. Before I did this I made certain that my neighbor, a wholesale dress manufacturer, did not object to my practicing.

"Make as much noise as you want to," he said, "I like music."

The Berkshire was on the same street with the Juilliard School. I invariably took some musician back to the hotel for luncheon or dinner, and usually had the meals served in my room. After we had eaten there was always music. I look upon this period as a very happy one. My books and short stories were bringing in fabulous sums; I was free to play the piano as much and as often as I wished, and I was having a share in the development of music in this country. At the same time I was lecturing and playing with symphony orchestras. Occasionally I felt weary, and when I did I thought of France. Some day, I told myself, I would live in Beaune. But that was only a dream. The activity of the present always awakened me.

I sailed on the *Paris* on July 18, 1931. I was bound for the Second Anglo-American Music Education Conference at Lausanne, Switzerland. Percy Scholes, the English educator, had thought up the idea as a means of spreading culture and good will among Anglo-Saxons. He was a rare breed of musician—an optimist. His fellow accomplice was Paul J. Weaver, professor of music at Cornell University. He had coaxed me to the second conference. I was to be co-chairman with Sir

William Henry Hadow, editor of the *Oxford History of Music*.

When I boarded the *Paris* I wondered why I had said that I would go. Five days later I knew. On the last morning out a steward interrupted a chess game I was having with Edward H. Blanc, a New York attorney. Would I give Captain Pugnet the pleasure of lunching with him?

I finished the game and left for the luncheon several minutes late. Among the guests was Helen Worden of the *New York World-Telegram*. After a very rich meal the Captain suggested music. He was an extraordinarily versatile man. In addition to being a great sailor, he was an amateur boxer and musician. He not only made music but had built the instrument on which to play it—an upright piano which stood against one wall of his cabin.

I tried out its tone with César Franck's Sonata. Captain Pugnet accompanied me on a violin of his own manufacture. The combined effect was just what you might expect. I had not noticed Helen Worden particularly until the Captain and I began our din. She not only turned the pages, but asked for an encore.

Next morning on the boat train I changed my ticket from second to first class to breakfast with her. That night we dined at Chez Francis, a typical French restaurant close by the Seine. Over a chateaubriand, *pommes frit*, and a bottle of Chambertin I told her about Beaune and my dreams of returning to it. She listened attentively. Here was a girl who did not take my dreams lightly.

At Lausanne I found myself among many musical friends at the Palace-Beau-Site Hotel: Paul Weaver; Mrs. W. L. Mc-Farland, president of the National Music Supervisors Conference; Harold Vincent Milligan, president of the National Association of Organists; Russell V. Morgan of Cleveland, head of the National Music Supervisors Conference; and John P. Marshall, professor of music at Boston University.

Among the British musicians were Stanley Roper, organist

of the Royal Chapel at Windsor; Ernest Bullock, organist
and choirmaster of Westminster Abbey; Sir Henry Hadow;
W. G. Whitaker of Glasgow; and Ernest MacMillan, principal of the Toronto Conservatory of Music, who was later
knighted by the King for his fine work.

I was disappointed to find no French, Russian, Italian, or
German musicians. It was strictly an Anglo-Saxon affair. I
particularly missed Isidor Philipp, greatest of all French
piano teachers. I longed for Leopold Godowsky and Ossip
Gabrilowitsch. They were in Paris. It was only a day's ride
to Lausanne. Their humor would have brightened the work.
Together they were irrepressible. A few weeks before they had
gone to the Salle Playel to hear an American pianist, the
daughter of a mutual friend.

After the first number Ossip reached for his hat. "I can
stand it no longer."

"But you must," said Godowsky. "How will you explain
it later?"

"I don't care what you tell her," said Ossip. "I've never
heard anything quite so bad as this before."

With that he walked out. In the evening he and Godowsky
met at dinner.

"How long did you stand it?" he demanded.

"Oh, I stayed until the end," said Godowsky. "I even
went backstage to see the girl."

"What on earth could you say to her?"

Godowsky grinned. "I said, 'I congratulate you, my dear.
Your playing is unique. Mr. Gabrilowitsch says there is nothing like it.'"

When the Lausanne Conference ended I could understand
why Gabrilowitsch and Godowsky did not attend.

I do not believe in conferences on the arts. They may
demonstrate that artists can be friends, but they stultify the
creative.

To produce great music, great pictures, or great literature

an artist must have solitude. After his work is finished he needs an audience, not a debating society.

I will admit, however, that beautiful music livened the conference. Inga Hill, a young Minnesota girl who was studying at the Juilliard, sang gorgeously. Ethel Bartlett and Rae Robertson, the two-piano team, performed brilliantly in the hotel's Old World grand ballroom. The Prague String Quartet, Yves Tinayre, and Beryl Rubinstein also delighted us with fine music.

But aside from pleasant meetings and numerous exchanges of good will, I doubt if the situation in international music was much affected one way or the other.

An English delegate and correspondent for the *Nottingham Guardian* reported the conference very fairly after his return to England. In the October 7, 1931, issue of his paper he wrote, "Though the results of the Conference were by no means unfruitful, they would probably be of little public interest. My object is rather to give some of the impressions I formed of the condition of music in America and of American musicians themselves."

He found the educational systems of Great Britain and America entirely different. Although our native tongue was English we each spoke another language, particularly in music education. He felt English church music was far superior to American church music. On the other hand secular music in America counted more to the average person than it did in England. The reporter concluded by saying that the conference proved musicians from other countries could rub elbows without spatting, but it didn't do much for the cause of music itself.

In retrospection I agree. No conference ever will.

CHAPTER FIFTEEN

✯✯

Back to Morningside Heights

I

WITH the Institute of Musical Art now officially under the Juilliard's wing, the three miles of city blocks separating the two schools became a nightmare to those of us whose duty it was to keep an eye on both.

My personal feelings in the matter were secondary. If the East Fifty-second Street building had been adequate, I would have ignored the nerve strain of bucking New York traffic, but, as the Juilliard continued to develop, a real concert hall was becoming more and more of a necessity.

Something had to be done. Should we build? Should the Institute be moved downtown or the Juilliard go uptown? The Institute was in a fine building designed for the purpose for which it was used. The plan of house in which the Juilliard functioned had no relation whatsoever to a music school.

Rehearsals were held in the large room on the ground floor, and concerts of any size had to be given in whatever hall could be rented for the purpose, such as the Engineering Building at 25 West Seventy-ninth Street. It seemed obvious to me that an adequate concert hall was the School's chief

116

need, but the original faculty of the Graduate School did not altogether agree with me. They enjoyed the intimacy of their teaching and their association with their pupils in the quite inadequate Fifty-second Street building. Since the School could afford to rent Town Hall or the Engineering Building hall, most of the faculty would have preferred to leave the situation as it was. But a proper hall in which to give operas, and still more in which to rehearse operas, seemed to me essential. That hall should be something of a laboratory where the students could sit in on rehearsals. It should be part of the school. The only way we could get all this was to put up a new building. Where?

As far back as 1926 President Butler of Columbia was thinking out loud to me on paper about music and the University. While I was still at the University, he wrote the following letter:

My dear Professor Erskine:

I have been reading in the newspapers of the general plan in the making for the development of technical and professional work in music and have learned with great satisfaction that there is to be a combination or union of interests and movements in a way that ought to strengthen both. Every year makes me a stronger believer in the necessity of the economies and increased efficiencies which come from a smaller number of stronger agencies for intellectual undertakings of every sort.

It occurs to me to suggest that you keep in mind the possibility and desirability of effecting as time goes on such co-operation between the work in music and the University as exists between Union Theological Seminary and ourselves. The University could contribute a large body of intellectual material and a large group of cultural opportunities to students of music, and doubtless there are not a few university students who would like from time to time to take advantage of the exceptional opportunities of a more technical and highly specialized kind than the University could furnish.

Faithfully yours,

Nicholas Murray Butler

The Institute was close to Columbia. Adjoining it were two vacant lots. If the Juilliard put up a new building on these lots would Columbia back us up?

I went to see Butler. I quote his very words, "By all means bring the Juilliard to Morningside Heights. There are many things which the University, already established, can do for students of music without new expense or overhead cost to the Juilliard Foundation. This will leave your school's funds free to care specifically for musical art."

This was one of the reasons I insisted on building the new School at 130 Claremont Avenue, an enlargement or extension of the old Institute of Musical Art. This satisfaction was hastened by one or two attempts to produce opera while we were at the Fifty-second Street site.

II

The architects of the new and enlarged school were Shreve, Lamb, and Harmon, who as I remember were suggested by George Davison, who had had some dealings with that excellent firm. The preparation of plans, and referring them to the faculty for their opinion, consumed a longer time than I expected, but we took all the time that was necessary, and the building when it was finished promised to give complete satisfaction—a promise which has been well fulfilled.

When the rooms which were to serve as offices for the president, the dean, and the assistant dean were well on the way to completion, Helen Worden and I mixed a cocktail one evening, took it up to 130 Claremont Avenue, and drank to the health of the new building and to the happiness of all who were to work there. We considered the ceremony as equivalent to breaking a bottle over the bow of a ship. After that, until my later collapse of health, Helen attended with me every concert we gave in the School, and followed the progress of all the promising students.

My offices on the second floor overlooked the lovely little

park which separates the Riverside Church from International House. Above the trees I could see the roof top of the old Claremont Inn where I often lunched with visiting musicians. Beyond the inn loomed the Palisades. On clear days I fancied I could see the very road along which Aunt Nanna and my sisters and I used to drive with Bess, our faithful horse, when I was a child.

I liked my office. Elsie Sloan Farley, the decorator for the School, had used my favorite color scheme: light blue-green walls and Mexican red carpet. On the walls I had hung a couple of my favorite paintings, one a landscape by Rubine, the other a French beach scene by Keisling.

My desk faced one wall, Miss Miller's the other. Ernest Hutcheson's office adjoined mine on one side, Oscar Wagner's on the other. I never closed my door. I wanted the faculty and students to feel that I was always on hand ready to discuss any problem. For a retreat I had a study on the third floor. Here I gradually moved my library from Wilton until all four walls were lined with books, and here I had my piano and did my practicing.

My study was only one aspect of the many splendid features in the new school. It took us months to get used to the luxury of our own music library, a spacious quiet room on the fourth floor. Miss Gwendolyn Mackillop functioned there for fifteen years as librarian.

Already the school was acquiring its characters. One was Felix Goettlicher, orchestral and instrument librarian. He became a permanent member of the Juilliard staff in October, 1931, though he had assisted Mr. Stoessel in previous years both at the School and at Chautauqua. He was formerly assistant music librarian and transportation manager of the New York Symphony under Walter Damrosch until its merger with the Philharmonic, having toured the United States as well as Europe with that orchestra. He remains a very important member of the Juilliard staff and probably takes his work more seriously than anyone else at the school.

He is something of a landmark now. He is the squarely built, kindly-faced man who moves solemnly about the stage before and after each performance, collecting music, shifting instruments.

Another loyal and valued member of the School is our comptroller, William J. Bergold, who was engaged by Dr. Noble in October, 1926, and who has remained in charge of the steadily expanding accounting department. When we moved uptown, he was in the seventh heaven over his handsomely equipped new offices.

But to me the most thrilling innovation at the new school was the new Casavant organ. I was remembering my Grace Church days. The Institute of Musical Art gave instruction in the organ on several small practice instruments and on an excellent organ in its own concert hall. Gaston Dethier had charge of this instruction until the year of his retirement in 1945. But—until the Casavant, the Juilliard had nothing!

While the Institute was being enlarged the practice organs became a difficult problem. A place had to be found to locate them temporarily. We were very grateful for the timely help of the Jewish Theological Seminary, which at the moment was completing its own handsome new building, and generously it let us have the use of several rooms for over a year. Here our practice organs were installed, and instruction and practicing went on undisturbed. When the final enlargement of the Institute was completed, the practice organs were set up again in our own building.

The new Casavant organ was ingeniously installed in the large space in two of the upper floors where the tuners can get at it conveniently. The sound comes down into the hall through a spacious grille in the ceiling.

Shortly after the installation I invited George Bonnet, the French organist, during his last visit to America, to come to the School and play on the Casavant. He had fled from Paris to this country when the Germans occupied his city. It was our good fortune. He was one of the great organists of the

world. An editorial I wrote for *Collier's* magazine—"Be Fair
to France"—caught his attention. We soon became good
friends. I had high hopes of persuading him to head the organ
department at the Juilliard. To that end we invited Bonnet
to lunch at the School. On the day of his visit I called for him
at a church on the west side where he was practicing on the
organ. Bringing him up to the School, I had many of our
faculty meet him in the little private lunch room in the
School cafeteria. He and Mr. Hutcheson engaged in animated
conversation about the proper way to judge an organ and
the proper use of organs in the modern world. Mr. Bonnet
had no use for electrical organs. After lunch he played for us
marvelously, and at the end of the visit Ernest had a complete
understanding with him that we should invite him to be the
next head of our organ department, but only a few weeks
later his sudden and tragic death put an end to our plans.

We then engaged David McK. Williams, organist at St.
Bartholomew's, to head the department, but his long illness
prevented him from entering upon his duties. Our beautiful
Casavant organ is still without a great artist like Bonnet to
teach it and to play it.

When we moved the Juilliard to Morningside Heights,
only one member of the faculty voted against the change.
He was of the opinion that the Juilliard should not become
too involved with Dr. Frank Damrosch.

But the faculty on the whole was well pleased when the
new auditorium was opened on November 7, 1931, by an orchestral concert conducted by Leopold Stokowski, and on
successive evenings by a piano recital by Rachmaninoff and
a series of performances of Louis Gruenberg's opera, *Jack and
the Beanstalk*, for which I wrote the libretto.

CHAPTER SIXTEEN

❧❧❧❧❧❧❧❧❧❧❧❧❧❧❧❧❧❧❧❧❧❧❧❧❧❧❧❧❧❧❧❧❧❧❧

My Flyer into Opera

I

FROM the moment the Juilliard School opened its newly built concert and opera hall at 130 Claremont Avenue, I have been associated with various criticisms of old-fashioned or purely conventional opera.

Dullness and tragedy are certainly not synonymous, but in opera librettos I have usually found them so. The music of *Tristan* I love beyond measure, but personally I find the libretto beneath contempt and should enjoy the opera just as much if the singers vocalized from one end to the other. That may be a peculiar aberration of mine. I think most operas survive, if at all, in spite of dull and gloomy stories. I did not say "all" operas.

Mr. Juilliard emphasized opera in his legacy. If we were to respect his wishes, opera singing and opera production must be an important part of the school's curriculum. We had excellent voice teachers. We must give their students a chance to sing new operas. Old-fashioned European opera with its preposterous plots, its tiresome recitative, and its remoteness from American culture and American life, never has been and never can be interpreted properly by American singers.

Most young singers approach operatic roles or arias in much the same way they would sing the ordinary classical song. Interpretations of the song simply require creating the mood of the words and the music. An opera, however, should express not only the mood of the particular dramatic situation but also the point of view of the country and the time in which the opera was written. The singer must acquire a sympathetic understanding of the modes of thought and feeling involved. Sometimes the excuse is given that Wagnerian roles are too heavy, especially for young voices, but I feel the real trouble is a pretty general absence of interpretive skill.

Albert Stoessel was familiar with my views on this subject. In 1930, while the Juilliard was still in its old building, he mentioned a new opera which Louis Gruenberg, a young Russian composer, had in mind. Ernest Hutcheson and I called him up. He was getting a divorce; he needed money. He would be happy to discuss his opera. Perhaps he could work on it during his enforced stay in the West.

I liked Gruenberg—in fact, I have always liked him. He was eager, impulsive, and friendly. With his words tumbling over one another, he poured out his ideas. He wanted a fantasy on which to superimpose his delicate, lacy music. In the West, where he would find leisure, he'd write the libretto himself—basing it on Peter Pan—J. M. Barrie's whimsical story. But to do this he must have money on which to live.

I asked him to come back the next day. That evening I repeated our conversation to Paul Warburg and Ernest Hutcheson. When Gruenberg returned the following afternoon I told him that three friends of the Juilliard would endow him for a year if he could give all of his time to the opera and if its première could be at the Juilliard. This offer held only if the opera was something which the students could sing. Gruenberg signed the contract that day. He never asked who were the three friends of the Juilliard. They were Ernest Hutcheson, Paul Warburg, and myself.

Shortly before Gruenberg left for the West he dashed into my office in the East Fifty-second Street building. He couldn't write the opera. He had no libretto.

"But you are using Peter Pan," I protested.

"Barrie won't give me permission to use his story."

He had sold us the idea before asking Barrie's consent!

I was frankly worried. My friends had joined me in this plan on my say-so. Gruenberg stared at me. Why didn't I write the libretto myself?

The administration of the school was a full-time job. A half-finished novel waited in the desk of my hotel room. I was already doing more work than I should. But to save the venture in which I had involved my friends I promised to write a libretto for Gruenberg's music. It wasn't easy. Gruenberg was Russian. I suggested "Jack and the Beanstalk." He had never heard of the story. When he read it he said there weren't enough characters to support his music.

"We'll make the cow the chief character," I replied.

He looked as if I had lost my reason. "Who ever heard of a cow singing?"

But in the end he approved of my libretto and supplied it with charming music. When the new school was dedicated, *Jack and the Beanstalk* had its première. The critics liked it. After playing November 20, 21, and 23, 1931, at the Juilliard, it moved to Broadway for a two-weeks run at the Forty-fourth Street Theatre. We wanted the students to face Broadway audiences. The experience was undoubtedly valuable, but the cost was so tremendous we said we would never do it again.

However, *Jack and the Beanstalk* made money for Gruenberg. It was produced by professionals at the Chicago Opera House. Later Alma Milsted, the young soprano who sang the part of Jack at the Juilliard, organized a small opera company of her own when she graduated. Among the operas she and her troupe performed on their tours was *Jack and the Beanstalk*.

Many of my personal friends came for the dedication of the new school, among them Bill Donovan—now General Donovan, director of the U.S. Strategic Service—Efrem and Alma Zimbalist, Ruth Draper, Mrs. Charles F. Mitchell, and Professor and Mrs. William Bigelow of Amherst. Our mutual friend, Professor Woodbridge, was in Berlin lecturing on philosophy. Biggie and I missed him. At the end of the evening when we were sitting around the living-room fire in my apartment, we raised our glasses to Sheddie, in affectionate memory of our triple friendship.

II

Another year Professor Woodbridge and his wife saw my second opera. My creations, I fear, were always a sore trial to him, but I persisted in enjoying his criticisms. I know by experience that anyone who takes part in making an opera wants to do it all over again as soon as he has a performance before an audience.

Instead of doing *Jack and the Beanstalk* over, I wrote the book for an opera by George Antheil. It was called *Helen Retires*.

George liked to refer to himself as the Bad Boy of Music. He later used this for the title of his autobiography. He wasn't bad and he wasn't a boy when we met. He was a gifted musician who both charmed and exasperated all who had any dealings with him.

His extraordinary reputation in the musical world began, for better or worse, with the performance of his *Ballet Mecanique* in Carnegie Hall, New York City, on April 10, 1927. The *Ballet* was only one number in a program of his compositions, but it stunned the audience into complete incapacity to notice anything else. In private conversation

George would now admit with a cheerful smile that the
audience didn't have a fair chance.

All of his music is composed in the modern idiom, but,
with the exception of the *Ballet*, it is music. The *Ballet*, however, was composed as a sound accompaniment for a motion
picture in which the rhythm of sight is sharply opposed to
the rhythm of hearing. This contrast between the visual and
the audible called for something which is not music in any
ordinary sense, and Antheil supplied what was needed. For
some reason the entire work, film as well as sound accompaniment, could not be produced at the concert, and Antheil was
overpersuaded by reckless advisers to exhibit the sound accompaniment without the film which gave it meaning. The
audience saw some pianos and heard them produce noises;
in addition they saw and heard lawn mowers and other useful
machines which seldom come on the concert stage. The
grotesque incident became an indestructible legend. I said as
much in *Omnibook* at the time George's autobiography was
published.

I heard of George Antheil first over thirty years ago when
he was a boy in Trenton, and a schoolmate of his in one of
my Columbia classes used to talk to me about the genius
temporarily concealed in New Jersey's capital but destined
to astonish the world. I got the full blast of the *Ballet
Mecanique* at the Carnegie concert, and, however unfortunate that concert was, it left on me the conviction that Antheil really was a genius. When years later he asked me to furnish him a libretto for an opera, I was flattered. The collaboration remains one of my happy memories. My own part in it
was not all I could wish, but the beauty of Antheil's music, its
daring and its vitality, made an impression which has not
dimmed.

After he had played some of this music on the piano at a
meeting in Philadelphia, I asked Josef Hofmann what he
thought of it. His reply indicates something of Antheil's
quality as a performer. "The music is modern—I should have

to hear it several times. Besides, my attention was on his playing. He must have a wrist of India rubber! He was doing impossible things all evening."

In my study at the Juilliard George played over parts of *Helen Retires* for Leopold Stokowski.

"Why do you bang out the pianissimo?" asked Stokowski.

George had no mercy on the human voice. Sembrich and Schoen-René refused to let their students sing in his opera.

"That music is awful," said Schoen-René. "It will ruin any voice."

Only two girls in the entire school could sing the part of Helen.

In spite of this, Stoessel and I agreed that Antheil's music was brilliant and provocative. It must be heard. On March 1, 2, and 3, 1934, the Juilliard presented "*Helen Retires*—libretto by John Erskine, music by George Antheil." We were damned and praised.

George's music was both beautiful and irritating. I saw serious faults in my libretto. I found none in the settings. Alfredo Valenti and Frederic Kiesler, although diametrically opposed by nature, collaborated happily on them.

Valenti came into the Juilliard picture through the operatic performances given at Chautauqua, where under the guidance of Ernest Hutcheson and as an extension of Stoessel's training a season of opera was given by Juilliard pupils every summer.

Mr. Valenti had been trained on the British operatic stage and had all the advantages of experience in an old tradition. Fearing that he might lack some modern ideas, I sent him to study for two seasons with Madame Ouspenskaya. Her training he naturally appreciated and he always spoke of it with special gratitude, though perhaps his work as stage director would have been remarkable in any case.

George Antheil introduced me to Kiesler, stage architect and artist as original as George himself strove to be. The School engaged Mr. Kiesler to collaborate with George in

the staging of *Helen*. The costumes and the settings of the
opera were altogether Kiesler's work. He got on admirably
with Mr. Valenti, and they continued in happy collaboration
at the School until the emergencies of World War II practically interrupted all the Juilliard operas. Now that the
School has resumed its complete program, in which opera
production begins again to take its place, I am glad to say
that Fred Kiesler, to my great delight, continues to design
and arrange the stage settings. His is one of the most original
minds with whom the work of the School has come in
contact.

III

In 1935 Mr. Beryl Rubinstein, pianist-composer and director of the Cleveland Institute of Music, discussed with me
a possible libretto for an opera. He wanted a story based on
folklore or on some old fairy tale. We agreed at last on the
version of *The Sleeping Beauty* which I had already published as a short story under the title of "Cinderella's
Daughter."

Kiesler's designs for *The Sleeping Beauty* expressed my conception of the opera. The libretto in its final form was typical
of my writing, being a combination of the poetic and the
realistic, the naive and the sophisticated. Begun in January,
1936, I resumed work on it in the spring of 1937 and finished
the opera the following August.

The Princess, you remember, was to sleep one hundred
years and to be wakened by the kiss of the Prince Charming.
All the folk in the castle fell asleep with her, but not the
people outside. The sleep was for precisely one hundred
years, and if the King and Queen wasted time arguing with
the Good Fairy they must have been a little late in coming
to. I preferred to have them escape the century charm altogether and to assume that the delayed waking would apply
to the rest of the household.

Why did the Princess prick her finger with the spindle?

I assume that she was a little absent-minded at the moment, thinking of the boy with whom she had a tryst in the forest that evening. After the hundred years the Prince appears and is about to kiss her when she murmurs in her sleep the name of the boy. The Prince, temporarily discouraged, goes home.

The Princess on waking goes to the forest to keep her engagement. She finds her lover's great grandson waiting there to meet another girl, his sweetheart. For the Princess, of course, he has no use at all, and she returns to the castle, with a glimpse of the meaning of the flight of time.

The Prince, after all, was not discouraged, not really. He called at the castle again to inquire after the health of the Princess.

The autumn of the year I completed the libretto for this opera, I worked out a story for another opera—an unpublished score of Victor Herbert's. It proved an exciting challenge to make the words fit the music. I decided that the right way to make the music effective would be to find a play laid in New York about the time the music was composed.

I used the Hudson-Fulton celebration as a general background. One element in the plot was a fantastic but real incident of that commemoration. A Sultan from some obscure corner of northern Africa heard of the celebration and decided to attend it—to the great embarrassment of Mayor Seth Low. The Sultan came along with several wives, a cortege of slaves, and I believe some animals to amuse himself with.

Mr. Low engaged Professor Vladimir Simkhovitch of Columbia University, a singularly adroit man, to provide special entertainment and distraction for the Sultan—the general purpose being to keep that embarrassing potentate as much as possible out of sight. Mr. Simkhovitch once told me of his grotesque adventures with the Sultan. I got his permission to play fast and loose with the facts and dress them up for my own purpose. I had many pleasant meetings with Mr. and Mrs. Arthur Bartlett over the story. She inherited the score from her father, Victor Herbert. I'm sorry to say nothing ever came of the book I wrote for his music, but I had a grand time doing it.

That was the last opera I had any share in writing.

But from the day I became president of the Juilliard up to this very moment, I have never let up in saying what I thought about opera. My critics call it my overdeveloped talent for speaking out of turn.

IV

The *Nation* for October 1, 1930, carried this news item:

John Erskine, president of the Juilliard School of Music, made a rather surprising statement the other day in the course of an interview giving out the plans of the school for the coming year. Mr. Erskine was discussing European opera and its presentation, with all the furbelows of elaborate scenery, a splendiferous ballet, and grand opera stars singing in a foreign tongue.

"I see no future for it," he said, "and I don't think it has even a present.

"If there are any music lovers left in the audience at the Metropolitan—and one suspects that in the galleries at least there are many—this will sound mournfully upon their ears, and will not lack, moreover, a note of truth. Except in New York City, where it furnishes an occasion for an evening of social splendor, and at the same time gives an opportunity to a large foreign population to hear their native tongue and their native music, grand opera finds small support in America, and subsidy for it is harder to obtain every year. It is a rare bird that the average citizen knows nothing about and cares less. The radio is daily spreading, along with its programs of heart songs, a knowledge of fine music among thousands of new listeners. A healthy American opera might catch its share of them, but not, one suspects, European opera with its preposterous plots, its tiresome recitative, and its remoteness from American culture and American life."

Mr. Hutcheson had arranged with the help of Oscar Wagner to entertain all the music critics of the city one day at lunch and answer questions about our plans for the new school. One of the critics, I forget which one, had asked me casually what I thought of the future of opera in New York.

In a very few hours I knew that my reply was reckless and might be hard to live down. The newspapers picked up the phrase, repeating it with different degrees of seriousness. Within forty-eight hours I had an invitation from Otto H. Kahn to lunch with him, if I could do so, immediately, in the private dining room of his bank. I accepted the invitation fully aware that I might be spanked or scolded for lack of respect for the Metropolitan Opera. Mr. Kahn, though courteous as always, had a touch of grimness about him when we met. My remark had been printed in newspapers everywhere, he said, and he found it more difficult than usual to get promises of aid for the Met for the new season. Why on earth had I taken such an attitude toward opera?

I told him that my words did not deserve the attention they received, but I could say this much for them—they were entirely sincere and spontaneous, and I believe they were also entirely defensible.

We had opera performances at the Metropolitan, of course, and some of the singers were extremely fine, and often the individual performance was remarkable, but none of the operas were American. Few Americans could be named among the singers, practically none in the management. The Met in my opinion was an Italian opera house. I knew by personal observation that Italian was the official language spoken, and if I or any other American wished to converse with Gatti-Casazza it would be necessary first to learn Italian.

Then, warming to the theme, I went somewhat deeper. I said I could see no future for opera anywhere except in those places or those countries in which the art was permitted and encouraged to express the ideals and the taste of the people.

Opera is not the kind of music one associates with energy. That's why it is so difficult for an American to write opera.

There won't be any solution unless we produce contemporary American operas based on stories that arise from American life so that our singers will thoroughly understand the text and the music.

I thought then, and I think there is much more reason to think now, that American opera will evolve in a direction pointed by the American taste, as in such works as Jerome Kern's *Show Boat*. If I were expressing the same opinion to-day, my illustrations of the American spirit would be Oscar Hammerstein II and Richard Rodgers.

To my amazement, after one or two protests against my failure to admire the Metropolitan just as it was, Mr. Kahn told me he agreed with my opinion entirely. His children would agree with it. American youth in general would agree with it. He confessed that his own training and his European taste rather disqualified him from guiding the American taste in opera or in any other form of music. But he would say frankly that from what might be called an American point of view, I was right; there would not be an American opera at the Metropolitan until the opera we produced there expressed entirely the natural tastes of the American people. He had little faith that any American would compose operas in the European tradition which would give satisfaction to those trained in that tradition. Opera would have to start fresh with whatever raw material the American temperament supplied. He hoped the opera of the future would not be jazz, though at the moment he feared jazz was what his children and their friends were interested in.

After more talk of this kind we agreed to meet often and see what we could do to effect a cordial relation between what he called traditional opera and the American kind.

But we never discussed the subject again, and I had few further occasions to meet him, though Mrs. Kahn's interest in the National Music League, an organization which she actively encouraged as a kind of booking agency to develop concert opportunities for young American artists, might have brought us together.

CHAPTER SEVENTEEN

✿✿✿✿✿✿✿✿✿✿✿✿✿✿✿✿✿✿✿✿✿✿✿✿✿✿✿✿✿✿✿✿✿✿✿✿

Summer School

I

THE OPENING of the new building of the Juilliard School naturally attracted the attention of all the institutions in the neighborhood which to any extent or in any way taught music. During the winter of 1931 I received a letter from Professor Peter Dykema, the head of the music department of Teachers College. I had known him for a number of years. He was famous for his audacity. Now he was making the amiable suggestion that since the Juilliard had this fine building, with complete equipment of Steinway pianos, and since this equipment would be standing idle during the summer, Teachers College would be glad to make use of it in order to install a summer session.

The proposal rather took my breath away, but I telephoned to George Wedge, the head of the theory department of the Institute. Wedge came to my office and in a very few moments he and I had worked out a complete scheme for our first summer session. It was entirely my idea. Wedge agreed to head the school. We selected our faculty from the Juilliard and Institute teachers, and the program for the new summer term was announced in February, 1932.

I have always been grateful to the Teachers College people for precipitating this action. I did not admire educationally what Teachers College was doing in its musical or even in its other courses, and I had no idea of turning over the Juilliard equipment to them lock, stock, and barrel. Their suggestion of a summer school carried with it no hint that any rent should be paid for the use of this costly equipment.

On the other hand, if it seemed preposterous that the equipment should be handed over to Teachers College, why should it not be used by us?

George Wedge, a graduate of the Institute, came to my mind because Dr. Damrosch had employed him as a sort of dean at the Institute, and he had proved himself resourceful and I knew him well. He immediately made a success of the summer courses, which were designed for music teachers from distant parts of the country who might wish to do advanced study at the Juilliard School but who were not free to come during the winter term.

Wedge ran the summer school, but as long as I was president I never failed to be on hand for those sessions. I lectured, I gave piano recitals, and I made it a point to know all the students.

George Wedge had plenty of experience in music and organization. Among other things he had been associated with the Herbert Witherspoon studios from 1917 to 1925.

He began his teaching career at the Institute under the inspiration, and later under the somewhat repressive influence, of Mr. Percy Goetschius. Wedge held a post as organist in a New York church, and he also did some composing. His interest in music at first was alert and vital. In time he was the author of several textbooks on harmony. Still later after the death of Dr. Frank Damrosch, when George had become dean of the Institute, the fashion of studying and teaching harmony moved far beyond the rather formal and mechanical methods which he believed in and still followed at the Institute. I have always felt that his work as director of the Sum-

mer School brought him in contact with music teachers everywhere with benefit to him as it was to the school. His chief
interest, however, was the composition of textbooks, and by
this work he perhaps fastened himself to a routine which
could hardly be defended from the point of modern composing or of modern teaching.

Having taught English composition for most of my life, I
was somewhat perplexed to learn when I went to the Juilliard
that musical composition in that institution and many other
music schools was taught by the repetition of set exercises
rather than by the composition of anything that by the pupils
or their teachers could be considered musical creation. In my
youth English composition in some places was taught through
exercises in grammar and the incessant correction of errors.
The student was not encouraged to have anything to say, and
it did not occur to many students to become writers. The
change toward the creative approach to composition is now
becoming as marked in music as in the English classes.

When William Schuman was elected president of the
School in 1945, Wedge not unnaturally retired from the Juilliard, since Schuman was one of the youngest and most vigorous exponents of a kind of composition and teaching methods
to which Wedge was altogether opposed.

II

The Institute of Musical Art, and the Juilliard Graduate
School afterwards, were closely associated for obvious reasons
with the great Steinway firm of piano makers and with the
music publishers of the Schirmer family. The Steinway piano
has always been the instrument used by the School, and Dr.
Frank Damrosch established in the Institute building for the
convenience of the students a branch of G. Schirmer, Inc.
Both these relations have continued most happily in the later
development of the combined school.

When we opened the new building at 130 Claremont Avenue we bought 125 new pianos. Today we have 167 Steinways at the School. Schirmer's continue to supply us with sheet music. It is a concession we have for the convenience of the students and, of course, Schirmer's is happy to sell its music. In return it gives the students ten per cent discount, and beginning last year (1949) it contributed six annual scholarships to the school—a sum amounting to about three thousand dollars.

During my presidency Theodore Steinway was the head of the famous piano firm, the constant encourager of young musicians, and a faithful friend of the veterans.

He was and is a great actor. I always thought his heart lay in the theater rather than in the piano business. He adored character parts and usually had a leading role with his wife Ruth in the Comedy Club shows. I never heard him play the piano, but I have heard him make magnificent speeches on music and many other subjects.

III

When I headed the Juilliard, our dealings with Schirmer's were chiefly through its president, Carl Engel, one of the most delightful characters I met in the course of my musical adventures.

Carl spent most of his life in thankless toil for music. Every musician in our country owes something to him, though probably unaware of the debt. He succeeded Oscar G. Sonneck as head of the Music Division of the Congressional Library, and he maintained the standard of Sonneck's remarkable work in that position, building up the collection, one of the greatest in the world, devising new ways to make its treasures available to students and to the public, and increasing the respect of musicians for their profession and their art. Service of this kind demands a technical equipment, an administrative ability, and a self-effacing devotion such as you'll rarely find in one man.

Before and after this achievement at the Library in Washington, Carl directed the policy of music publishers, picking out talent before others had recognized it, building up catalog lists of compositions the value of which is permanent. Music publishing, of course, is a business, but it is also a venture in an art, and it is one business which depends on a critical understanding of that art. Unless the music can be sold, the business will go under, but unless the music sold is good music, the reputation of the house will go under.

Carl Engel was a great scholar and an admirable writer. I loved him for his personality and for what I've called his temperament. Character, perhaps, is the better word. The most casual incidents of an afternoon spent with him in his home on East Thirty-sixth Street were lifted to unforgettable importance by his whimsical comment and interpretation. He seemed to attract to himself people and happenings who brought out his playful, impish, but deep wisdom. I call to mind three illustrations.

Some years after World War I a Viennese baron, Carl Ferdinand Tinty, brought to this country an amiable project for furthering good will among the intellectuals of all nations. He had an old castle outside of Vienna which could accommodate, he said, a hundred guests. Why not invite a well-selected hundred for a fortnight at the castle every summer? There would be no program of speeches nor any other inconvenience; the great men would merely talk to each other, admire each other, realize the idiocy of ever disagreeing with each other—and peace would ensue. The Baron took this happy thought to Professor James T. Shotwell of the Carnegie Endowment for International Peace, also of the Committee on Intellectual International Co-operation of the League of Nations. Professor Shotwell, dear colleague though he was, wished Tinty off on me, and I assembled a group of writers, scholars, painters, musicians, and sculptors to see what could or should be done with the Baron and his castle. We had some wonderful meetings, overflowing with idealism and

good will, but more than a little poisoned by a doubt of the
Baron's sanity. There was even a doubt that the castle was in
existence. The Baron had pictures of it on a film, but how
could we be sure the edifice was still standing, or whether—
horrible doubt!—the Baron owned it?

I can still see Carl Engel moving around one evening at the
old Beethoven Association rooms fairly glowing with mis-
chievous delight at our predicament. All of us, I suppose,
except Baron Tinty himself, were wondering if we couldn't
delegate someone to go look at the place. The thought was
transferred to Carl, who out of a clear sky volunteered, since
he would be in Vienna anyway that summer. He went, and
brought back the reassuring news that the castle was entirely
as the Baron had represented it. This was in the autumn, of
course, the Baron having removed himself from the New York
scene during the summer.

He never returned to us. Just when we were willing to talk
with each other or with other great men on his premises for
the benefit of the millennium, the news reached us, through
the daily press, that he had got married in Chicago. In that
city a short time later he also got pneumonia and died. We
should have felt the undiluted tragedy of his death, but I fear
it struck us as fantastic, even a little funny.

IV

Some years later when I was at the Juilliard School, a musicologist from Vienna called on me. He was on his way to
Hollywood. Only a month before he had decided one evening
that the Socialist party in Vienna had no future. Being a man
of action, he started to mix some drugs in a glass. A friend
happened to drop in. "What on earth are you doing there?"

"I am about to commit suicide," said the musicologist.

"Don't do that! I can lend you some money."

"Money?" said the musicologist sadly. "I have three thousand dollars of my own."

"You commit suicide with three thousand dollars in your pocket? Have you ever been to New York?"

"Never."

"Why not visit America? If you don't enjoy yourself you can still commit suicide at your convenience."

So here was the musicologist talking to me. On the voyage he had seen a motion picture and conceived the idea that motion pictures could be improved. He was going to California to show Hollywood how to do it. Hollywood must have thrown him out as soon as he knocked at the door, for he was back in my office within a fortnight. The motion pictures were altogether out of his mind—he had a new idea. In every railway station across the continent, at least in those where his train stopped, he had seen books displayed by authors of whom he had never heard. There should be an agent on the Continent to represent *all* American authors, not simply the top-flight ones who, he assured me, were in most cases merely the luckiest. In another fortnight he was back in Vienna, and I had a letter from him requesting the privilege of peddling my books around. Evidently he didn't think me lucky. I told him I already had an agent, but he could go ahead with the blessing of all concerned. I never heard of him again.

Since he was a musicologist, I was consulting Carl about him throughout this episode. Carl's opinion of him, as of the Baron, he expressed in the story of the German and the Viennese, comparing notes on the postwar situation. "With us," said the German, "it is serious but not yet desperate."

"With us," said the Viennese, "it is the reverse, desperate but not yet serious."

The picture of Carl is not quite complete unless it includes his large dog. The creature embodied Carl's scholarly and business talents; it listened patiently to deep talk in the library and it went with Carl to business, waiting for him outside the office door. I often wonder what the poor fellow did after Carl died in 1944.

CHAPTER EIGHTEEN

✚✚

Parties

I

WHENEVER I called on Ernest and Irmgart Hutcheson I was impressed by the beauty and by the location of the white stone apartment house in which they lived at 11 West Eighty-first Street. The rooms were large and the ceilings high. From the front windows one could see the pleasant green of Manhattan Square and the red turreted roof of the American Museum of Natural History. Also visible were the tree tops of Central Park and, to the south, the skyline of New York. At night when the glow of Broadway silhouetted the big buildings the view was incredibly lovely.

Returning to my room at the Berkshire after a Sunday luncheon at the Hutchesons', I knew I must have an apartment in Number 11. The entertainment of musicians—a very real part of my duties at the Juilliard—was becoming more and more of a problem. A hotel restaurant and a single hotel room were no answer to the situation. I repeated this to Irmgart. She spoke to the owner of Number 11—a Mr. Jackson. There wasn't a single inch of available space in the house. She conferred with him again. He had an idea. What about building

140

me a penthouse on the roof? He was an optimist. So was I; and I had forgotten the difficulties of remodeling the farmhouse at Wilton. I liked Number 11. In addition to the charm of the building, it was far more convenient to the Juilliard than the Berkshire. Besides there was the view. I could breakfast on my balcony. From it over after-dinner coffee I might watch the lights of New York. I have always adored space. My idea of a perfectly proportioned room is the old King Cole Room at the St. Regis.

Mr. Jackson built me a room almost as large. It ran the entire width of the house and practically half its length. Three enormous French windows opened off three separate balconies! At one end of the room there was a huge fireplace, at the other my piano. I had special shelves built in for my books. There was ample space for my paintings on the light green walls. For contrast I used earth red rugs and black and silver aluminum furniture. I carried this color scheme into the compact dining room. I've never seen the necessity of a large dining room. Mine was just big enough for the long black and silver table, buffet, and black patent leather upholstered chairs. Off this dining room was a wonderful kitchen. The cheerful brown face of my maid, Iva Ford, broke into a broad smile when she first saw that kitchen. It and the dining room had outside doors leading to a terrace which extended along three sides of the apartment. Also opening off this terrace were the three bedrooms and my study. On top of my penthouse perched the water tank. I mention the terraces and the tank because of later developments.

II

I took possession of the apartment just before the opening of the Juilliard's new home. At the première of *Jack and the Beanstalk* I gave a midnight party for faculty and cast. Everyone exclaimed over the unique charm of the penthouse. With fifty or sixty people in the living room there was still no sense of crowding.

I like people and I like parties. By that I mean special company and special entertainment—not the least of which is good food, good wine, and good talk. Iva was a fine cook with a couple of *chefs-d'œuvre*—breast of chicken baked in cream, and planked salmon. We alternated between these two dishes —building our dinners around them. Not a week end passed that I did not have some party.

The month I moved into the apartment—October, 1931— Mrs. Nicholas Murray Butler wrote me that a friend of hers, the Countess von Bethman, wife of the Premier of Austria, would be in New York for a fortnight. Would I be nice to her?

I located the Countess at the Plaza. She was delighted to come to dinner. Mary Pickford happened to be in town. I invited her, also Martha Dickinson Bianchi, Leonora Speyer, Fannie Hurst, and Helen Worden and her mother. I've forgotten the names of all the men who came but one—Jack Monroe. Mary Pickford asked if she might bring him. He had composed some light music and he played the piano.

I remember him because he forgot his hat when he went home. Miss Miller, my secretary, phoned him the news next morning. He thanked her for the information, but never came back to pick up that hat—a brand-new black felt.

Dinner was at eight. Everybody arrived punctually on the hour but Martha Dickinson Bianchi. At quarter past eight she still had not put in an appearance. Because she was the niece of Emily Dickinson, the poet, and because she had lived abroad and was witty in her own right, I thought the Countess von Bethman might enjoy meeting her. My friendship with Martha dated back to an October Sunday afternoon in 1903, when she had bidden me, then a young associate professor of English at Amherst, to high tea with her and her mother at the Evergreens—the Austin Dickinson family home. Martha, flaming red hair piled high on her head, wore a light summer dress and served us lobster Newburg on the side porch. I shivered in a heavy tweed suit. I had accepted the invitation because I was curious to learn more about Emily Dickinson. Later I learned that in the office directly behind the little library were Emily's piano and other souvenirs connected with her. But not once during my visit was she mentioned. Not that it mattered. I enjoyed Martha and her mother for their really remarkable conversations.

Such was the beginning of a friendship which weathered many an eccentricity of Martha's. I thought of all this the evening of the dinner for the Countess von Bethman. At twenty past eight I telephoned Martha's New York residence, the National Arts Club. She was in her room. Had she forgotten the dinner?

"Certainly not. I've been sitting here waiting for you to call for me." The tone of her voice implied that she considered herself, and not the Countess von Bethman, the guest of honor.

Because it was Martha I dashed down to Gramercy Park and personally escorted her to my home for dinner. Rude? Yes. Eccentric? Yes. She was an incurable Dickinson, but, in her own imperious fashion, a grand friend. I doubt if the Countess von Bethman thought so. I never saw her again after that evening.

Leonora Speyer understood, perhaps because she appreciated the artistic temperament, having plenty of it herself. Before her marriage she had been a violinist—one of the youngest and most talented in all Europe. Next to her violin her cherished possession was a Tourte bow. It had cost her a pretty penny and she had paid for it with her own money. One evening in London she gave a private recital at the home of a wealthy friend. After the last number, a guest, Sir Edgar Speyer, came up to congratulate her. As he started to shake her hand she dropped her bow. He stepped on it, breaking the bow into a million pieces. She blew up and said in so many words that she hoped she would never see him again. The

next afternoon Sir Edgar called on her with a present—the
finest Tourte bow in all London. A month later they were
married. Leonora told me this story herself. Sir Edgar loved
her music, but she never played again after she was married.

III

Among the many friends I associate with those happy evenings at Number 11 West Eighty-first Street was Paul Kochanski. He had taste in everything: music, people, wines, food,
and living. He loved life. I can see his short, squarely built
figure, violin tucked under his chin, as he stepped the length
of the living room to the Chopin minuet he was playing to
illustrate the tempo. He and Zosia had been very rich. During
the Russian Revolution they lost everything—everything, that
is, but his violin, a Stradivarius. Even when they were hungry
they clung to it. In New York he earned a comfortable living
with his teaching and his recitals. Their home, an apartment
on East Seventy-fourth Street, possessed an Old World ele-
gance. But in their eyes were memories of the tragic experiences they had endured.

When Paul died in 1934 we held his funeral at the Juilliard.
Zosia asked me to speak. Difficult though it was, I did. The
concert hall was crowded with his friends—the great musicians
of the world. As the casket was carried from the building to
the hearse the wonderful carillon on the Riverside Church
began to ring out the Chopin funeral march. Another friend
of Paul's, Kamiel Le Febre, carillonneur of the Riverside
Church, was saying good-by to him.

Driving home from the cemetery I sat beside Mrs. Alexander Siloti. She remembered the day in Russia that Paul
married Zosia.

"Zosia's parents begged Paul to take care of her," Mrs.
Siloti said. "She was so young and unprepared for life. 'Be
gentle with her, Paul,' they said. He always treated her like a
child. How will she get along without him?"

He left her little else but his violin. The income from its sale has helped her to live.

IV

The second year of my occupancy at 11 West Eighty-first Street I noticed a slight dampness in the hall ceiling. I put it down to a crack in the tin roofing and a prolonged period of rainy weather. I might have given it further thought if my attention hadn't been diverted by a far more insistent irritation—an enormous klieg spotlight which made daylight out of my bedroom from dusk till dawn. It was fastened on the terrace of a penthouse on top of the adjoining building and, in addition to illuminating my own apartment, it lit up the entire north side of the building as far down as the courtyard.

The second morning at breakfast I mentioned the maddening searchlight to Iva.

She grinned. "Don' you know what that's for, Mr. Erskine?"

"To keep me awake all night?"

"No'm. That terrace next door belongs to a gangster. Some other gangster is out to get him. He might climb up the fire-escape leading from the courtyard to our terrace, shinny over onto the other gangster's terrace, and shoot him daid."

After hearing that I turned my face to the wall and gave thanks for the klieg light. A night came when there was no light. I couldn't sleep. Again I mentioned the fact to Iva at breakfast.

She nodded. "The gangster next door don' have to worry any more. He was shot daid last evening on his way home."

That night sitting in the living room trying to concentrate on the evening paper I heard a gurgle. I'm not naturally scary but I jumped. With my eyes still on my newspaper I listened intently. This time it was a gush and a swoosh. I leaped up. A young flood was rippling through the hall into the living room. A few seconds later, as the water hit the electric wiring, the lights failed. In the darkness I groped my way to the outside hall and elevator. The water tank on the roof had burst!

For hours afterward the building superintendent and I waded about in overshoes desperately trying to salvage my books and piano by the flickering light of candles. Water still rained down from what was left of the hall ceiling. I kept an umbrella handy.

At two o'clock in the morning we were interrupted by a violent pounding on the front door. Opening my umbrella I made my way under it to the door.

There stood Helen. "Thank God, you're safe!" she cried. "I've been trying to reach you for five hours. Something's wrong with your phone."

I nodded. "I know. It's been drowned."

She wiped her eyes. "I was so worried. Mother read about that gangster who lives next door being shot. When I couldn't get you on the telephone she was certain you'd been killed too."

At this point Helen gave a wild shriek of laughter.

"And why, may I ask, are you laughing?" I demanded.

"You look so funny." She pointed to my overshoes and opened umbrella.

The next day I returned to the Berkshire, where I remained until I could move into a thoroughly dry apartment at 471 Park Avenue. It was a duplex and quite the most handsome home I ever had.

CHAPTER NINETEEN

✠✠✠✠✠✠✠✠✠✠✠✠✠✠✠✠✠✠✠✠✠✠✠✠✠✠✠✠✠✠✠✠✠✠✠✠✠

Cross Currents

I

AMONG the guests at many of my Juilliard music parties was Paul Cravath, the lawyer. He could look and act, on occasion, like a bear, but he was very nice socially. He was at his best in improving the condition of the Negro. Here he carried on the wishes of his father, Erastus Milo Cravath of Fisk University.

In music affairs he was apt to hedge, then be a law unto himself, as I had occasion to learn when William Mathews Sullivan, an attorney for several opera singers, attacked the Juilliard in the newspapers.

He demanded to know whether the Juilliard Foundation was fulfilling the intention of Mr. Juilliard's will; to what extent Mr. Juilliard's wishes had been carried out with reference to the Metropolitan Opera Company; whether it was Mr. Juilliard's intention that the Foundation should take over the Institute of Musical Art, or that the building on East Fifty-second Street should remain unoccupied and unproductive of income; whether the Juilliard School should employ a very expensive faculty or that foreign instructors should be employed; and finally whether it was Mr. Juilliard's intention that the public should be asked for $300,000 for the Metropolitan Opera Company when that Company had not received the financial aid to which it was entitled under Mr. Juilliard's will.

This was not the first time that the charge had been made that Mr. Juilliard left something to the Metropolitan which his trustees failed to deliver.

I was as much responsible as anyone for the policy of the Juilliard in those years. I believed that what the Juilliard had done had been true to Mr. Juilliard's wishes in spirit and in letter.

We had no difficulty in learning what Mr. Juilliard's wishes were. He left his trustees free to encourage American music as they thought best, but he expressed three wishes which his trustees tried to respect scrupulously. The first was that this Foundation should provide for the training of musicians, and he named among possible methods of procedure the establishment of a school. The second was that free concerts might be given of such a quality as to educate public taste.

The third was that the Foundation might aid out of its income in the production of certain operas at the Metropolitan.

John Perry, who drew Mr. Juilliard's will, was a trustee of the Foundation and a director of the Juilliard School of Music. Allen Wardwell, counsel for the Metropolitan Real Estate Corporation, was chairman of the directors of the Juilliard School of Music. Cornelius N. Bliss, one of the trustees of the Metropolitan Real Estate Corporation, was a director of the School. And Paul D. Cravath, chairman of the Metropolitan Opera Company, was also one of the directors.

There had been, therefore, on our two Boards no predisposition to neglect the Metropolitan.

Mr. Juilliard wished the Foundation to assist in the production of operas which otherwise might not get a hearing at the Metropolitan—operas of historic interest to students and operas written by American composers.

As soon as Mr. Juilliard's trust was founded, the Metro-

politan was approached with an offer to carry out Mr. Juilliard's wish. The offer was declined, on the ground, I understand, that the normal programs ought not to be disturbed.
The Juilliard Foundation then suggested that it pay for a supplementary season of opera at the Metropolitan for the production of unusual operas and American compositions. This
offer the management of the Metropolitan declined.

The Foundation then proceeded to carry out Mr. Juilliard's
other wishes.

Mr. Sullivan implied that we should not have any foreign-
born artists on our faculty, or any who were not yet American
citizens. I could answer for our teachers, that they were devoted to the cause of American music and to the interest of
American musicians, and that they all spoke English. I said
as much in reply to Mr. Sullivan. I added that I should wait
with interest to see how he applied this principle to the Metropolitan. I suspected that he had raised a ghost which would
not soon stop walking.

To have proper facilities for the training of opera students
and the production of operas, as well as for other advantages,
the Foundation had moved the School from East Fifty-second
Street to its present location.

II

The myth that Mr. Juilliard left an emergency fund on
which the Metropolitan was entitled to draw appeared first
in print, so far as I know, in an article by a music critic. He
said, "The days of the Maecenases and of gifts of millions to
opera companies are flown. Augustus Juilliard planned otherwise when he left his millions to be employed as a musical
foundation, but *the part of the funds which he intended for
the Metropolitan in a POSSIBLE TIME OF NEED* have
gone into bricks and mortar, and they are not available."

The plain meaning of these words was that the Foundation
neglected its trust and diverted to improper uses part of Mr.

Juilliard's money. My reply to the critic appeared in the *New York Times*.

In conversation with Ernest Hutcheson and me, he offered the somewhat original argument that he was absolved from all responsibility in making that charge, because at the time that he made it he had not read Mr. Juilliard's will. He said he had got the idea from Otto Kahn. I wrote Mr. Kahn, asking why he had made such a charge. He replied that he had never made it, that he always understood Mr. Juilliard's warm interest in the Metropolitan, and he had never criticized the way in which the Foundation had executed its trust. I then asked the critic whether he didn't think it best to retract his statement. He wrote me that he did not owe the Juilliard the slightest apology. When I answered his charge, I took occasion to speak of certain differences between the practices at the Metropolitan and Mr. Juilliard's ideals for American opera, as I understood them. For over half a year we had been discussing informally the problem of the Metropolitan at each monthly meeting of the Juilliard directors. I hoped from the first that, if the Juilliard was to save the Metropolitan, the Metropolitan would cease to be a foreign opera house, would take a more cordial attitude toward American composers and singers, and would bring down its salaries.

When the crisis became acute, Mr. Cravath and Mr. Bliss asked me to join the committee to raise $300,000. They asked me, they said, because I was a critic of the Metropolitan, but Mr. Cravath encouraged me to believe that if the Metropolitan could carry on, its work would be developed as we all desired.

III

At a meeting of the Foundation we agreed in principle to see the Metropolitan through on certain conditions. I submitted definitions of the purpose of our gift:

To enable the Metropolitan to give further encouragement to American singers and composers, according to Mr. Juilliard's wish.

1. To secure educational opportunities at the Metropolitan, such as the privilege of attending rehearsals, for properly qualified students.

2. To enable the Metropolitan to serve a larger audience, by a supplementary season of *opéra comique*, or by other supplementary programs.

3. To enable the Metropolitan to introduce modern stage methods.

4. To insure the production next season of American operas already commissioned, such as the work by Howard Hanson and Richard Stokes.

Mr. Sullivan spoke of the high salaries paid to teachers at the Juilliard School. The average salary was well under $10,000 for a school season of eight months. What the salaries at the Metropolitan were I did not know. I understood, however, that a few of the stars had refused to take cuts and had insisted on their full contracts.

I was sorry to see Mr. Juilliard's money go into those particular pockets, especially at a time when the artist-teachers at the Juilliard School had voluntarily taken heavy slashes in their already moderate salaries so that more aid might be extended to students and to musical enterprises outside the School. To start the ball rolling I had deliberately cut my own salary in half.

I concluded my statement with the hope the Juilliard Foundation would put through its plans for the Metropolitan. But, I added, if the money were handed over to the Metropolitan without such conditions as would insure Mr. Juilliard's intention, I should not care to be connected with either the Foundation or the School.

Before releasing this statement to the newspapers I sent it to Paul Cravath for approval. He okayed it.

The afternoon of the day my reply to Mr. Sullivan appeared in the newspapers I went to a performance at the Metropolitan Opera with Helen Worden. During the intermission two members of the Metropolitan Opera Board, Lucrezia Bori and Cornelius Bliss, appeared in our box. Both were very angry. What had I meant by implying that the Juilliard would aid the Opera? Didn't I know that this would kill the Met's drive for $300,000?

I replied that Mr. Cravath had approved my statement before it went to the newspapers.

CHAPTER TWENTY

✼✼✼

My Last Concert

I

THE FIRST evening in my new apartment I invited Helen Worden to take dinner with me. She said she would rather go to a tea room. I took her, none too graciously. As usual, the tea room Helen suggested was jammed with elderly females from neighboring apartment hotels. We had to wait in line, roped off from the restaurant like so many lunatics. I began to think we were crazy, when we were finally let in and allowed to sit at a table with a strange couple. But Helen seemed cheerful enough, so I tried to make the best of a bad evening and put down her passion for tea rooms as an aspect of her character which I had not yet encountered. To my horror she not only lingered over her lemon pie but said she would like another pot of coffee. It was nine o'clock when we left the place.

My new home, 471 Park Avenue, was on the southeast corner of Fifty-eighth Street and Park Avenue. Helen suggested returning to her hotel by way of that street. This seemed odd, but I had now come to the conclusion that she was beyond all understanding, so I said nothing. As we reached Park Avenue I automatically glanced up at my windows.

There was a light in the living room. I remembered carefully switching off all the lights before I left. I had also told Iva that, since there would be no dinner to prepare, she might have a free evening. I snatched Helen's arm and pointed to the lighted windows. "Someone has broken into my apartment!"

"It looks that way," she agreed.

By now I was half across Park Avenue and she running to keep up with me. The doorman greeted us calmly enough. When I told him that my apartment was being burglarized he said he would investigate the situation with me. As I started to fit my key into the lock the door opened. There stood Ernest Schelling's butler!

"Good evening, Mr. Erskine." He bowed. "Welcome to your new home."

Behind him I could see the smiling faces of our friends, Ernest and Lucy Schelling, Ruth and Theodore Steinway, Irmgart and Ernest Hutcheson, Mrs. Charles Dana Gibson, Fannie Hurst, Hulda Luschanska, Oscar Wagner, Margaret and Walter Damrosch, Helen and Felix Salmond, Florence and Schuyler Smith, Julia Steinway and Edward Johnson.

Iva poked her head out the kitchen door. "You didn't know you was goin' to have a surprise party, did you, Mr. Erskine?"

My first reaction was one of relief. I had misjudged Helen Worden! Now I could understand why she had been so loath to leave the tea room!

Ernest and Lucy Schelling had organized the entire party. Their butler had brought food, drinks, china—everything. Lucy had written a couple of witty skits in which Ernest and Theodore acted. I have never heard Ernest Hutcheson play so gorgeously.

Several times during the evening I gave a mental prayer of thanks for the new apartment. Six floors were between me and the water tank. The rent was less than that which I paid at 11 West Eighty-first Street and the living room far more impressive. It had a thirty foot ceiling height—perfect acoustically. There was a balcony and an open grate fire.

And in addition a splendid dining room, a butler's pantry, a library, and an upstairs study! With such a noble setting, I should fulfill my destiny in music. Long after the last guest had gone I sat in front of the open fire dreaming of the happy future which lay ahead.

II

I had now assembled a faculty at the Juilliard with a remarkable knowledge of the American music situation. Across my desk came most of the major problems and projects which are now part of the history of American music in the years between 1928 and 1937.

Chief among these problems was the Metropolitan Opera. Mr. Gatti still cast his spell over its Board of Directors.

Otto Kahn died in November, 1934. Paul Cravath succeeded him as president of the Metropolitan Opera Association. Cornelius Bliss was chairman of the Board. Both men were making a valiant effort to save the Opera. But Gatti was still reporting a frightening deficit.

David Sarnoff, a recently elected member of the Board, asked for the auditing sheet. There was none. When an accounting was ordered, Gatti resigned. The season of the year ending 1934 had cost $3,000,000, leaving a deficit of almost a million dollars.

Over a cocktail at the Century Club Allen Wardwell told me the Board had about decided to close the doors of the Metropolitan. The only alternative was for the Juilliard to take charge. In Allen's words, "They want to leave their baby on the Juilliard doorstep. You criticized the Opera management by implication, John, when you said that with a different management opera might succeed. Can you tell us now what kind of management to set up?"

I promised to have a plan on his desk the next day. At 1:00 A.M. in the study of my new apartment, I typed out the following plan, which the Juilliard and Metropolitan trustees accepted:

Allen Wardwell, Esq.
  15 Broad Street
    New York City
Dear Wardwell:

Here are my suggestions for the Metropolitan Opera, following our conversation last night.

1. Since the main difficulty seems to be the falling off of subscriptions during the last ten years, there ought to be a very energetic effort to secure additional subscribers, and to keep those the opera already has. There ought to be some underwriting to provide a safe margin in what must be a year of transition.

I would propose, therefore, that the Juilliard Foundation underwrite the opera for next year to the extent of $150,000, that the Metropolitan Company, or the Association, or both, underwrite the year for a further $100,000, and in addition that the Metropolitan groups secure subscriptions to the amount of at least ten per cent more than the subscriptions of the current season.

If these additional subscriptions cannot be secured, I should not be in favor of the underwriting by the Juilliard Foundation. But with a new administration, and with an attractive program, I believe the subscriptions could be secured.

2. I think there should be a main season of Grand Opera lasting fourteen or fifteen weeks. There should also be a supplementary season of six months or more, at popular prices.

3. The control of both seasons should be vested in a committee appointed by the Metropolitan Board. I think the committee should consist of Mr. Cravath, Mr. Bliss, Mr. Brewster, you, Mr. Hutcheson, and myself.

4. The Director should be Herbert Witherspoon, with Edward Johnson as Assistant Director in charge of the supplementary season. Mr. Ziegler should be the business manager.

5. This Committee of Control, and this direction, seem to me essential. My plan will not work unless it is carried out by those who understand and agree with it. Mr. Witherspoon and Mr. Johnson, I know, would be entirely sympathetic, and I have no doubt of Mr. Ziegler's co-operation.

If the plan is entrusted to Committee and this direction, there ought to be no deficit.

6. We ought to plan the season, so far as finances are concerned, as though we were starting a new company. Roughly speaking, we might assume that we begin with an opera house, scenery, costumes, and other equipment, with certain fixed charges and with a reasonable prospect of taking in $1,000,000 or slightly more. We ought to plan a budget of not more than this sum, offering the artists and the staff what money we have after fixed charges are cared for. If the artists and staff would not accept the best we can offer, I would let them go. In these times they can be replaced by others of first quality.

7. Personally, I should be glad if most, if not all, of the present company stayed with us. Much as I'd like to see American singers on the American operatic stage, I would displace nobody of competence who has been loyal to the Metropolitan and who has thrown in his lot with us.

8. The main season of the opera should include the great classics, not only those with which we are familiar, but also, so far as our resources permit, certain additional classics which to the New York audience would be novelties. Mr. Witherspoon has practical plans for securing such novelties at small cost. Each production, even of the most familiar operas, should have in it some element of novelty and freshness.

9. The Metropolitan should set up a laboratory to invent new types of scenery less costly, using perhaps lights rather than materials. The Juilliard School might be used as such a laboratory and might share the cost of the experiment.

10. There should be more adequate rehearsals for performances. Here the Juilliard School might co-operate.

11. For the supplementary season, running through the summer months, air-conditioning should be installed. It would not need to be undertaken until the end of the main opera season of 1935-1936.

For this supplementary season the proscenium should be reduced in size and the orchestra pit partly covered, so that a small company and a small orchestra could be used. The singers here should be young Americans, occasionally aided by an experienced artist. The salaries should be very small, but there should be frequent appearances. The operas should be given in English. From the young singers trained in this group we should hope to select the future artists for the main season.

12. The top price for the supplementary season should be three dollars or less, the lowest price fifty cents.

13. New American operas under consideration by the Metropolitan might be tried out first at the Juilliard School at no expense to the Metropolitan. An opera which in performance proved promising might then be assigned to the repertory either of the main season or of the supplementary.

14. Skeleton companies might be sent out, where the cost is guaranteed, to collaborate with small opera companies through the country, using the local chorus and orchestra and some of the local singers.

15. Such collaboration, as well as a supplementary season at the Metropolitan, would cultivate an audience for the great artists during the main season.

16. The main season, I repeat, ought to pay for itself. The supplementary season would, I believe, make a profit.

When and if there is a profit, I would devote, roughly, one third of it to the improvement of the equipment, one third to increase the salaries of the artists and staff, and one third to lowering the price of admission.

This suggestion as to the division of profits seems to me most important. Perhaps I don't make it in the best form, but I am thinking of the advantage the Managing Director would have in dealing with the orchestra, the stage hands, and the artists, if the Metropolitan would hold out some prospect of profit-sharing. The same advantage would be enjoyed by those who solicit subscriptions. The public would be more cordial if there were an ultimate possibility of lower prices. At the same time, of course, the opera ought to reserve a certain amount for new equipment and for safety.

Faithfully yours,

John Erskine

The plan, accepted by the Boards of both the Juilliard and the Metropolitan, is, in substance, still used.

III

What the Metropolitan needed was a practical musician—
if such a man existed—thoroughly experienced in grand opera
and preferably an American. I felt we had found the answer
in Herbert Witherspoon.

I met him through Ernest Hutcheson. He had known
Witherspoon many years. Herbert was tall, white-haired, and
distinguished and looked more like a member of the Union
Club than an opera singer. I approved of him because he had
a grasp of the arts and because he had gained his experience
in many countries. He studied drawing and painting at Yale
Art School. He studied singing in New York, London, Paris,
and Berlin and acting in Munich. He had toured America
with Theodore Thomas' orchestra and for many years he had
sung first bass at the Metropolitan. He had also directed the
Cincinnati Conservatory of Music. More recently he had run
his own vocal studio in New York.

His third wife, Blanche Sternberg Skeath, had been educational director of Schirmer's, the music publishers, before
their marriage in 1934. She and Herbert came often to my
home and I went to theirs at 911 Park Avenue. She had
great executive ability, was a charming hostess, and an inspired
cook. She had taught Herbert's Chinese servant some of her
best gourmet dishes. Most important of all—she adored Herbert.

The Juilliard and the Metropolitan Board congratulated
themselves on having found the answer to prayer in Herbert
Witherspoon as general manager.

But, as the weeks passed, both Allen Wardwell and I became keenly aware that Herbert was very tired. We were re-
lieved when he told us that he and Blanche expected to sail
for Europe in May. The relaxation of an ocean voyage would,
we were sure, give him the rest he needed.

IV

Until the spring of 1935 I continued to write and to play, and it isn't much of a boast to say that the playing continued to improve. On February 19 I played with Ossip Gabrilowitsch and the Detroit Symphony, on February 24 with Eugene Ormandy and the Minneapolis Symphony, and on May 11 with Frederick Stock and the Chicago Symphony at Cornell College, Mount Vernon, Iowa.

I'll never forget that date. I admired Stock tremendously and was excited over the opportunity to play with his orchestra. On the evening of May 10 just as I was about to sit down to dinner with some members of the faculty I was summoned to the telephone. New York was calling. Herbert Witherspoon had died while sitting at his desk in the Metropolitan the day he and Blanche were to sail for Europe.

I didn't sleep a wink that night. Herbert's funeral would be the day after the concert. I played the Schumann Concerto and caught the midnight plane for New York.

Once again the Metropolitan was without a general manager. I felt sure that Edward Johnson was equipped to carry on. His professional experience paralleled Witherspoon's. He had sung in light opera, studied abroad, been leading tenor at La Scala, and created numerous new roles at the Metropolitan.

A week after Witherspoon's death, I invited Johnson to come to my apartment to discuss the Opera. After we had gone over the situation pretty thoroughly I asked him if he would like to be general manager of the Metropolitan.

He was silent for a few minutes. Then he said nothing would make him happier. He hesitated only because he wondered whether or not he would be equal to the job. I said I thought he would.

That week he was appointed general manager to succeed Herbert Witherspoon.

V

On the evening of November 5, 1935, I lectured at Lansing, Michigan. There was a piano on the stage, and after the lecture the audience asked me to play. The piano proved to be in tune, so I played. Next morning, the brightest of fine days, my friends, Mr. and Mrs. Edgar Harlan Clark, drove me to Detroit, where I was to lecture at noon. When we were about half-way, near Brighton, a heavy truck came around a curve, straight at us, on the wrong side of the road. It looked like death for us all. I remember one quick thought, that I had had a grand time and life owed me nothing. Then we struck. From the back seat I pitched forward into the unshatterable glass of the windshield, driving my head through it without pain, having had the forethought to fracture my skull at the same time. It's a good anesthetic while it lasts. I also broke my nose and the little bones of my right hand, which are useful in piano playing, and I damaged other important areas, with results which for a year or so were unpleasant and never will be quite cleared away.

The truck which tried to pass the line on the wrong side of the road was a state vehicle, and Michigan at the moment had a campaign on for more careful driving. That campaign was a good idea and I wish it had been successful.

CHAPTER TWENTY-ONE

✦✦✦✦✦✦✦✦✦✦✦✦✦✦✦✦✦✦✦✦✦✦✦✦✦✦✦✦✦✦✦✦✦✦✦✦✦✦✦

I Learn to Live Again

I

BRIGHTON, Michigan. I had never heard of that town before November 6, 1935. Ever since it has been deeply impressed upon my mind. It was in the Brighton Hospital that Mr. and Mrs. Edgar Clark and I lay on stretchers until the ambulance from the Henry Ford Hospital in Detroit picked us up. The Michigan State Highway truck had demolished the Clark car and all but killed us that morning. I didn't lose consciousness once. The doctor had been frank. He couldn't tell how badly injured I was until X-rays were made. He knew my nose had been broken and my right side damaged, particularly my right hand. It was very possible that I might never play again. It was entirely possible that I might not live.

It has often been said that a drowning man's entire life flashes before him in a matter of seconds. My failures and successes paraded before me as I lay on that stretcher. I appraised myself as I would a character in one of my novels. I card-indexed the main reasons for my failures; overromanticism, supersensitiveness, pride, a quick temper, and refusal to admit life as it was. My marriage had been a failure because I pinned on Pauline all the attributes of a Greek goddess. When the poor woman didn't express them, I blamed her. But in another sense our marriage had been a success. For Pauline had borne me two wonderful children in Anna and Graham.

I had been hurt because Amherst let Columbia have me. Yet, lying there staring at the ceiling, I knew it had been right for me to go. But it might have been handled differently if I had been less proud.

When Ashley Thorndike and not I was made secretary of the English department at Columbia I felt a deep injury. My lectures were a source of substantial revenue to Columbia and, judging from the registration figures, I knew that my classes were the most popular on the campus. Yet President Butler had deliberately named Thorndike my superior. Again, if I had stifled my pride and talked it out with Butler, my career almost certainly would have taken another turn. When I asked Butler for a leave of absence to devote my time to music, I was openly being discussed as his successor.

Did I ever honestly want to be president of Columbia University?

No. The very size of the University put the emphasis on business rather than scholarship for any chief executive. Of necessity its president was removed from real personal contact with students and teaching. His job was that of executive of a big corporation. Money, not education, was his concern. Yet I had loved Columbia more rather than less with the passing years. Now I was sorry I hadn't had a chance to lecture there more often.

At the Juilliard I had met with nothing but understanding and appreciation. Yes, I was glad I left Columbia. I still had much to do in music. I prayed for a few more years to live. I wanted to see Helen Worden and my children.

My recollection of the ambulance ride to Detroit is hazy. I remember vaguely worrying about my lecture that night at the Detroit Town Hall Series and insisting that I could give it. After that I lapsed into unconsciousness. The doctors evidently gave me a sedative, for I knew nothing until next morning when I was awakened by a tap on the door of the big room where I lay in bed. A white-capped nurse tiptoed softly to the door. A whispered exchange of words and she was back.

"Miss Worden wants to know if you would like to see her."

I cried. It was the first time I had broken down since the accident. My face was so swathed in bandages that I could not speak. I nodded my head.

The news of my accident had been flashed over the wires to the newspapers, the *World-Telegram* among others. Helen got it at the office. Her editor, Lee Wood, was a man with a heart. He told her to send in her next column from Detroit. It was snowing in New York and the planes were grounded. She left on the first train. Graham, my son, followed at midnight. He and Helen lived in the hospital until I was well enough to travel home.

The night I arrived at the Henry Ford Hospital Dr. George Kreutz, the nose and throat specialist, did his best to repair my damaged nose. Not having any photograph of me to go by and never having seen me before, he set it as best he could. When he got through I breathed as well as ever, but the beaked bridge which had been very much a part of my rugged countenance was gone. In its place I had the straight regular profile of a Hollywood matinee idol. As much as I appreciated Dr. Kreutz' skill I have never been too happy over the alteration. It wasn't in my character.

During my stay at the Henry Ford Hospital I had dozens of X-rays taken. It seemed to me every single part of my anatomy had been photographed. This was not altogether true. When I returned to New York my physician, Dr. Harold Keyes, suggested more X-rays as a precautionary measure. One revealed a fracture in my skull! I must remain quiet for a whole year. That was easier said than done for one of my temperament. Aside from a slight limp in my broken leg and the broken knuckles of my right hand, I felt better than ever. The month's enforced rest in the Henry Ford Hospital had got in its good work.

II

I picked up my life where I left off. In an effort to limber up the muscles of my right hand I practiced long hours on the piano. Once the news of my recovery spread, I also had plenty to occupy me with the Juilliard and the Metropolitan.

Mrs. Kathleen Snow Stringer, who was in charge of the Detroit Town Hall Series, wrote that members of her group were eager to have me return for the lecture I was scheduled to make the day my accident intervened.

That was a challenge. I never wanted to see Detroit again, but I disliked unfinished business. I talked it over with my doctor. He advised sticking to my rather strict schedule, which permitted me one night a week at the opera, one hour a day for writing, and one afternoon a week at the office. The balance of the time was to be spent in bed.

I improved rapidly. The last of January I was able to send the following wire:

Mrs. Kathleen Snow Stringer
Detroit Town Hall Series
533 Detroit Leland Hotel
Detroit, Michigan
    The doctor says I may come April first.

John Erskine

In the audience that night were my companions in disaster—Mr. and Mrs. Edgar Clark. Like myself, they still carried scars of the accident. Mr. Clark had been hit the hardest—the steering wheel was pressed into his chest by the force of the collision. I understand that this injury subsequently caused his death.

Since the state of Michigan was bankrupt, neither the

Clarks nor I were able to recover more than $1,000 damages apiece, despite the fact that their car was completely demolished by a state highway truck on the wrong side of the road. My medical expenses and loss of time as a result of that accident amounted to over $10,000.

When Fulton Oursler, then editor of *Liberty* magazine, asked for more François Villon stories, I jumped at the chance.

III

The Detroit return engagement was one of a lecture series that took me as far south as Chattanooga and New Orleans. My stay at the University of Chattanooga was a great success but tiring; dinner at President Alexander Guerry's, followed by my address to an immense audience, a reception at the Guerrys', and a party with the students which lasted till after midnight. I had turned my back on the doctors' advice.

The noon after my Chattanooga speech I spent at the University's music department. It was enormous. I think the registration must have been three or four times that of the Juilliard. I spoke to the students, then lunched with the faculty and more students at the President's home—a hundred guests!—gave a talk to the undergraduates at three o'clock, attended a cocktail party at Colonel Kimball's, and then, thank heaven, the train at four forty-five. I had had a grand rest coming down and foolishly thought I could keep up the mad pace of my pre-accident life.

I was still pouring out François Villon stories for Fulton Oursler. When that was done, I told myself, I would write novels based on great Americans. One of them would be about Walt Whitman. The setting would be New Orleans —during the years he worked on the *Times-Picayune*. Having this in mind I was delighted when an invitation came to lecture in New Orleans. It was my next stop after I left Chattanooga.

I stayed in the Vieux Carré at a picturesque hotel—the

Monteleone. I reveled in the charm of the old French Quarter. The women went shopping with net bags, as in Paris; the banana sellers had street cries; there were an extraordinary number of perfume shops and bookstalls and antiquary shops; at night the colored boys who sold hot tamales pushed low carts with lanterns on them. It was a dream world, somewhat dilapidated but lovely. I explored the Vieux Carré until I knew it by heart, especially St. Louis Street on which the famous French Opera House had once been located. It was destroyed by fire. I saw its ruins.

Reporters who had heard that I intended to use New Orleans as the setting for my novel on Walt Whitman were waiting at the Monteleone for me. As a consequence of their stories I had an invitation to lunch with the Gustav R. Westerfeldts on their plantation. Mrs. Westerfeldt was president of the Poetry Society, and a niece of hers had studied with me at Columbia. She was excited over the Whitman novel. I'll never forget her lovely colonnaded home on Prytania Street—the oldest house in the "Garden District."

I went back to my hotel filled with a longing to see New Orleans the Salzburg of America. As a start the French Opera House should be rebuilt. That night I poured out my ideas to Fulton Oursler in a letter written at Antoine's.

His reply was a wire. "I'll give you all the space in the world for an open letter urging the people of New Orleans to get busy."

I spent the next day composing the letter. I suggested that New Orleans establish a music festival in the Vieux Carré. "If you offer us the right things we'll all be here—" I said. "And by we I mean the art lovers of Central America as well as the United States."

I advised the city to start by rebuilding the old Opera House—"designed in the spirit of the Vieux Carré." As a program I offered: "First, a week or a fortnight, or a month of opera, and let it be exclusively pre-Wagnerian opera. Confine yourselves to the musical expression of that Latin culture—French, Spanish, Italian—which produced the charm of old New Orleans. A house large enough for Wagnerian performances is too large for proper performances of the old French and Italian operas. At present Wagner dominates the great opera houses of the world. Make it your province to give perfect performances of the music which your citizens loved long before most other American towns had any opera.

"When you have concluded your opera program, or perhaps during the intervals of it, bring together in a series of concerts the artists and the orchestras of Central America, as well as those from the Southern part of the United States.

"When your entire musical program is concluded, give us a season of French, Spanish and Italian plays."

The letter was scheduled for the November 21st issue of *Liberty.*

In August I went to Bar Harbor to visit Mr. and Mrs. Walter Damrosch. It was a gay whirl from the moment I arrived, with swimming, mountain climbs, music, and much sociability. I met old and new friends; Felix and Helen Salmond, Mr. and Mrs. Atwater Kent, the Howard Auchinclosses, Mr. and Mrs. Clement Moore (Joseph Pulitzer's daughter), the John D. Rockefellers, and I don't know how many others. I also lunched at a music club where Arthur Train was the leading spirit. It was pleasant to be made much of!

IV

In October I traveled for the Juilliard, stopping at Des Moines, Louisville, Birmingham, and Atlanta.

On October 22 I spoke at the Iowa State University in Des Moines. I have the precise date because I kept a copy of the President's introduction. His conception of me is what I long to be, not what I am. That is why I am giving it to you:

"I have a special formula of words, a kind of ritual, which I use in introducing John Erskine. I used it in presenting him to the campus audience in June and I shall use it in presenting him this evening. It runs something like this:

"Science is knowledge and Philosophy is wisdom; while Art is the communication of the ecstasy of both knowledge and wisdom through the forms, colors, rhythms and tones of the beautiful. And in the universe of discourse called Education, Art is most meaningful when communicated through a personality radiant with the beauty of literature, the rhythm of poetry, the harmony of music, the colorfulness of drama, and the charm of speech. That, ladies and gentlemen, is why John Erskine is now presented as the premier lecture guest of the State University of Iowa."

I lectured as well at several towns in South Carolina and Tennessee. I met many interesting people and learned much about that part of the country. I found it growing prosperous again. In Birmingham the audience at Phillips Hall insisted I play something before my lecture. I discovered that I was much stronger. The traveling didn't bother me at all—so I thought. My hand was better. I proved that by playing and writing.

At Memphis I saw newspaper friends of Helen Worden's —among them Edward Meeman, editor of the *Press-Scimitar*, and Mary Raymond, women's editor of the same paper. I also met I. L. Myers, a pulp paper manufacturer. He invited me to lunch. Fine paintings hung in every room of his apartment. I recall Hogarth originals on the walls of his bedroom. His taste in music was equally discriminating. Offhand I would say that Ike Myers has done more for music in the South than any other one person. That first meeting in Memphis was brief. I was to see him often in years to come.

From Tennessee I turned north, heading for Chicago. I was to speak at Rudolph Ganz' music school on November 11. While I was there my open letter on local opera to the people of New Orleans appeared in *Liberty*.

Newspapers all over the country applauded the idea. The

Montgomery, Alabama, *Journal* said, "It is not surprising that John Erskine, the philosopher, should make the suggestion that the United States should have a great music festival rivaling anything of its kind held in Europe, but it is surprising that he should have mentioned New Orleans as the most appropriate place in America for such a festival. Northern men do not usually concede that much to Southern communities."

The *New Orleans Times-Picayune* granted that "John Erskine presumably has no ax to grind and no special increase of either honors or income to expect from his suggestion. Apparently it is from the heart, or apparently from the reasoning of a logical and most incisive mind. His idea is not new but seldom has it been put in more concrete and forceful form. The Erskine letter has had the immediate effect of stimulating interest among public leaders. . . . But even the brilliant mind of John Erskine cannot lay down, in a space of 500 words, a plan that could be used as a working diagram."

I was bombarded with letters, telegrams, and long-distance telephone calls for and against my proposal.

"Your letter in *Liberty* and the encouragement given by the magazine's editors in presenting your idea so forcefully have given New Orleans just the impulse needed to bring into active unison the scattered forces which have hitherto been talking about a revival of the old culture," said H. Van R. Chase, of the New Orleans Association of Commerce.

Dr. H. W. Stepher, head of the music department of the Louisiana State University, feared that my suggestion of a festival might interfere with the development of his music department.

Roy Alciatore, proprietor of the famous Antoine's restaurant, wrote, "In the old days of the French Opera, my father has often told me of how he himself brought hot consommé to Sarah Bernhardt. Steps are being taken to make your suggestion an established fact."

R. W. Leche, then governor of Louisiana, said, "I hope John Erskine's suggestion will spur the citizens of New Orleans into action."

And a group of interested citizens did indeed invite me to return and help them organize the festival. I promised to do so in February, 1937.

I had much to occupy me in the intervening months, including more music and another lecture trip: Atlantic City, Detroit, Rochester, Albany, Troy, and Bennington College in Vermont.

At Atlantic City I made what the assembled educators said was a good speech. But my head wasn't working as it should. I found it hard to write.

At Detroit I had a great reception and Dr. and Mrs. Kreutz, the nose man, gave me a dinner. I returned from Bennington just in time for a big party at Ernest Hutcheson's. He had some forty people to a buffet supper and afterwards lectured on *Tristan and Isolde*. It was quite superb and his playing of the music marvelous. The list of guests included the Allen Wardwells, the Myron Taylors, Felix and Helen Salmond, Olga Samaroff, Blanche Witherspoon, Paul Cravath, Mr. and Mrs. William Francis Gibbs, Mrs. August Belmont, and many others. Oscar Wagner sat off at one side and napped, in spite of himself, having played golf all day. I sympathized with him for I too was extremely weary— more tired than I remembered ever having been in my entire life. I wondered how I could keep all the engagements on my calendar.

CHAPTER TWENTY-TWO

✦✦✦

That Poison in My Tea

I

FOR THE first time since the publication of *Helen of Troy* I was beginning to feel the turn of my successful literary tide.

As the financial crash of 1929 hit the country, the Juilliard trustees, like other financiers, realized that we ought to retrench and economize. Our salaries for our best teachers were somewhere around $20,000 a year. The Board thought we had better reduce this sum to at least $15,000. My own salary was originally $20,000. Voluntarily, and against some protests on the part of the treasurer of the Board, I cut my salary to $10,000, feeling that it would be easier to break the news to my colleagues that their own incomes must be reduced if I had taken a serious cut first. At the moment my writings were in considerable demand. The year that my son Graham was studying at the Sorbonne, I crossed the ocean four times to see how he was progressing. During each crossing I wrote a short story which I disposed of at the end of the voyage in New York to a magazine that had given me a blanket order for a number of stories. The price I received for a single story was only slightly less than half a year's salary.

Those were halcyon days for writers as well as for other folk. But ever since the crash of '29 the picture had been changing. I didn't get the full impact until 1937. I knew only that I must earn more money. The children were growing up. Anna wanted to study dramatics. I wanted Graham to have a final year in Europe for his architectural studies. The expenses were still going on at Wilton. In spite of warnings from my doctor I kept forcing myself to do more work. I was also conscious of the size of my apartment. Although my rent was not exorbitant, I felt I was living on too lavish a scale, at least to appearances. My wife had said as much to my relatives. I was having too good a time. I gave up my apartment, stored most of my books, gave away most of my furniture, and moved into two rooms, a bath and kitchenette on the top floor of 540 Park Avenue. I was penny wise and pound foolish. At the time I did not think so. I planned to spend my life either at the Juilliard or lecturing across the country. I told myself that I no longer needed a home.

II

During the weeks at the turn of the year, though I didn't realize it at the time, I was getting ready for the big crash.

Looking over the record I have been setting down here, I am not surprised that my nervous system was collapsing. All the years at the Juilliard I had been carrying the administrative work of the president's office, attending faculty and board meetings, visiting various parts of the country where we had stationed Juilliard representatives, playing with orchestras and chamber music groups, making numerous speeches before musical organizations, and—last but not least—writing one novel a year and several volumes of essays and short stories.

I wistfully thought of my peaceful days at Columbia. It was something of a shock to get word from Frank Fackenthal that I was to be retired as professor emeritus. On the heels of his letter came one from President Butler.

Dear John:

You have received formal notice from the Secretary of the University of the action of the Trustees yesterday in designating you as Professor Emeritus from the date of your retirement on July 1, 1937. I am writing to express my great personal pleasure in this action, which ensures that your name will be carried on the University rolls and that you will continue as a member of the University family in which you have been for so many years.

Nicholas Murray Butler

Butler was a great administrator and a great man in many respects, but he had his peculiarities. The uncle for whom he was named, Nicholas Murray, librarian at Johns Hopkins, understood him better than anyone I have ever met.

When I first returned to teach at Columbia, I went to take tea with Mr. Murray and his wife at their home in Paterson, New Jersey.

Our topic of conversation was Nicholas Murray Butler. His aunt said, "When Nicholas was very young he wanted to be a missionary. I'm sorry he didn't follow his desire."

"It's a good thing he didn't," said the uncle. "He would have made a terrible missionary."

"I think he would have been a very good one," said the aunt. "He would have converted the natives."

"And if they didn't agree with him he would have burnt them alive," said the uncle.

III

That I carried on my literary career side by side with the attempt to equip myself as a musician, practicing two or three hours a day, needs some explaining. I was crazy to attempt it, but that it ended in disaster for me is entirely my own fault. I was thoroughly happy with my life and paid no attention to many warnings that I was doing too much.

I discounted the fact that our nervous energies are strictly limited. By constant practice I had brought my right hand back into flexibility. Ernest Hutcheson said I was playing better than ever.

On January 11, 1937, I pushed Fate too far. The Bohemians, the musicians' club of which Ernest Hutcheson was president, gave a party that night. Ernest planned an American program of piano music, and invited me to play it. There was also a performance of some American music by the Gordon String Quartet. The pieces I chose were:

Sea Pieces   Edward MacDowell
    a) To the Sea
    b) Song
    c) From the Depths
Serenade   Howard Brockway
Polonaise Americaine   John Alden Carpenter

Most of this music I had played before, but I found some of it inexplicably difficult. I did not realize I was on the verge of a complete nervous breakdown. At the last moment I abandoned all hope of playing properly Beryl Rubinstein's *Arabesque*, which he had dedicated to me. To my horror I couldn't remember it. I realized I was even forgetting the familiar MacDowell pieces. I put it down to the extremely heavy schedule of that day.

Theodore Steinway had asked me as a favor to him to make a speech on January 31 at the Pipe Night of the Players Club. He was presiding. I planned one speech and gave another, on opera—improvising it when I saw a number of opera stars were among the guests. After the evening was over the men told me they had never heard me make a more brilliant speech. I credited their enthusiasm to the good will of the occasion. Next day Frank Mason, who had been present, asked me if I would send him a copy of my speech.

I didn't remember a word of what I had said and I couldn't have told, if I'd been shot the next minute, what my subject was. This terrified me. A week later I was to start out on a lecture tour which would take me as far as the Pacific coast.

The afternoon of my departure I stopped at the Drake Hotel to discuss last minute matters with a friend. I found it increasingly difficult to think. As I was talking my entire right side began to tingle. The last thing I remember saying was "Call Helen Worden."

Helen and her mother were living in those years in an apartment at 449 Park Avenue. By some good fortune she happened to be home that noon. I believe Zosia Kochanski was lunching with her. At any rate, when the telephone brought the news of my collapse she rushed across the avenue to the Drake diagonally opposite her apartment. The doctors told her I had suffered a paralytic stroke. Until I could be moved she stayed at the Drake keeping an eye on me, the doctors, and the nurses.

Graham was in Italy. As soon as I could talk I made it clear that I didn't want him to come home. Everything was being done for me that could be done. My recovery was in the hands of the gods. When I was moved back to my apartment, Helen rode in the ambulance. From the moment that I was carried into that little apartment I hated it. What with day and night nurses, the doctors, and Iva, my maid, there wasn't room to turn around. I regretted with all my heart the loss of my comfortable and spacious duplex. The one bright spot was the friendliness of my neighbor, Mrs. Henry Lott. Hot broths, delicious salads, and cooling desserts helped Iva over rough spots.

The doctors said I was an ideal patient—by which praise, though they didn't know it, they were paying a tribute to my Scotch stubbornness which refused to be downed.

IV

This illness had been for me the most profound experience of my life. The automobile accident in Michigan showed me what it was like to expect to meet death—a very useful discovery—and now for the second time I had been taught the adventure of not knowing whether one is good for months or days. That of course is our condition at all times, but in this kind of illness the chance was sharpened. And with the shock to the nerves had come a blessed release from concern with all but the important things.

During that second bout with illness I read a great deal. I hadn't read so thoughtfully for many years, perhaps not since Amherst days, and I flatter myself that my thoughts now go deeper because of that reading.

The doctors said I must have something to hope for. Was there anything I wanted to do? Yes—and this was a surface irritation—move to a larger apartment. The two rooms in which I had been cooped up for months were a prison.

My doctors thought it a healthy sign that I worried about my apartment. Harold Keyes, my own physician, had asked Livingston Hunt, a noted brain specialist, to share the responsibilities of my case. Dr. Hunt said I must lead as normal a life as possible. He encouraged me to try to walk and to write. In less than two weeks I was stumbling around the block with the aid of Helen and my nurse. I was also pecking out, with the forefinger of my left hand, the final stories eventually to be put in a book, *The Brief Hour of François Villon*. I also tried to practice the piano. But at best it was a sorry performance. At the end of two months I could see little progress.

In the long hours of lying half-paralyzed on my bed, I had plenty of opportunity to face myself. The thought of complicating my own life as well as the lives of those I loved by being a helpless paralytic was frightening. Enough morphine to settle the problem rested in my medicine cabinet. Wouldn't it be a kindness to myself and to others to swallow an overdose of the stuff?

I argued the question all through the night. Mother regarded this life as an apprenticeship. She was not one to quit. When she was all but dying and looked it, she kept on. Tossing and turning in bed, it seemed to me I could hear her say, "My dear boy, you are to do your best in everything. It isn't your business to say when you are to die. Don't try to do it all yourself. Leave something to God."

Whether my imagination credited her with these words or whether her spirit really spoke I do not know. But I knew that what she said was right. As I lay in my bedroom watching the dawn paint the Queensboro Bridge pink, I thought of the day I went to war.

Mother had entered upon her last long illness, but she raised herself to a sitting position and put her hand upon my shoulder. "John, my dear, you have grown up. I didn't think you were strong enough to say good-by to your son, but I should have remembered that you would say good-by to anything if it was necessary."

When I came home after the war ended and the University at Beaune had been closed, Mother, by some miracle, still lived. I hurried, as quickly as I could, from the boat to the street, but every taxi was gone. I had to take a surface car. Two blocks this side of 115th Street I took off my medals and put them in my pocket. I had quite a number. When I saw Mother I lifted them out of my pocket and spread them on the counterpane for her to see. She never looked at the medals.

Instead she kept patting my arm and saying, "My dear boy. You're back safe and sound. I've waited for you to come home."

Remembering all this, I knew Mother would be ashamed of me if I attempted anything so cowardly as suicide. That morning, when the nurse left me in the bathroom to shave myself, I threw the morphine down the drain. I had made up my mind to stay and take whatever life had in store for me.

That day I sent word to Mr. Perry that I had an announcement to make to the Juilliard Board—could its members meet at my apartment? When the eight members gathered in my small living room, I announced my resignation as president of the Juilliard School and recommended that Ernest Hutcheson be appointed in my stead.

There were protests, of course, but when the men, all my friends, realized that my decision was final, they asked Allen Wardwell to voice for them the understanding and regret with which they were forced to accept my resignation.

At a reception held in the Juilliard School, the faculty presented me with a handsome wrist watch and an oil painting of Lower New York. I still cherish a copy of that farewell speech. Here is my favorite paragraph:

"John Erskine, President of the Juilliard School, has had our trust, our admiration and our pride in his manifold achievements. John Erskine, the writer, has lent the power and vision of his creative imagination to the building of the institution we love and serve. John Erskine, the speaker, has often given us inspiration for our work. John Erskine, the man, has made us his friends, and John Erskine, the musician, has made us his colleagues."

I still cherish another message from my old friend, Fred Keppel. It reads:

Dear John:

Some thoughtful eye in my office picked out the notice of your resignation, and mailed the clipping to me here, rightly judging that I would be deeply interested.

You have made musical history in the ten years of your service, and your friends have been very proud of what you have accomplished.

May the years to come give you rich opportunities.

Affectionately,
Frederick P. Keppel
The Carnegie Corporation
522 Fifth Avenue
New York City

I met Fred when we were both college students, he a senior, I a sophomore. But it seems to me that I must always have known him, he has been such a close and loyal friend. His great abilities were enough to make him a remarkable man, but I admired even more his zest for life, his shrewd humor, and his quickness in understanding the changing problems of the years when he played so brilliant and so public a part. He was dean of Columbia College when I returned to Columbia to teach, and he was in the War Department when I went to France in the educational work. Subsequently he headed the Carnegie Corporation. At the Juilliard I found many opportunities, thoughtfully contrived by him, to set up some co-operation with his Carnegie group, and always furthering the cause of music. The last time I saw him was in St. Paul's chapel at the funeral of Columbia's dean, Herbert Hawkes. Keppel died in 1943.

I resigned from the Juilliard primarily because of the condition of my health. I also dreamed of finding time to write and to study and to think.

I had not been able to keep my engagement with the New Orleans' festival enthusiasts, nor could I help them for some time to come. Politicians, seeing the popularity of the idea, seized upon it. They eventually went to jail for other reasons.

✦✦✦

I Speak for Music

I

IN FEBRUARY, 1937, I moved from my small apartment on the top floor of 540 into a more spacious one on the sixth floor. Fate had again given me a reprieve. I was to have another chance at life.

The owner of the building obligingly let me put in all the bookshelves I needed. That meant covering most of the walls in the living room, study, dining room, and hall. I still had a day and night nurse and I still felt a little wobbly on my feet. But I was coming along. By March I was strong enough to let both nurses go. A couple of days at my brother Bob's in Scarsdale, two weeks at Mrs. Harry Hamlin's wonderful inn, the Hedges in East Hampton, and I was ready to continue my life. One thing was certain. I would never play again. The accident, plus the stroke, had permanently crippled my right hand. It looked as though, music having educated me, I should give myself from now on to literature.

Much as I loved writing, I refused to give up music entirely. I loved it too well. As long as I could speak I intended to raise my voice in its interests. I remained chairman of the Metropolitan Opera Board, a director of the Juilliard School Board and a trustee of the Juilliard Foundation. I also continued to lecture—chiefly about music.

Roughly speaking I would say that I have given about five thousand lectures. Of this number more than half were on music. I enjoyed best two series, one at the Carnegie Institute of Technology in Pittsburgh, the other at Cooper Union in New York. Each had an entirely different approach to music.

In the autumn of 1938 the President of Pittsburgh University asked me if I would care to make a weekly appearance at Carnegie Tech. with Fritz Reiner and the Pittsburgh Symphony.

This Music Appreciation course attempted to do something which, so far as I know, had not been tried before. The orchestra was present at each session—with Fritz Reiner conducting. I would ask it for the single movement of some symphony, or some other important piece of music which takes ten or fifteen minutes to play. We played the piece at the beginning of the hour and a half, and again at the end, to see how much we had gained in the capacity to listen.

Nothing was said about the biography of the composer or about critical opinions of the music. I tried to do for the ear what a competent painter can do for the eye when he stands by your side as you look at a picture and points out to you the good things in it.

Of course we paid much attention to the tone and the uses of the various instruments.

The course was possible because five universities or colleges in Pittsburgh co-operated with students from the institutions electing the course, and there were also registrations from the general public. The finances therefore took care of themselves. The co-operation between educational institutions was, so far as I know, an innovation, and it still seems to me a most promising idea. I wonder that more schools and universities don't do it.

Instead of their wearing me down, I thrived on those weekly trips to Pittsburgh. I met people who loved music. I was thrilled at the response of the audiences and I thoroughly relished the marvelous midnight suppers served Fritz and myself by Carlotta Reiner.

I reminded myself of a line which the *New Yorker* once printed in a profile on me: "John Erskine bloomed late and he's making up for lost time."

That work with the Pittsburgh Symphony involved an immense amount of study on my part to reach the point of saturation necessary. But, even if I never played again, I would now enjoy a real facility in score reading and could impart this knowledge to others as I explained the various instruments taking part in a symphony.

II

I found the same satisfaction in the Cooper Union series which I gave in 1940. Houston Peterson, then in charge of the lectures, gave me an opportunity to talk on music. In the first lecture I discussed the ancient modes and scales and the different systems of tuning and various agreements as to pitch. I then sketched the development of polyphony and the principles by which harmony has developed and is still developing. These matters I illustrated on the piano with my undamaged left hand. I then reminded the audience that until very recently music was chiefly a matter of the voice, and instruments held a secondary position. And I explained why, in a vocal world, polyphony could easily develop and why an instrument like the piano encouraged new discoveries in harmony, since on such an instrument the overtones could be recognized and reinforced.

Polyphony survived in the concerto grosso, but when the solo interrupted there could be only a melody. So long as music was written primarily for the church, the melody submitted more or less to the restraints of decorum; but the individualistic principle is expansive, and when voices were displaced by instruments, and when instrumentalists went in for technical fireworks, the concerto became what we now understand by the term: a show piece for virtuosity. The concertino, concentrated and dramatized in the soloist, monopolized the attention; rudimentary vestiges of the concerto grosso survived in the accompaniment and the tutti.

Many of the great concertos in the past were written by composers who were also performing virtuosos. Mozart and Beethoven are in the list, also Rachmaninoff. The earliest pianists were competent violinists as well, and prolific composers are likely to write for all the instruments they know. In our specializing age the composer isn't likely to be a brilliant performer, but he will have a respectable acquaintance with many instruments, and he can always have the advice of virtuosos in the various fields.

The concerto for human voices, ancestor of all other kinds of concerto, has ceased to exist. We still use the solo voice against a choral background, but we also use the orchestra to support the chorus. The instrumental concerto supplanted the vocal for several reasons, one of which is quite sufficient: the number of instruments is large, and when used for solo purposes against a rich accompaniment each is capable of new effects. Composers have always been fascinated by the possibilities. A modicum of courage is needed, apparently, to try out any instrument hitherto not admitted to the best concerto society. The saxophone is improving its status; in time we shall be ready for some banjo concertos. They will probably receive a serious welcome, since the banjo in the hands of a virtuoso creates beauty as well as astonishment.

In the second lecture I began by reminding the audience that Palestrina did his work just a few years before Shakespeare did his; that Bach and Handel preceded by several decades the American Revolution; that all the modern development of music is very recent indeed. After this I sketched the development of the orchestra, of symphonic and operatic music, and of piano music, trying to make the point that, aside from the undoubted evolution of the piano and of the orchestra as an instrument and the enrichment of harmony, the last century and a half has been not so much a development as a constant shifting of emphasis. The experiments made in the most forward-looking operas, for example, are not different essentially from the problems raised by old Peri in 1600—whether to combine the dramatic sections with the lyrical by pretending that dramatic parts were lyrical, or to emphasize the dramatic by speaking the dialogue and going in for realism. As another example I pointed out our contemporary neglect of the voice and the consequent eclipse of good song writing and opera composing.

I concluded by outlining the essentials of music form—of form in any art where the main statements have to be emphasized by repetition. I suggested also some of the changes which may occur in our way of presenting music if amplification is developed and used, and if we are willing to depart from the traditional orchestra.

III

The rhythms which even the masters have used are pitifully few. One reason that our age, studious and experimental, returns with such enthusiasm to Bach is that he availed himself of all he inherited and added inventions and novelties of his own. After him the art has had more than one moment of what might be called economical success—a shrinkage of its tradition. Even though you yield to nobody in admiration of Chopin, or Schumann, or Brahms, you must admit their effects are less rich and varied, as their technical material is poorer, than those of Bach and Beethoven.

Theoretically music rests on popular impulse, like the other arts—popular we call it, not vulgar. To retain its hold on the mass of humanity it must continue to express, in however refined a form, all sides of that basic impulse. If it doesn't, the popular impulse will take its revenge—humanity will express itself somehow.

Swing at the present moment is perhaps a popular revenge

on music for forgetting to express all it has to say. In music
the popular impulse is all for rhythm, then melody, and finally
harmony. If your learned and traditional musician gets the
cart before the horse, emphasizes the harmony, squelches the
melody, and suppresses the rhythm, he will lose his audience.

Jazz seems to me normal and healthy. Of course you can't
make perfect music out of rhythm alone, but you also can't
make it out of melody or harmony alone.

Of all the arts music has still perhaps the greatest number
of undeveloped possibilities. It has been slow to use the har-
monies which it knew of, and still slower to discover additional ones. Even now we cling faithfully to the major and
minor modes, as though there were no others, and complain
about the poverty of the medium. At a moment which is
producing no sublime composer in any style, it seems rash to
blame the medium on the materials. To justify our sterility
we say many fine musical compositions could be improved by
rewriting. That is quite true. But in this art the difficulty is
much greater than in literature. The rewriting has already
been done in the case of old composers or of composers not so
well established in fame as to seem sacrosanct. There are
dreary passages in a good many of the classics which I should
like to see stricken out, but any such improvement would raise
a dreadful howl from the pious.

And there would be danger, of course, in starting the practice of rewriting masterpieces unless it were possible to confine the activity to exceptional people. If a MacDowell wishes
to shorten and arrange Alkan, the result is first-rate, but I
shouldn't like all the pianists and composers to have a free
hand in cutting out whatever they happened not to appreciate.

Composing music has always fascinated me. I wish now I
had done more of it. Running through old sheet music the
other day I came upon the Columbia "Marching Song,"
"Stars of the Summer Night," and "My Love Has Come."
The marching song was entirely my own. I set Longfellow's

Stars of the Summer Night" to music for the University Glee Club; Rossetti's "My Love Has Come" I set to music for Father.

I collaborated on four light operas but actually wrote the music for only one—*The Governor's Vrouw.* In all I composed two hymns and two Christmas carols. The hymns were "Abide with Me" (privately printed) and "St. Paul's," which was used in Protestant hymnals. I am not proud of the carols. I liked best the music for my first hymn, "Abide with Me."

I enjoyed composing hymns. I don't mean that in a do-good sense. To me, anthems are the noblest of all forms of music. Fine hymns are pretty close to anthems. I am speaking of the simple old-fashioned hymns uncluttered by false trimmings. I have in mind Father's favorite hymn, "There Is a Green Hill Far Away." I always liked best those great hymns which were common to many sorts of people. Of course not all hymns have the dignity of these. Some are liked just because they are well-known. But there cannot be great hymns unless the composer knows great anthems.

Perhaps because of my early background I have always been drawn into church music. In 1914 President Butler asked me to be on the Columbia Hymnal committee. We were to collect and edit the material. It was work I understood and thoroughly enjoyed. Those serving with me were John B. Pine, clerk of the trustees, Raymond Knox, chaplain of the University, E. D. Perry, professor of Greek, James C. Ebert, professor of Latin, and Walter Henry Hall, Columbia choirmaster and organist.

Pine didn't know the first thing about hymns; Knox, Perry, and Ebert little more. Hall, of course, was thoroughly experienced. Butler couldn't carry a tune, but he had plenty to say about what he wanted in that Hymnal. He listed his requisites:

Include the most noteworthy hymns of each of the following classes:

1. Hymns familiar throughout the English-speaking world

because of their substantially universal use by the Protestant churches and in family worship.

2. The most noteworthy Latin, German and English hymns that have scholarly or academic associations. The great hymns of the ages are, with very few exceptions, written in one of these three languages. I think that some of the most noteworthy Latin and German hymns should appear in both the original form and in the standard translation.

3. Hymns of great literary beauty and spiritual significance which because of the fact that they lie outside of the ordinary theological formulas are not included in the well-known collections. I have in mind hymns by Cardinal Newman, Keble, Faber, Frances Ridley Havergal and John Greenleaf Whittier.

A collection of this kind uniting in one group the familiar hymns of childhood with the more stately and noble products of the hymn writers of all times would, I think, make the collection unique of its kind and in every way worthy of the University.

With all this talk President Butler amiably approved our choices—many of which were not his.

CHAPTER TWENTY-FOUR

Old Friends

I

D URING the spring of 1939 I renewed old friendships in the South. On February 10 I lectured at the historic Dock Theatre in Charleston. The following week I was to give three lectures at the University of Miami.

The invitation from the University had come through Walter Scott Mason, director of its Winter Institute, but I felt certain it was at the instigation of Hervey Allen, a trustee of Miami University. I first met Hervey and DuBose Heyward when I lectured at Charleston in 1923. They were struggling young poets living on a houseboat. While Hervey cooked incredibly delicious food, he entertained me with an exciting account of some murder involving prominent Charlestonians. When he was all through he calmly informed me that all the characters involved had been dead more than a century. He made history live.

Five years after we met, Lawrence Langner of the Theatre Guild produced *Porgy*, which DuBose and Dorothy, his wife, had dramatized from DuBose's novel. In 1934 Mr. Langner called on me at the Juilliard. Would we dare put on an all-

Negro opera? If I had been a wise man I would have raised objections. My obvious belief in the success of such a venture convinced Langner that it had possibilities. In 1935 the Theatre Guild produced the first all-Negro opera on Broadway. It was *Porgy and Bess*, the opera about which I had been so enthusiastic. The Heywards had done the book, George Gershwin the music.

I never doubted Gershwin. From the first moment I had heard him play his *Rhapsody in Blue* at Ernest Hutcheson's, I knew he was a first-rate genius. I learned to know him intimately and I never changed my opinion. Overstudy and overwork snuffed him out while he was still young. Anything that happens to wrecks like me is all right. But it is heartbreaking to have a fatal illness overtake youngsters who are needed so desperately to save the world from our mistakes. George Gershwin was a fine citizen as well as a great composer. His music will never die.

I have that same belief in *Porgy and Bess*. In the years to come it will be heard many times wherever good opera is given.

That February evening in 1939, when I spoke at Charleston's old Dock Theatre, DuBose and his wife were in the audience. Success hadn't changed him. He was the same soft-spoken, thoughtful boy with whom I had so many fine talks on the houseboat.

II

After his tremendous success with *Anthony Adverse*, Hervey Allen moved to Florida and built himself a handsome home at Coconut Grove.

At Miami University I was one of several speaking for the Institute. On the same program was Leonard Liebling, the music critic. I liked him as a person, but I always felt that his sister, Estelle, knew more about music than he.

I have been hammering for years at the one requisite for music criticism: the critic ought to know what he is about.

In so far as the newspaper critic tries to serve as a kind of scorekeeper for the maker of concerts, noting that this or that musician played or sang better or worse, has this virtue or that defect—I see no particular value in his services. The concert has already been given when his criticism appears, and it is impossible for the audience to argue with him or check up .on his opinions by any reference to the performance, of which almost certainly no record has been made.

A great service could be rendered, sometimes it is rendered, by telling the public in advance why a certain performance is likely to be worth hearing, why certain numbers on the program are important in musical history, on what grounds the performer has a special right to claim our attention. The daily criticism in the newspaper should, I think, play up the news by discussing in some such fashion the concerts which are to be presented to the community in the immediate future.

Our present custom of rushing a criticism into type directly after the performance is, I think, unfair to the critic, to the performers, and to the public.

In other words, I think the good music critic should serve the community in two ways: first, by educating the audience in advance toward a more discriminating enjoyment of what they are to hear; second, by discussing the performances after deliberate reflection.

Undoubtedly a music critic, to be effective, must be a good writer as well as a good musician. By good musician I mean that at some time in his life he should have enjoyed first-rate professional training as a performer. Unless he has this background he probably cannot take the point of view and understand the ideals and problems of those he may be called upon to criticize. But most of all he should be a sincere music lover.

I have the warmest sympathy for newspaper music critics since their papers, at least in large towns, overwork them, and they have too little time for study. Their work too often becomes for them drudgery. Rather than submit performers—and the audiences—to the criticisms of the jaded and un-

sympathetic critic, we probably should be better off with no
criticisms at all.

Several months after the Miami University Institute meetings, I said as much to Leonard Liebling. I couldn't have said
it if he hadn't understood and loved music. Perhaps that is
why he agreed with me.

My first lecture at the University of Miami was a success,
judging from the size of the audience. Afterwards came a reception at the home of the University's president, Bowman
Ashe. However pleasant, it was a crowded and tiring day. I
found myself slipping into the nerve strain I had been trying
to avoid. Next morning I put on my bathing trunks and sun-
bathed in the backyard of the University guest house at Coral
Gables. That noon Hervey Allen took me to lunch at the Surf
Club. We talked the afternoon through. He had all sorts of
splendid ideas for the University. At heart he was a teacher.
His years in the English Department at Columbia had proved
that.

Next morning he showed me through the music department of Miami University. The head of it was Arnold Volpé,
founder of the New York Stadium Symphony concerts. More
than anyone else, he was responsible for the success of the
music department of Miami University. He was a famous
conductor and he knew what he was about. Unfortunately,
he died in 1940.

A reassuring number of colleges and universities across the
country have good music departments. Columbia, for example, has an excellent one headed by Douglas Moore. The
music department at the University of Arizona is unusually
good. But very few of them can ever approach what is offered
at a good conservatory.

The final day at Miami University was a test of my strength.
I reveled in the fact that I not only stood it but had a good
time. In the morning I looked over my notes for the night's
lecture. Then I was taken to a large luncheon, then to a rehearsal of the University orchestra, then to a reception and

tea, then to dinner with President Ashe and Hervey Allen and Robert Frost, the poet, at the home of the widow of Ambassador Robert Bingham. She had married one of the University faculty. After dinner came the lecture, then a farewell party, and at midnight the train for New York.

III

April of 1939 found me lecturing in Texas. I discovered in 1928 that Texas was a country, not a state. It hadn't changed. A memorable experience of my stay in 1939 was a visit to the King ranch. I was a voluntary guest of the sheriff. On the morning of the first day we crossed the northern boundary line. On the evening of the second day we were still on King ranch land!

Paul Kochanski once told me that of all the states in the Union he considered Texas the most advanced musically. Its people demanded the best. He admitted that oil fortunes helped. His favorite Texas story was about the daughter of a Texas farmer who wanted to be a violinist.

Paul had given a recital in Houston and was headed for San Antonio. At the first stop he noticed the station agent wig-wagging the conductor with a yellow envelope. A moment later the conductor stuck his head in the car. "Telegram for Paul Kochanski. Answer requested."

Paul ripped open the envelope. The enclosed message read, "Missed your show in Houston. Will you repeat it for my daughter? She wants to be a fiddler. Means overnight stop three stations down the line."

Hastily Paul scribbled "No," on the back of the telegram. He had never heard of the man.

At the next stop another telegram was handed him. It read, "Name your price."

He laughed and wrote "$5,000" on the envelope. That would settle him. At the following stop he got a third wire. "Okay. Cars meeting you at next station."

His San Antonio concert was two days off. The fee was
fabulous. Besides it might be fun. But what on earth did the
man mean by cars? There must have been a mistake in trans-
mitting the message. He had the answer when he left the
train. Two Rolls-Royces were waiting, one for him, the other
for his violin.

His host, a kindly faced old man, stood at the ranch gate
with his daughter, a young girl about thirteen. They had read
about Paul's concert the day after it had been given.

"The one thing my girl wants to do is play the fiddle," said
the old man. "She thinks it's going to help her if she sees how
you do it. After we give you some stout Texas ranch food we'll
let you try."

When the meal was over they led him into a big raftered-
ceiling living room warmed by an open fire. On top of a huge
concert grand rested two violin cases.

The old man walked across to the piano. "If your fiddle
goes sour we can fix you up." He opened the cases and held
up the violins for Paul to examine. One was a Stradivarius,
the other a Guarnerius.

Paul played until midnight by the light of the open fire for
the old man and his daughter. Oil had been struck on the
farm six months before. The one thing the girl wanted to do
was play the violin. Paul said she could do it surprisingly well.

IV

By now you've probably guessed that I like to travel. I was
to have plenty of it for the next half dozen years.

On the last day, or rather night, of June, 1939, I boarded
a plane at Newark airport. Hollywood was my destination. I
was to be master of ceremonies for the next six weeks on a
West Coast radio program; also, Fulton Oursler had ordered
ten articles from me—interviews with movie stars, directors,
producers, and musicians.

Lawrence Tibbett occupied the berth beneath mine on the

sleeper plane. He was one of the stars on my program. I hoped
to discuss the program on the trip, but he didn't wake up. He
was still asleep when breakfast was served out of Fort Worth,
so I joined a man across the aisle, a circuit-riding preacher
from the Tennessee Mountains. At El Paso the preacher was
replaced by an American who had lived in Mexico City for
fifteen years. He was in the purchasing department of the
Mexican Government and going to Los Angeles to buy freight
cars and locomotives.

Tibbett was up in time for the landing. Rudolph Polk, the
organizer of our program, met us. A news photographer took
several shots of Tibbett, now wide awake, descending from
the plane with me. He and I were to make our first appearance on the radio program the next evening. In addition to
Tibbett, my supporting cast included Madeleine Carroll and
Groucho, Harpo, and Chico Marx.

Within the next twenty-four hours I found myself a whirl-
ing vortex of offers and counter offers to do this or that script
if . . . I knew Hollywood well enough not to take it too
seriously. What about my writing a picture for Tibbett? He
couldn't do it until 1940 but, and if . . . I smiled and went
on about my business. So did Tibbett. We were rushed here
and there by rival producers. One afternoon it was a garden
party given by Mr. and Mrs. Mudd, chief backers of the Hollywood Bowl concerts. Every musical person was there—Matze-
nauer, Pierre Monteux, Richard Bonelli, and several others
from the Met. The Mudds' beautiful estate adjoined Harold
Lloyd's.

At five we went back to the studio. Frank Forrest came in
to say hello, also Harpo Marx, a double for his brother, Chico.
The broadcast went to everyone's satisfaction, though the
script seemed to me pretty feeble.

The tentative bids from picture companies for scripts were
exciting me. Sam Goldwyn wanted to see me in a hurry. So I
went over. He was in urgent need of a picture for Merle
Oberon. We had an enormously enthusiastic meeting discuss-

ing possibilities. While I was conferring with him, another movie company was trying to reach me for more talk about the Tibbett film. Hollywood!

That evening Groucho Marx gave an enormous party. The guests were the speakers on our last program, the radio people, the script writers, and all the Marxes except Harpo. By now I knew there were five Marx brothers. They went on the stage together as the four Marx Brothers. In 1939 there were three still in business. The nicknames of the three, Groucho, Chico, and Harpo, were used only in the family until Alexander Woollcott persuaded them to use the names on the stage.

We sat at card tables and enjoyed an excellent buffet supper. Tibbett and Madeleine Carroll sat with two of the radio people. I sat with a radio man and his wife and Groucho's daughter, Miriam, aged twelve, I believe. The talk was general through the room, and as Groucho's house had a full-sized bar and there was a professional to attend it the evening was not inhibited. But everybody was working hard at pictures or radio programs, so we broke up before eleven.

Groucho and Chico were married to extremely nice women, Chico's wife being especially intelligent. I liked Chico best of the brothers, not that Groucho wasn't a grand fellow, but he was introspective, restless, and melancholy. After meeting him I felt that what he did on the stage was not himself, whereas Chico was a born trouper with an immense natural talent, and though he was the eldest brother he kept his enthusiasm and his youthful spirit. He loved what he was doing. He had an extraordinary talent for the piano, though he used it in bizarre ways.

Stokowski once took the Philadelphia orchestra to a Marx picture to see the way Chico played a run, and when Artur Rubinstein was in Hollywood he called on Chico and asked for a demonstration. After dinner I asked Chico to show me, and we sat by the piano the rest of the evening convulsed by brilliant stunts that would shock some conventional pianists.

When I said I was dining with Stokowski Tuesday evening, everybody laughed. I confounded them all. Next afternoon I drove to Stokowski's exotic little place on the high Beverly Crest Drive, with the most superb view I have ever seen. He suggested that I dismiss my car and he would drive his. We went to the Beachcomber, an imitation Chinese-Hawaiian spot, which was the rage at the moment. After a fine meal and a good talk he drove me home about ten thirty.

He spoke of Walt Disney with unbounded admiration; otherwise he spoke of himself and his plans—which was what I had asked for and come to hear. After he had told me that only universal geniuses should direct pictures, I waited a discreet interval, then asked if he would ever direct a picture. He said he was directing one at the moment.

The next day I saw Walt Disney, so far the most interesting person I had yet met. He was an extraordinary genius who made me feel his energy and enthusiasm the moment he spoke. Yet he was thoroughly practical and modest, giving credit to all of his associates. He said of Stokowski that, having done the recording with the Philadelphia orchestra for the Mickey Mouse film, he had fallen in love with pictures and was hanging around trying to be useful when there really wasn't anything for him to do right then.

At the Disney studios I saw some preliminary tryouts of the film Stokowski had been working on. I was shown the whole process of making an animated cartoon, then the fragments of film ready out of the whole Stokowski enterprise. I described it in detail for an article in *Liberty* which I called "Mickey Mouse, Supported by the Philadelphia Orchestra."

V

Two nights after the Marx party Frank Forrest gave us a beefsteak fry in his patio under the clear stars. Earle Lewis of the Metropolitan and his family were there. Also Mr. and Mrs. Mario Chamlee and the Gene Lockharts. We had a wonderful talk until all hours. Frank cooked the steaks himself on a charcoal brazier. I reflected that California was as good at cooking steaks as Texas was bad.

I was constantly meeting musicians in Hollywood. Lunching on the Paramount lot I ran into Arthur Loesser, the pianist—Beryl Rubinstein's colleague. That afternoon Ernest Toch, the Viennese musician, called on me at my hotel. I dined at his home the following night with only him and his wife. Vicki Baum came in afterwards. Next day I went to see a studio run of *The Cat and the Canary*, Hornblow's picture for which Toch wrote the music. I wanted to hear the music, not only because of the articles I was writing for *Liberty* but because I thought Toch was the man we should have at the Juilliard to head the composition department. He was fairly young and a real person. We didn't get him for the School then, but I still hope he will come.

I heard much financial gossip about Jascha Heifetz' picture *They Shall Have Music*. Curiosity took me to that preview. It was superb for the playing of Heifetz and the high-school orchestra, and the best recording of music I have ever heard. The plot was silly, but perhaps nothing better could be done, with the Heifetz records finished before the story was written and with the girl soprano who had to be included. Another preview I saw was *Starmaker*, an awful picture, awful that is with the exception of Walter Damrosch. He was making his Hollywood debut at eighty! And doing it with style too.

The town glittered with bright young conductors. In our radio show Robert Dolan, the orchestra leader, took a large part in the dialogue. His intelligence and charm were extraordinary. I marked him down as one of the coming orchestra leaders.

Shortly after I had settled myself at the Château Elysée, Clara Gabrilowitsch telephoned that she was now living in Hollywood. Could I lunch with her the next day. I had a happy time. Among the guests was Doris Kenyon, who immediately invited me to dine at her home. I went two nights later. Igor Gorin, the singer, was there. Also John L. Balderston, who wrote *Berkeley Square* and worked on *Gone With the Wind.*

The possibilities of life are so numerous in Hollywood. That may be the effect of the sunshine. For one thing the sun brought out a distressing tendency in nudism. A crackpot on my street cut his lawn every week in nothing but shoes and shorts. He was thinner than Bernard Shaw and twice as old. Ladies of all ages went shopping in bare feet and a two-piece swimming suit: brassière and skeleton panties. God must have laughed.

But it was not so mad a world as it sounds. You simply had to be a real person, able to hold your own in the swift stream.

I was getting disturbing news about the Juilliard. Ernest wrote that he would resign in October, on the ground that he wouldn't have taken the presidency if I hadn't been ill, and now that I was well he wanted to give it up. I wrote back that he ought to talk with John Perry and other friends before he decided. Frankly, I was beginning to feel that the Juilliard needed a younger man than either of us.

VI

It was a gay life for me up to the very day I left Hollywood. The last evening the Lockharts entertained in my honor and invited Dalies Frantz, the pianist, Rosa Ponselle, the Frank Forrests, Alec Templeton, the blind pianist, and thirty or forty others. The party was staged on all three levels of the house. It began with cocktails on the first level, the playroom, then wandered up to the tennis and badminton courts and garden where dinner was served in a night-club setting. The final sequence was on the third level—in the enormous living room where Alec Templeton played the piano, Marek Windheim sang, and Ernest Charles gave us songs of his own composing.

The Hollywood climate was marvelous and I could easily find excuses for dawdling longer, but my health was wonderful and I felt ready to face the rush of New York once again. I returned in September.

For the next few years I was to commute back and forth between New York and California. Because of the big salaries and the climate, Hollywood was to be the musical capital of America until television became the Pied Piper. Artur Rubinstein, Heifetz, and many other musicians had bought beautiful homes there. Members of our Juilliard faculty began making it a summer resort. Despite all this great talent, I regret to say that little music history was written in Hollywood. It may have been that the musicians were too prosperous. I think it went deeper. I didn't find one moving-picture person in authority who cared a rap about real music.

CHAPTER TWENTY-FIVE

French Musicians

I

HISTORY amounts to a cycle of renaissances. Predominating is the desire to excel. Sometimes, as in the Athenian period or the Elizabethan era, this is expressed aesthetically. Then there is an about-face, and the desire is expressed materially, or physically. That was the cataclysm the world was being torn by when I returned from Hollywood. Hitler had declared war in Europe.

That trip convinced me of the futility of attempting to regiment the nation as a whole in cultural matters, especially where local needs and impulses must be reckoned with. In those early war years our country was full of grandiose schemes with imposing letterheads and worthy intentions. I happened to be a target for most of the music do-gooders, simply because I raised my voice so often in music's behalf. A few, such as placement committees for refugee musicians, I willingly joined. I had already been considerably mixed up in that problem, but the worst of it, as I soon found, was that so many of the people involved were not first-rate musicians. Nevertheless they were in trouble. It required a great deal of wisdom to provide help for those who needed it as human beings, without letting the poorer artists pretend to a place in music to which they were not entitled, and without letting any of them displace earlier arrivals who honestly deserved to get on.

However, we usually managed to find pupils or concerts for the best musicians. And the best, in those early war years, was very good. One of the first to ring my doorbell when I returned from Hollywood was Isidor Philipp, the French pianist.

Nobody is so hard to help as a composer unless it is an author. Philipp was writing his memoirs, but it wasn't easy for him to take advice. For most of his long life he had been professor of piano at the Paris Conservatoire, one of the half-dozen outstanding teachers of great artists. He devised new and remarkably effective methods of imparting and acquiring technique, and it is probably a very moderate statement of the truth to say that few piano virtuosos today have not at some stage of their development profited by his famous exercises. He had a great deal to tell, but it was hard for him to put it on paper.

His fame as a teacher had been carried so far that until very recent years, when he has played over the radio in the United States, some of us have perhaps forgotten that he is in his own right a great artist. His brilliant contribution to technical pedagogy served always the larger cause of good musicianship.

It was at a recital of his pupils that I first met Philipp. Leopold Godowsky took me to the Salle Playel in Paris to hear what he described as a young pianist who would some day be very famous—an American boy. He had been studying in France several years. His name was Beveridge Webster. We were tremendously impressed. After the concert I discussed with Philipp the possibilities of Beveridge eventually teaching at the Juilliard. But it wasn't until Mr. Siloti's retirement in 1942 at the age of seventy-nine, that Beveridge

Webster's name was added to the roster of brilliant pianists
who taught at the Juilliard. He was appointed by President
Schuman in 1946, at the age of forty-seven.

Beveridge maintains the best standards of a French conservatoire. His reputation grows fast as one of the finest performers of our day, one of the most distinguished teachers,
and altogether a fascinating personality—part of which I
think he owes to Philipp.

II

It was as a magnificent artist that Philipp won his place
among world musicians. The number and the range of his
friendships, the extent of his travels, his thorough understanding of the musical achievements and the musical problems of his day were astounding. He was famous in happier
days for the French, or let us say the Parisian, quality of
his wit, but his close friends prefer to praise him for deeper
qualities of heart. Our talks recalled a tragic epoch—the years
of his hope and happiness, filled by him with tenderness and
thankfulness, and with much of that pity with which those
who strive to add beauty to the world must contemplate the
condition which from century to century the world seems to
prefer.

All conversations had in them more than an undertone of
sadness, yet they expressed undiminished, with no suggestion
of defeat, the passion for music which long ago dedicated this
man to a single-hearted career. His memoirs will be an in-
valuable record of one noble aspect of modern France. A
nation puts its best foot forward when it produces lovely
music, and since the traditional enemies of France have
understood this truth we have been somewhat overwhelmed
by propaganda which distracted attention from the French
genius. We have been taught by those interested in such
doctrine that the French genius is not for music at all, but

for drama—or rather, for the theatre, and even there for
the theatre in only its lighter aspects. We shall in time, no
doubt, recover our wits and our sense of humor; the Paris
which Mr. Philipp knew, the Paris of Gounod, of Saint-Saëns,
of Widor, of César Franck, and of all their comrades was a
kindly home for music and for musicians. Posterity will de-
termine at its leisure whether any other capital in any other
country during the same epoch produced so much music
which will give pleasure so long.

Mr. Philipp had a large part in the French music of his
time. Now he is having his share in the American music of
our time. New York has become his permanent home.

When he came to me he was in exile from his land, en-
countering all the hardships and handicaps of the world
tragedy. His property, his books, and his music were in
France, and, what was worse, some of his relatives were
still there. Uncertainty about them would have completely
discouraged any ordinary man. But Mr. Philipp re-established himself on our shores in a most gallant fashion. He
found many friends: Carl Engel, Walter Damrosch, Kousse-
vitsky, Ernest Hutcheson, Josef Lhevinne, Olga Samaroff
Stokowski, Carl Friedberg, and other pianists and piano
teachers.

America is lucky to have him. He lives at a small hotel
within sight of Broadway, brushing elbows with the gaudy
characters of New York's theatrical district. None guess that
the white-mustached old man with chin buried in muffler
is France's greatest living pianist.

I often tried to persuade him to tell me about the Paris
of each period—the city as he first knew it, as it was toward
1900, as it became later. But he said he did not like to recall
the past.

I have always been interested chiefly in people. I hope
in this book to give an account of all the interesting musicians I have met. Of course events and ideas are essential

to a story, but in these pages I am attempting to group them around musical personalities and try to do what will be in essence a portrait gallery of musicians who lived in my own time.

A rough list of the worth-while artists I have known numbers already three hundred. Of these Philipp was one of the most picturesque. Among the most amusing was Florent Schmitt, also a French pianist. Theodore Steinway and I happened to be sitting in the front row the night he gave a recital in one of the private rooms at Town Hall. At least we were seated there when the concert began.

The piano, the usual concert grand, had been elevated on four large wood blocks to form a small platform. Promptly at eight fifteen Schmitt, a dignified Frenchman with a silvery Louis Napoleon beard, stepped from behind a red curtain, bowed to the audience, and mounted the platform. Parting the tails of his full-dress coat, he seated himself at the piano and struck a resounding opening chord. At the blow, a block on which the piano rested slid from position. A sharp crack of splintering wood and a rear leg of the piano plunged into the gap between blocks, leaving Schmitt at a listing keyboard. There were anxious cries from the audience. Theodore Steinway remained calm. It evidently wasn't his piano. With a couple of other men we tried to lift the piano back in place. The leg was wedged between the blocks. There were shouts for the janitor. Presently a man in overalls sauntered in carrying an ax. Schmitt shrieked. After all, a concert grand costs money. We quieted him by explaining that the ax was simply to pry the blocks apart. The janitor separated the blocks—we raised the piano. Once more it was in position.

Schmitt peered nervously under. What was to prevent the block from slipping again? As he glanced up his eyes fixed on Theodore and myself. Our combined weight was almost four hundred pounds.

"Would you gentlemen be so kind as to keep the block in place by sitting on it?" he asked in his precise English.

For the balance of the evening Theodore and I held down the end block while Schmitt banged away on Debussy, Ravel, and Stravinsky.

CHAPTER TWENTY-SIX

✳✳

In the Cause of Music

I

OLGA SAMAROFF called me in the autumn of 1939, shortly after I returned from my second visit to Hollywood. She had an interesting music project to discuss. When could I drop around?

We lunched together the following noon in her apartment on West Fifty-fourth Street. Had I ever heard of the National Committee for Musical Appreciation? Only vaguely. Why did she ask? Because its backers had invited her to direct it. She was already standing on her head in an effort to conduct her two classes—one at the Juilliard, the other at the Philadelphia School of Music. In addition she was doing private teaching and lecturing at the Layman's Music Courses. She believed in the National Committee for Musical Appreciation. Its purpose was to popularize symphonic and operatic music in the United States.

Would I take the chairmanship?

Olga knew that popularizing good music had long been a pet cause of mine. Music is a language, not an accomplishment. It can be learned by using the ears and the eyes. I have always insisted that if more people spoke it the concertgoers

wouldn't have to wait until they read the critic next morning
to know whether they had a good time. I said as much to
Olga. She suggested that I meet the head of the advertising
agency managing the project. The idea had originated with the
Washington Star. Its owner, the late Frank B. Noyes, called
in the agency which had been distributing good records at
cost for another newspaper as a circulation stunt. Noyes
didn't care about circulation. He wanted to promote public
interest in the National Orchestra. The dinner announcing
all this was to be held at Washington in February.

I spoke at that dinner and similar occasions in Indian-
apolis and Cincinnati. In August, 1940, I assumed the post
of chairman of the National Committee for Musical Appreciation. The *New York World-Telegram* described it as
"culturally, the most important musical job in America."

I hesitated for some time before accepting the office. It
meant more traveling. As one reporter put it, "Dr. Erskine's
lecture tours in the interest of music would whiten the face
of a trunk-born trouper. He tosses off one-night stands with
the ease of a honky-tonk circus."

He was right. But because I believed so strongly in popularizing the language of good music, I said yes. It meant work.
We went to twelve orchestras and recording companies,
asked them to play the major symphonies for us, the records
to be issued without names and to be made at a cost to
permit us to sell them for $1.75 a set. One million sets
were sold the first year. At least one million people were
familiarizing themselves with the best music.

On September 9 I spoke at the first annual dinner of the
committee. It was given in the Waldorf.

Over fourteen thousand musicians, artists, and well-known
professional people were guests of our organization. A former
pupil of mine, Ordway Tead, chairman of the Board of
Higher Education, acted as toastmaster. The committee's
first award, a silver plaque, was presented by Olga Samaroff
to Irving Berlin for his "God Bless America." Harry Wood-

burn Chase, chancellor of New York University, gave another plaque to George Sloan for his leadership of the successful campaign to raise $1,000,000 for the Metropolitan Opera. Chancellor Chase also gave to Mr. Sloan a check from the committee for $500 to be used in sending high-school students to the opera.

Leonora Speyer talked on the value of music as a language. Hendrik Willem Van Loon also spoke. In my speech I announced that the opera *Carmen*, first of a series of twelve sets of records, would be released in department stores the following Saturday to be sold without profit. Other operas were to follow.

The records were excellent. I have a complete folio of them which I still enjoy. But I was troubled because not all the selections were being made by the committee. The question rose in what sense were we sponsoring these records. After a series of conferences with the agency which organized the Committee, I resigned and subsequently the group of which I had been a part disbanded.

I wrote the experience off as one of my many adventures in the cause of music. Neither Olga nor I had any regrets. We had spread the knowledge of good music. And many organizations connected with advancing the cause of fine music had profited. One of the final things I did as chairman was to give to the Metropolitan Opera in the name of the New York Chapter the last of a sum totalling $8,360.35.

Many of my ideas had registered. William King of the *New York Sun* said, "A few of Dr. Erskine's pungent remarks about democracy in music, made in announcing the plan, will bear repeating." I pointed out that the first step toward appreciating good music is to hear it, and the next step is to hear it again. We need in music, as in the other arts, greater distribution, and if we spend more for gasoline than for symphonies and operas, one reason is that gasoline has more filling stations.

There was a time when a great artist was not at all a-

shamed to admit that every service in human society is on
one side an art, and on the other a business. To ignore this
fact and yet to hope for the spread of good music is absurd.
No art prospers if its potential audience is not reached. The
so-called crisis in music today rises chiefly, I believe, from
the slowness of the art to accept the democratic ideals . . .
If music can be brought to all who want it at a price the
audience can pay, the plight of musicians will be ended and
the art will enter upon a secure future, but before this democratic distribution of music is possible the artist must accept democratic ideas. The main problem of music today is
how to do away with that bottleneck which prevents artists
from getting at the largest audience, and prevents the potential audience from getting at the music they'd like to hear.

II

During these years Rudolph Polk, the agent who handled
my Hollywood broadcasts, was also interested in the production of music films. Through him I became editor and
commentator of the series. They were prepared for music
students rather than for the general moving-picture audience.
Since all young people are at heart music students, I hoped
these films would be used primarily in the schools. We tried
to present the artists as sincerely and simply as possible, adding to them and their performance no decorative distraction.
We intended to inflict no close-up of a gyrating insect upon
those who wanted to listen to Rimsky-Korsakoff's *Flight of
the Bumble Bee*. We wanted to leave the listener free to
give his whole attention to the music and the performers.

I felt certain that everyone who played or sang would enjoy
not only hearing but seeing the great artists, who though
they tour widely cannot visit every town in the world. After
the artist retires, or after his death, his art is usually lost for-
ever. Films such as those we planned would make possible
not only the sound but the visible technique and manner.

Precious as these films would be in the future, their present usefulness was obvious. Even though we attend a concert in person, we do not sit near enough the performer or the singer to study the technique in detail. The films which I had a hand in editing and commentating upon tried by skillful photography to make clear what the music lover and music student would like to see. The films would be a valuable supplement to what was being done throughout the country for music education.

I was deeply interested in the attempt, since the idea properly carried out would be of great value to the historical record of music in our time.

The first film was of the two-piano team, Victor Babin and Vitya Vronsky, pupils of Artur Schnabel. Babin, composer as well as pianist, made many of the arrangements which he and Miss Vronsky played. Though a number of masterpieces have been written for two pianos, the repertoire for this combination is not large.

To my deep regret, only six films were produced. The musicians we invited to play asked more than the producer could afford. It was another fine idea which did not work out as well as I had hoped. However, it had not been entirely a failure. Because of even those few films, the country was the richer for its knowledge of fine music.

Nineteen forty had been a hectic and in some ways a sad year. Professor Woodbridge had died in June. At his funeral in the University chapel my thoughts were chiefly on Amherst, and on the love he and Professor Bigelow had for each other. He was one of the greatest men I have known, and now that he was gone Columbia had lost something which isn't likely to come again.

The last commencement I attended at Amherst, I looked Sheddie up in the house where his class was holding their reunion, and we talked till a late hour about education and life and art and all the other things about which he could be so stimulating, and a great part of the talk was about

William Bigelow and the wonderful music we had in Amherst during our days there. Sheddie never outgrew the conviction that the best of Amherst was unique, and I have always had good reason to share his conviction.

III

It is my nature to be up in the clouds or down in the depths. I was feeling very low when I found the following letter in my morning mail:

DEPARTMENT OF STATE
Washington

December 30, 1940

My dear Dr. Erskine:

The Congress of the United States has made funds available to the Department of State for the payment of travel expenses for a small number of educational, professional and artistic leaders of this country to visit the other American republics. I believe that visits of this character may contribute most effectively to furtherance of the Good Neighbor Policy and promotion of a better understanding in the nations to the south, of the life and thought of the United States.

I take pleasure in extending to you an invitation to accept such a grant for a trip of approximately three months to one or two of these republics, possibly Argentina and Uruguay. During your trip you may wish to consider giving a number of lectures dealing with the literary and musical life of the United States. I believe that these lectures and the personal relationships which may be established should do much to develop deeper comprehension of this country among the intellectual and cultural leaders of the nations visited.

The travel grants will provide, subject to the Standardized Government Travel Regulations, for round steamship travel, a per diem of $5 aboard ship and a per diem of $6 during the stay abroad.

I shall be gratified if you find it possible to accept this invitation for I believe that the interchange of distinguished leaders among the American republics may prove a vital factor in assuring that community of interest which is essential to the safety and well-being of this hemisphere.

Sincerely yours,

Cordell Hull

I sailed on May 10, 1941, on the *Brazil*. My cabin was an enormous room. I had a marvelously comfortable bed and I slept till noon the next day, getting up only because I was hungry.

At dinner when the passenger list was distributed I noticed that a number of musicians were on board, and that Yehudi Menuhin would get on at Rio. After dinner I walked a while on deck and a Miss Smith introduced herself in order to introduce me to Baccaloni, the Met baritone, and his wife. His droll wit reminded me of Paul Kochanski. He told me that he bought a language record in London in order to improve his English, but unfortunately the record was of a lesson given on the radio, and the static misled an innocent foreigner like himself. He gave us an illustration.

The next evening at the Captain's cocktail party, I met a historian from Buenos Aires who had been visiting in the United States on such an errand as mine. He heard of my trip from his embassy and had been on the watch for me.

I gathered that the South Americans were puzzled at our sudden interest in them. I didn't blame them. Mr. Roosevelt had announced that he would give them fatherly protection before they asked for it.

At Buenos Aires Norman Armour, the American Ambassador, told me I was to lecture in French on "The Novel, The Stage, and Music in the United States." A happy command for me!

When I left New York I took along my half-finished manuscript of *Song Without Words*, the life of Felix Mendelssohn, thinking that I would complete it on the boat. Not until the day before I sailed home did I get that book finished. I had been on the go every minute. The days were crowded with meeting fascinating new people and seeing strange and beautiful places. Two of the most interesting friends I made were Victoria Campo, Argentine's leading woman in literature, and Allessandro Shaw, Buenos Aires banker and wit—a cousin of George Bernard Shaw.

I returned home in August, 1941. My trip had been like the days in France in World War I. Excitement made it possible for me to do more than I should have thought myself capable of. Aside from a slight limp and a weak right hand I was in better health than ever.

As a fine conclusion to the trip I valued this letter:

DEPARTMENT OF STATE
Washington

August 30, 1941

My dear Dr. Erskine:

The Department has received from its missions in South America most favorable reports on the results of your visit.

I want to take this opportunity to thank you for the distinguished services you have rendered in fostering more intelligent and friendly relations with the intellectual leaders in those republics. I believe that your visit has added to the prestige of the literary and musical attainments of the United States.

Sincerely yours,

Cordell Hull

⁂⁂⁂⁂⁂⁂⁂⁂⁂⁂⁂⁂⁂⁂⁂⁂⁂⁂⁂⁂⁂⁂⁂⁂⁂⁂⁂⁂⁂⁂⁂⁂⁂⁂⁂⁂⁂⁂⁂

The Metropolitan

I

AMERICAN OPERA

I WARN YOU that this is going to be an argument for American opera. My trip to South America convinced me that we should have more American and less European opera if we wanted to hold the attention of cultivated Latin Americans. In all the countries I visited the emphasis was decidedly on Old World music, literature, and painting. Italian composers had the edge on us.

I had been one of Edward Johnson's principal allies in his first year at the Met when he put on opera in an experimental way with young singers and with an unusual repertoire. One of the operas he gave that season was *The Bartered Bride* in English translation. Few performances which I have seen at the Metropolitan were ever a more uproarious success. The opera was always brilliantly funny, but until those performances the Metropolitan audience listened with the proper solemnity, never cracking a smile. The translation revealed what the opera really was about.

Of course this innovation met with many objections. One

of the best-known critics was loyal to the ideal of every opera in the original language of the libretto. He swore that *The Bartered Bride* had always seemed to him even more amusing in its original German. Several of his colleagues were so unkind as to point out that the original libretto was not in German. They congratulated their colleague on his familiarity with the Czech language.

In my early days at the Juilliard School I became accustomed to pathetic letters from Americans studying singing in Italy. The letter writers were not Juilliard pupils, but they had heard that Mr. Juilliard had somehow provided free instruction for talented Americans, and they wrote to say that they were extremely talented. They had already studied in Italy two or three years and they had no more money. Their plight, they quite frequently added, was particularly tragic since their teacher, the well-known Signor So-and-so, assured them that if they had another five thousand dollars to spend he could guarantee them an engagement at La Scala or some other famous theatre.

The scandal of these letters troubled the Italian authorities, and I am sure they did what they could to protect innocent foreigners from the humbug. Great singers are not trained in one or two years, and all singers need a general musical training, not simply an exercise of certain vocal cords. But we at the Juilliard, advising with our sympathetic colleague, Edward Johnson, did what we could to increase the opportunity for American singers to study at home and to find opportunities for extended training at the Metropolitan.

When Mr. Johnson assumed the direction of the Metropolitan, the importance of giving young American singers a new opportunity was great. World War I had interfered with our traditional dependence on Europe for musical training. Young Americans who wished to learn how to sing could still seek out Italian singing teachers if they could afford to go to Italy, but it was advisable from the Italian point of view that American singers should not begin to compete with the Italian. Italy after World War I needed American money. If an American student went abroad to study singing in Italy, the Italian singing teachers did not wish to let him go.

I was then of the opinion that the American opportunity in opera would come to those who could sing. The times have changed. At the present moment I believe the great opportunity in opera ought to be for young American composers. After having tried for some years at the Juilliard School and elsewhere to encourage young Americans to compose operas in the European tradition, imitating Verdi or Puccini, I doubt if any American educator who knows the temper of the American musician and the American audience expects any further return of the wave of the peculiar genius which impelled the production of French and Italian opera abroad during the nineteenth century. I believe the European manner and style have long since been succumbing to the new impulses in American music.

I say this from no silly wish to boost the American styles. I never cared for jazz as such, and if I had a chance of composing like Chopin or Debussy, I would jump at the chance, but George Gershwin belonged to our recent years and spoke for us as Debussy never could. Now there is a later development in the American taste. Even the lovely music which Jerome Kern put into *Show Boat* is somewhat too sentimental for us, decidedly too slow. The plain truth is that young America through recent years has discovered that music can be the total expression of our nature, and that it can be a beautiful expression, even though the American experience has been of wars and suffering and wounds and death.

Europe has not bequeathed to us any operatic masterpieces which adequately express the world that American and British youth have had to deal with in World War II. Yet literature through successful novels has furnished librettos based on the experience that a vast American audience, if they returned safely, can recognize as an old story. Americans who saw World War II would, I think, rather listen to the really beautiful lyrics of *South Pacific*, and watch the dancers, who intend no grand opera whatever. It is true of course that the cast of *South Pacific* contained Ezio Pinza, a fine singer who was well trained in opera, but before he could perform his part in that show he would have had to learn to waltz beautifully—unless even in his grand-opera days he had learned to dance as an extracurricular activity.

I certainly believe that the dance has a place in opera. In fact it takes a Wagner to keep me satisfied with opera if there is no dance, and he doesn't always do it.

I believe American audiences like dancing in opera, and wherever else they can find it.

I do not believe that there are many choreographers who understand how to direct dances as part of operas. I'm afraid I don't believe there are many choreographers.

The dance which is merely inserted into an opera is to me offensive, like any other interruption.

I believe that the day of static acting in opera is over. It will die hard because of tradition, but the public now wants the same vitality and movement in opera as in any other form of drama.

This means that the singers must pay attention to their persons, must look and act as well as sing like the characters they are representing.

I believe the music, the drama, the dancing, the scenery should be composed as a unit, to say one thing.

Opera should be a merger of dance music, painting, and singing. I should include also the libretto. Few operas illustrate such a harmony of the arts.

The problem of the dance in this country, like the problem of opera singing, is a question of education.

The average young singer is impatient with the years of study necessary for competence on the operatic stage. The average young dancer wants to get up and dance and be applauded. If you tell him or her that no one can be a great dancer who is not also a well-trained musician and a well-trained painter or sculptor, you will find yourself very unpopular. I hope that the Metropolitan will constantly strengthen its position as an institution—a place of amusement in the best sense, and also a center where training in the arts can be developed and synthesized.

I don't see why ballet should be the only form of dance in opera. It couldn't be if the opera were based on a subject to which ballet did not properly belong.

Since Wagner took the dance out of opera, he made the art form to that extent unattractive to youthful temperaments. Perhaps the Americans are very youthful. But I know that Isolde was predestined to tragedy. Even Hans Sachs was brought up in an atmosphere no more cheerful than might be expected if a company of kill-joy Beckmessers met in their lighter moments in an old church.

The stories which made up the librettos of famous operas were not cheerful, and quite often they celebrated murder and unspeakable horrors. It is for the continuance of this form of entertainment that our loyal contribution to our opera houses is asked, as though we should be untrue to our better natures to prefer something happier and more cheerful. It has been thought also that American patrons of opera would be interested only in individual singers, not in the music drama for its own sake.

I have visited few parts of the country where there did not seem to be a hunger for opera. Broadcasting the Metropolitan operas has helped no doubt to see grand opera, as it were, in the flesh. There are plenty of singers and directors in America today capable of giving us performances which would not creak.

The problem for the singers in American opera now is the question whether those who control grand opera, or in particular the Metropolitan, will attempt much longer to keep from the American public the kind of opera they enjoy. During recent years the finances of the Metropolitan have been

so shaky that no one would presume to prophesy a cheerful
future on Thirty-ninth Street.

The lover of the past day may, if he wishes, explain the
kind of shows Americans like to compose by saying they are
vulgar or that they are not real opera, but unfortunately for
this school of aesthetics it seems that the whole American
nation likes the kind of show the American composers like
to offer, and when the audience approves of the show and
is willing to pay for it the debate is practically closed. What
is still worse, we are less hopeful than we once were of a
continued supply of old-fashioned operas from Europe.
Europe too, even poor old battered Europe, has an eternal
supply of youth, and the youthful spirit in Europe is sympathetic to the spirit of youth in America.

In the summer of 1948 when the music unions were de-
laying the Metropolitan Board until we weren't sure that
we could get ready a season in time, Mr. Johnson, who had
just returned from a study of the European situation, suggested to the Board that there might be an advantage in
omitting the season for one year. He suggested that we might
profitably restudy the whole conventional repertoire of opera.
He had visited some important opera companies, he said,
one of which at the moment was staging *Show Boat*, and another was staging *Porgy and Bess*. It was not surprising to
some of us that both American operas were enjoying considerable financial success. Some of us were remembering,
with none too cheerful thoughts, that *Porgy and Bess* and
Show Boat are the only two operas composed by Americans
which invariably attract the American audience and make
money for the management. Neither would be permitted inside the Metropolitan Opera. They would not satisfy the
standards of the Old World opera.

It is not the composers who are likely to suffer from their
failure to satisfy Metropolitan conditions. Quite a number
of American composers are just now doing very well indeed
without the Metropolitan approval. But the Metropolitan

can have no future in a country which is entirely free to patronize the kind of opera it prefers. Oscar Hammerstein II and Richard Rodgers have developed their kind of musical entertainment until it is as elaborate as grand opera and quite as expensive, but they are able to produce it with a steady and gratifying increase in their wealth because the public are glad to pay for it. I can't escape the conclusion that the public would pay for all-year-round grand opera at the Metropolitan if they enjoyed it as much.

Naturally we use Hammerstein and Rodgers to illustrate the new kind of American opera because they are the outstanding team, and because practically every theatregoer knows their work, but there is much about their ideals and their methods which is shared by other composers and writers of lyrics and librettos. In one respect the best American writers of American operas are old-fashioned; they have this in common with the best of the older composers of Europe, that they are thoroughly at home in the show business. Instead of being ashamed of that fact, they realize that a knowledge of their profession from every practical point of view is essential.

When Bizet wrote *Carmen* originally he produced a masterpiece, but the practical men of the theater in his time felt that the opera could never succeed. Bizet loved the grim realism of Prosper Mérimée, and he had set all its grimness to his music. The managers of the theatre which wished to produce the opera decided to soften the text to suit the tastes of the audience. Bizet's music could remain as it was, but the audience would be spared a few murders and other unnecessary horrors. To make the required changes they engaged the most famous librettists in France—famous, that is, for their success in extremely light opera, Meilhac and Halevy, who had written the delicious libretto for Offenbach's *La Belle Helène*.

Few devotees of grand opera are aware in detail of what they are indebted, when they enjoy *Carmen*, to the two most skillful and experienced librettists in the field of *opéra bouffe,* or light opera.

During recent years at the Metropolitan I have more than once proposed to the president of the Board and to my colleagues associated with him that we should elect Oscar Hammerstein II and Richard Rodgers to the Board. I thought the Board should contain more members who knew something by practical experience about the show business. I was conscious that I knew nothing about it, and I was at no time led to believe that Charles Spofford, the president of the Board, or George Sloan, the chairman, had ever had the kind of training that Mr. Johnson or Herbert Witherspoon or Gatti-Casazza had to fit them for their post.

It's an extraordinary thing, but the American businessman, trained as lawyer or as executive, quite frequently has profound contempt or distrust for a musician who knows anything about the practical relation of the art to its audience. The officers of the Metropolitan seem to feel that they are preserving a high-minded attitude toward their trust if they contribute generously to wipe out financial deficits from season to season. Unblushingly they inform the public that there is a new opportunity for all truly cultural music lovers to contribute again, but apparently it does not occur to the old-fashioned supporters of opera that the goods which opera is trying to sell the customers are out of date, more than a little shopworn, and that a generation is growing up in America who know the kind of entertainment they want when they go to the theater. All theatrical entertainment, including opera, must first of all be satisfying entertainment. It can make no plea for support as though it were a religion or a church.

To be sure, music is for many of us in a true sense a religion, and we revere the art—when it deserves to be revered. But it is too late in the day for opera to preach the doctrine to its devotees that they owe it to their souls to pay for the support of their church, even when they don't care to listen to any more of its sermons.

Opera, to be vital again, must recover a sincerity it once had. American opera, the kind I have been speaking of, which unfortunately is not yet admitted inside the Metropolitan but which is developing rapidly to the satisfaction and the delight of millions of Americans a few doors from the Metropolitan in the theatrical district, has all the advantage of being primarily a sincere expression of the American spirit. It makes use of the most dramatic episodes in contemporary American history. It finds its librettos in themes which have demonstrated already their appeal to American interest.

Most American operas which American composers produce stand on their own feet financially. They call for no subsidies or subscription guarantees. They appeal for the support of the public at the box office, knowing well what it is that the public wishes to hear.

I make no claim to any practical experience gathered from a modern Broadway, but I have spent some years of my life trying to study the principles which control the success of theatrical entertainment in earlier Broadways, all of which have certain constant qualities. The most profound truth which can be learned from a study of the plays that William Shakespeare wrote for his Globe Theatre, undiscouraged by the fact that it was not very far from the Bear Garden, is this: that he invariably accepted the themes which his audience had already approved, and established his own genius for giving to those themes a memorable expression.

We must stop underestimating the intelligence of the average person.

II

AUDITIONS OF THE AIR

EDWARD JOHNSON not only gave a welcome to young voices, even though they might be American, but he did more than had ever been done before to take the public into the confidence of the Opera management, to put an end if possible to the secrecy and perhaps the skulduggery which to some extent, it may be, had formerly surrounded the application of young singers, especially of young women, to break into the opera world.

With the assistance of the Sherwin-Williams Company of Cleveland, the auditions for the Metropolitan were broadcast and were listened to by all who were interested. These auditions were made possible chiefly by the generosity of George A. Martin, the president of the Sherwin-Williams Company, who sponsored these weekly Sunday broadcasts from their beginning in 1935 until 1945. There were no auditions broadcast in the seasons 1945-1947, but in 1947, and up to 1949, they were put on the air again, sponsored by the Farnsworth Television and Radio Corporation.

Mr. Martin had unusual faith in American youth, and as long as he lived he liked to think that he and his company, though not engaged in any activity particularly associated with music, were making a central contribution to the opportunities which young Americans might find in the arts. Thanks to his additional generosity, the winners of the auditions received a cash prize. Mr. Martin knew well that, though an artist is supposed to be superior to cash, many a young American musician, especially if he is married, can learn quickly how to make use of an extra thousand dollars.

The final audition each season was to select the best voices which had been heard by the jury. The jury consisted of practically the same representatives of the Metropolitan each year. During the first season and several years thereafter it consisted of Edward Johnson, the general manager, Edward Ziegler, assistant general manager, Earle R. Lewis, the box office manager, and Wilfred Pelletier, one of the conducting staff. For several years I served as a judge. It was always exciting. Mr. Pelletier rehearsed with the contestants the numbers which they wished to sing. Both he and Mr. Johnson judged the voices not only for their absolute merit, but for their usefulness in filling roles which would be important in next season's performances.

Mr. Pelletier interested me particularly because he had many personal characteristics which strongly reminded me of my first music teacher, Carl Walter. He had a quiet French humor and a rich sense of humanity. He loved good food and enjoyed a bright story. He and Rose Bampton, his wife, gave unique parties. He was a pupil of Isidor Philipp. I should have liked to see him at the Juilliard.

I knew his commitments in Canada (he heads the Music Conservatory in Montreal) and his many other engagements, but I felt they were not insuperable obstacles. I knew how he, more than anyone else, could do for our youngsters what Albert Stoessel did, using them in various operas and concerts everywhere and generally giving them a hand up. He was thoroughly at home in conservatories and would fit into school life.

I have always dreamed of the Juilliard organizing small junior opera companies. Pelletier would have been ideal for such work. I had thought of this when Katherine Long died and left her sizable fortune to the cause of music. It was not left to the Metropolitan specifically, as some think, but to the cause of music *in general*. Since Mrs. Long was an American and since the Juilliard always championed the American musician in opera, I thought it would be an ideal challenge for us. Perhaps some day it will work out. It would be a perfect proving ground for young voices—even better than the auditions. Not that I'm belittling the auditions. They have been a tremendous success.

Mr. Johnson had listened to all the voices before they made their formal appearance before the entire jury. On him rested the chief responsibility for preparing the program for the following year. The jury were present in the large hall of the National Broadcasting Company with a very large invited audience. The singing of each piece was promptly recorded so that if there should be any dispute among the jurors it could be heard again.

Of course no matter how helpful the auditions wished to be, it was impossible to satisfy all the contestants and all their relatives. There would always be some complaints, at least with the choice of the winning voices. It was impossible, apparently, to make the contestants and their adherents understand that a first-rate voice is not enough to insure an opera career. Sometimes the accident of size, if tallness and shortness are accidents, would handicap the singer, but at least the public auditions gave many hearers a chance to judge the voices and also an opportunity to see the contestants in person.

I am sorry they were not continued. I hope they start up again. They offer an excellent show window for young singers.

The winners each received $1,000 and a contract with the Metropolitan. The runner-ups got a scholarship of $500 to further their musical education. In some cases in the past many of the runner-ups later received contracts after more study—Risë Stevens and Lucielle Browning, for example, both of whom are now nationally famous.

I remember the year Risë Stevens came to the Juilliard. From the very start we all knew that she would succeed. In fact, she was already a success. In her first school opera, *Maria Malibran*, she dominated the stage by her personality as well as voice. She could not only sing but act.

The *New Yorker's* music critic, Robert Simon, and Russell Bennett wrote *Maria Malibran*. It had its première at the Juilliard. I liked it and have always been sorry that the Metropolitan never did anything with it. The setting was old New York and the leading character, Maria Malibran, the young Italian opera singer.

III

VALUES

THE CHAIRMANSHIP of the Metropolitan Opera Board was a traditional post to be handed from one old New Yorker to another. It carried with it a mark of social distinction, like being a vestryman of Trinity Church. I know, having served on both. I have heard certain old New Yorkers who were vestrymen pointed out by admiring relatives as "having passed the center aisle plate at Trinity for fifty years as did his father before him."

I served as chairman of the management committee of the Metropolitan Opera Association from 1935 to 1939. Cornelius Bliss wanted it more than I. In 1939 I vacated the office, became a director instead, and Mr. Bliss succeeded me as chairman. George Sloan followed him as chairman.

Charles Spofford took Allen Wardwell's place as president. I came to know him as a fellow member of the Juilliard School Board. We soon began rubbing elbows and exchanging ideas at the Board meetings of the Metropolitan Opera Association. During the war he was in service abroad, but since his return I have been meeting him constantly, always, as it happens, on musical matters. He is a grand companion, forceful in character but gracious in manner, with a rich supply of humor and common sense. He is a member of Allen Wardwell's law firm.

Those serving with him as Opera Board members as I write

this chapter are George Sloan, Mr. Wardwell, John Morris
Perry, Ernest Hutcheson, Edward Johnson (retiring general
manager), Colonel Joseph Hartfield, Mrs. August Belmont,
Lucrezia Bori, Mrs. William Francis Gibbs, Mrs. Harold N.
Coolidge, Chancellor Harry Woodburn Chase of New York
University, Thomas J. Watson, C. D. Jackson, Mark Woods,
Carleton Sprague Smith, Philip G. Reed, Samuel Sloan Colt,
Lewis L. Strauss, Benjamin Strong, Morton Baum, Donald T.
Blagden, Thomas Sidlo, Curtis E. Calder, Dr. Charles H.
Straub, Rawlins Cottenet, General David Sarnoff, Clarence
Dillon, H. Wendell Endicott, Lauder Greenway, William
deForest Manice, Thomas H. McInnery, Henry Rogers Win-
throp, Cornelius Vanderbilt Whitney.

John Perry, Allen Wardwell, and I were very active in the
beginning. We presented a pretty solid front. Later on Ernest
Hutcheson joined us. Edward Johnson has never changed. He
was always honest in his love for the old operas, which he
knew thoroughly. He was familiar with the modern ones, but
his eyes never lighted when they were mentioned. He is an
easy guest—makes the party go and takes the lead in conversation.

Colonel Joseph Hartfield always sat on his feet curled up in
a chair, but this didn't prevent him from keen thinking. He
was quite a person, probably one of the most astute lawyers
in the country.

Mrs. William Francis Gibbs would talk at the end rather
than at the beginning of a session. Mrs. August Belmont
spoke more frequently. She looked, walked, and talked like a
person who has cultivated a position in life. She was at her
best talking. Her years in the theater had endowed her with
a very fine speaking voice and beautiful diction. Whatever she
said was so much music.

Lucrezia Bori was always entirely herself. She had natural
style in manner and dress.

The women seldom spoke until we all got up to put on our

coats and go. Then everybody helped everybody else and there was general conversation.

When I first became a member of the Metropolitan Opera Association our meetings were held on the first floor in a room right next to the main office. It was a little hot but dignified. I always liked it. Then the meetings were moved to a remote Opera Guild room inconveniently located high up in the building. The protests were so general that the Board meetings were shifted to a downtown luncheon club.

As a member of the Metropolitan Opera Board I soon learned that real estate was often more vital an issue than music at the board meetings. This is easily understandable when one remembers that the assessed valuation of the Metropolitan Opera building and land is $1,750,000. Many of the older members were frank to admit that their interest was purely financial. We saw them when there was an impending change of address. The only time I ever saw Clarence Mackay was at a meeting which involved real-estate issues.

Just after the administration of the Metropolitan Opera passed from the hands of Mr. Gatti-Casazza to Mr. Johnson, the members of the Board were much occupied, though it now seemed informally, with the question of whether a better site could be found for the Opera House. The present location seemed impractical. Thirty-ninth and Fortieth streets were too narrow to accommodate all the cars arriving at the beginning of a performance or again at the end of an evening. Many suggestions were made to locate the Opera House in some part of Central Park, perhaps in the neighborhood of Fifty-ninth Street, but the city was wisely jealous of any spare room which yet remained in the park, and after many suggestions the Opera House still is in what many regard as its obsolete and impractical location. Thinking in terms of present-day conditions, socially and economically, I wonder if it is so impractical.

Here is an interesting bit of information. The majority of the people who attend the Metropolitan Opera come from

Brooklyn. The Opera House in its present location is served by both the BMT and the IRT subways. An increasing number of opera goers are using these two systems.

In the course of time the Metropolitan Opera will undoubtedly move, but I doubt if that will be for another ten years. And where that will be is anybody's guess. John D. Rockefeller generously offered to shelter the Metropolitan in his Center Theatre but, because of its very size, the suggestion was not practical. Also many of us, including myself, regarded the Center Theatre as something of a Trojan Horse.

I cherished an idea which I discussed much with Jonas Lie when he was president of the National Academy of Design. We agreed that the right location for the Metropolitan Opera was at 110th Street, on the northern end of Central Park. If adequate space could be acquired between the northern outlet of Seventh and Fifth avenues—perhaps two blocks north from 110th Street—the Opera House would have an imposing location, easily accessible to traffic coming northward on Fifth Avenue or through the Park. It would also be convenient to bus lines, subways, and not too far from the 125th Street station of the New York Central Railroad.

Mr. Lie and I dreamed of an Opera House, modern in every respect and worthy of our city. If New York secured the necessary land for the project, we agreed that in the neighborhood of the Opera House should be located the High School of Music and Art, the Academy of Design, and other art schools.

My idea was to remove all the buildings on the blocks between Fifth and Seventh avenues and between 110th and 111th streets. This would provide a magnificent plaza. On the block north, between Seventh and Fifth avenues and between 111th and 112th streets, the Opera House should be placed. The setting, with the broad expanse of green park in the foreground, would be unbeatable, and the traffic problem could be provided for not only in the plaza but underground, and also by setting all the other buildings on 110th Street somewhat north of the line and so widening the street.

On the other blocks in this area the whole group could be designed to include the concert hall, convention auditorium, art schools, academies, and museums.

The City Museum is already near at hand on Fifth Avenue. With the College of the City of New York so near, as well as Columbia University, we should then have a district in the city in which the highest artistic and intellectual interests could be brought together.

I happened to describe the idea in some detail to Albert Spalding one day when he was about to call on Mr. La Guardia. Spalding relayed the idea to our impulsive Mayor, who wrote me an amusing comment, addressing me as Tiberius Caesar, and assuring me that he didn't have the financial resources which enabled the Roman tyrant to make architectural improvements or enlargements in the Eternal City.

So far as I know, none of my colleagues on the Board thought much of my idea, and they have probably forgotten all about it long ago. I still think, however, that opera in New York will never develop as it should until its future is planned with the utmost courage or even audacity. The history of the Metropolitan as far back as I have been able to study it has been consistently timid and unimaginative. New ideas are not at home in Thirty-ninth Street. They have often been suggested, but they perish as soon as they are exposed to articulate expression.

IV

THE LADIES HAVE THE LAST WORD

THE MOST important contribution to the Opera during Edward Johnson's administration may perhaps have been the organization of the Metropolitan Opera Guild by Mrs. August Belmont. In 1935 Mrs. Belmont, one of the most devoted supporters of the traditional opera, organized the Guild "to

promote greater interest in opera and to broaden the base of
the support for the Metropolitan." Mrs. Belmont is now
president emeritus of the Guild, having been succeeded by
Mr. Lauder Greenway as president.

Closely associated with her from the beginning have been
Mrs. Herbert Witherspoon, Guild director, and Miss Lucrezia Bori, chairman, who since the first days when Mr. Johnson took charge have been loyal supporters of the administration. Miss Bori is affectionately remembered by all Metropolitan patrons for the beautiful art with which she graced
the Metropolitan stage for many years.

When the ladies of the Metropolitan audience organized
so effectively the Opera Guild and on more than one occasion
presented generous gifts for the maintenance and improvement of the Opera, it went without saying that sooner or later
they would enjoy a much larger share in the control of Metropolitan destinies. So far as I know they never asked for such
a reward for their generous services, but the result was in the
nature of the situation. They had supported the Metropolitan
generously by actual gifts of money, and in the organization
and development of the Opera Guild they had shown more
imagination of the constructive kind than the men had been
able to bring to the Opera problems.

When Mr. Johnson felt that he must retire, after one post-
ponement in 1949, no doubt many plans were talked over
privately among all the energetic members of the Board,
whether they were men or women. Secrecy was the mark, as
we knew later, of all the preparations which led in the early
months of 1949 to the nomination of Mr. Rudolf Bing to be
Mr. Johnson's successor. I report the steps of this episode as
I knew them at first hand.

I first heard of Mr. Bing through the newspapers in March,
1949, when he came from England to explore the possibility
of bringing the Glyndebourne Opera to Princeton University
some time in 1950. The earliest reports of this move were
cheerfully optimistic. It was even suggested that the famous

English conductor, Sir Thomas Beecham, would come with the Glyndebourne company. Somewhat later, however, the newspapers reported that the Glyndebourne company would not come as they could not afford the trip.

The name of Rudolf Bing made no impression on me, and not a word was said to me by the officers of the Metropolitan Board, although I learned later that an interview had been arranged at that time with Mr. Bing to consider inviting him to take charge of the Metropolitan.

On May 12, 1949, I received the following letter with the accompanying enclosure from our president, Charles Spofford:

15 Broad Street
New York 5

Dear Dr. Erskine:

George Sloan and I are asking a few of the Directors of the Opera Association to lunch at the Century on Wednesday next, May 18, at 12:30, to meet Rudolf Bing, the General Manager of the Glyndebourne Opera and Artistic Director of the Edinburgh Festival, who is to be in New York for several days next week.

We hope very much that you can join us. Would you let me know whether we may count on you.

With best regards,

Sincerely yours,

Charles Spofford

While waiting for this Century Club meeting with Mr. Bing, I heard the sad news that Mrs. Otto Kahn, the widow of Otto H. Kahn, had died in London. Mr. Johnson asked me by telephone if I would write a resolution which the Board could adopt for the next meeting. Some speed was necessary since the people who were to illuminate the scroll were to be asked to prepare also a much longer resolution in tribute to Mr. Cornelius Bliss, who had just died. Casually, as though in passing, Mr. Johnson remarked that Mrs. Kahn went very suddenly; she had been conferring with Mrs. August Belmont only a few moments before she died in London, from where she was preparing to proceed on a visit to the Continent. I did not think at the moment of the coincidence which had brought Mrs. Belmont and Mrs. Kahn together, but the next day Mr. Johnson suggested that the memorial I had sketched out might very well be shorter, and perhaps the reference to the meeting with Mrs. Belmont might be omitted. So I omitted it, but laid up the incident in my memory for further study.

At the meeting of May 18 at the Century Club, the following members of the Board were present to meet Mr. Bing: President Harry Woodburn Chase of New York University, Mr. Allen Wardwell, Mr. George A. Sloan, Mr. C. D. Jackson, Mr. Mark Woods, Mr. Thomas J. Watson, Mr. Carleton Sprague Smith, and Mr. Philip G. Reed.

Only a few of these gentlemen had met Mr. Bing before, but I believe they were all impressed with his pleasant manner. Apparently he had accepted the account of his history which Mr. Spofford sent out to all of us in typewritten form. Obviously there was no reason why he should not accept it, since he had furnished the facts to Mr. Spofford. It was perfectly clear that he was present to be looked over as a candidate for Mr. Johnson's post. He mentioned the advantage there would be in spending some time at the Metropolitan next autumn to observe Mr. Johnson's methods. He made several friendly suggestions for the enrichment of the Metropolitan's offerings to the public. He suggested that we ought to have a summer season at the Opera, but since the house is not air-conditioned he asked why we did not rent each summer a small air-conditioned theater.

He also suggested that the Metropolitan or any other opera needed far more rehearsals than they at present have. If he could follow his own custom in England he would put the singers into rehearsal fully a month before the curtain was to go up.

The members of the Board present passed over the suggestion of the air-cooled theater with a smile at his ignorance of New York conditions. An air-cooled theater is hard to find waiting for a tenant in the New York summer season. I asked how his budget could provide for rehearsals for at least a month before the curtain went up on his Glyndebourne season. Mr. Bing cheerfully explained that the English labor regulations did not require a manager to pay his company for their rehearsal time.

Mr. Bing made a very amiable impression on me, and I liked him. I doubted if he knew much about his business; perhaps I should say I questioned what he knew about theatrical conditions in New York, but perhaps he would learn more with time. He was obviously very eager to accept the Metropolitan post if we offered it to him. At one or two points in our friendly discussions I wondered if he had reason to think we had already offered it to him.

Shortly after the luncheon the Executive Committee was called for a lunch meeting at the Broad Street Club. Colonel Joseph M. Hartfield, the chairman of that committee, presided. Miss Lucrezia Bori, Mr. Sloan, Mr. Spofford, Mr. Johnson, Mr. Colt, and I were present. The meeting was hurried, and I had the strong impression that we had been called to elect Mr. Bing general manager of the Metropolitan, and that extended debate would not be welcome just then. Mr. Spofford read to the Committee from numerous letters which he had received from Mrs. Belmont. Here for the first time I learned that Mrs. Belmont had gone to England, apparently with the knowledge of some members of the Board, to select a general manager of the Metropolitan. It was quite obvious that she had been satisfied with what she had learned about Mr. Bing, though it didn't seem to me that she was yet well informed about the gentleman. She had been aided, however, by the opinions and advice of an English friend. I did not know who the lady was or whether she had ever been in New York, but Mrs. Belmont seemed to think she was well qualified to select a general manager for the Metropolitan.

Mr. Spofford and Mr. Sloan, backed up by Mr. Johnson, assured the committee that Mr. Bing was altogether the most eligible candidate whom they had found. They discouraged a further search for any other European candidate. Until I made myself a nuisance by asking about successful American musicians, nothing was said to imply that America possessed any good musicians. The chairman of the committee, Colonel Hartfield, questioned each one of us in turn as to where we stood on Mr. Bing. I replied that I liked him personally, but I had never met him before and I was aghast at calling as general manager for the Metropolitan someone whom I could not certify was even a musician.

Until this stage of our quest for a manager, we had discussed several times the possibility of dividing the management of the Metropolitan by electing a business manager in association with an artistic manager. So far nothing had been said about Mr. Bing's artistic equipment; nothing, that is, except that Miss Bori had testified that she had talked to him about his opinions of opera, and he seemed entirely orthodox. I told Colonel Hartfield that if the President and Chairman of the Board had no one else to bring before the directors, it would be very difficult to vote against Mr. Bing, but I could not vote for him happily on the basis of nothing but our present information.

A few days later there was a general meeting of the Board, and Mr. Bing was elected to succeed Mr. Johnson on June 1, 1950.

The situation at the Metropolitan is, to say the least, confused. For the first time in Metropolitan history the general manager has now been chosen not by the men of the Opera Board but by the ladies of the Opera Guild. The final vote is still cast by the men, but Mr. Bing seems to have been selected for us by Mrs. Belmont, who made a special trip to Europe for that purpose, and by Mrs. Otto Kahn, who immediately before her death conferred with Mrs. Belmont in London; also by an English lady of title, better known to music circles in London than to us, who assisted Mrs. Belmont in making her choice and whose help she acknowledges graciously in her letters to the President of the Metropolitan Board.

I would be sorry indeed to seem unappreciative of Mrs. Belmont's work for the Metropolitan. I am one of her warmest admirers, but that fact does not prevent me from feeling that every member of the Board should have been informed on what the ladies were up to when they went to England. I wish I were more thoroughly convinced that even the most loyal supporters of opera among the members of the Opera Guild have such a range of acquaintance among European opera directors that they can be trusted to select the next general manager of the Metropolitan. I also wish I could feel sure that the ladies of the Opera Guild are competent to choose, or are even willing to choose, an American for a general manager if such a person exists.

❧❧

The MacDowell Colony

I

MRS. EDWARD MAC DOWELL formed what is now known as the MacDowell Colony by converting the property which she and her husband had begun to develop at Peterborough, New Hampshire, into an institution where young artists of every kind could find leisure and quiet during the summer months to pursue their creative work, whether in music or in painting or in sculpture or in literature.

The Colony was inaugurated August 16 to 20, 1910, by a memorial pageant performed in the amphitheater built in the grove of pine trees. The orchestra which accompanied this pageant was made up of Harvard students and was conducted by Chalmers Clifton, at that time studying at Harvard.

Mrs. MacDowell gathered as directors of the property well-known musicians and extremely successful businessmen. When I came back from World War I, even before I went to the Juilliard I joined the group of directors—not that she ever considered me a businessman or yet a musician, but she had heard me say that I had studied with Mr. MacDowell at Columbia, and my admiration for him was well known.

The Colony in his name has naturally attracted many musicians. Ernest Schelling was an early president. Albert Stoessel was also an officer.

The officers and directors of the Colony as this is written are: president, Cecil Smith; vice-presidents, Carl Carmer, Mary Howe; treasurer, Lewis M. Isaacs, Jr.; executive secretary, Louise Fillmore; John Taylor Arms, Miss Esther Willard Bates, Mrs. Hugh Bullock, Mrs. George Edwards Clement, Chalmers Clifton, Laurence Vail Coleman, Aaron Copland, John Erskine, Barry Faulkener, Rudolph Ganz, A. Erland Hagedorn, Ernest Hutcheson, Mrs. Edward MacDowell, Mrs. Howard Mansfield, Walter S. Marvin, William McCleery, Douglas Moore, Henry B. Nevins, Hobart Nichols, Mrs. Robert L. Popper, Mrs. Benjamin Prince, DeForest Porter Rudd, Mrs. Eugene Coleman Savidge, Carleton Sprague Smith, Thornton Wilder.

In 1947 we, the trustees, were warned by competent inspectors that the original pageant amphitheater through neglect was disintegrating, and either the stone seats should be rebuilt or no further performances permitted.

With others of the directors I felt that the Colony should undertake the expense of restoring the stone seats in the amphitheater. We had been advised that the dilapidated stone structure might cause an unfortunate accident. Someone climbing over the broken stones might damage an ankle. We decided, therefore, to put the amphitheater in first-rate condition and then to build a small shell and platform so that concerts and other forms of entertainment might be given, the purpose being to make enough money eventually to pay for the repairs.

I hoped also that in time the young composers at the Colony might wish to use the shell for the presentation of some of their compositions.

This was almost entirely my own idea, and I felt responsible for getting up the programs. In plain words, I felt responsible for the expense. The Colony paid for the building of the shell and for the repairs of the old amphitheater. I personally paid for all the musical expense except for the appearance of our good friend, Albert Spalding; he and his accompanist both donated their services.

The restored amphitheater was reopened September 2, 3, and 4, 1948, with three recitals given by Albert Spalding, Mary Davenport, and Beveridge Webster.

For two years these concerts were my gift to the Colony. If Carl Carmer and Louise Fillmore had not been on hand loyally to back me up, I doubt if I would have repeated the experiment. It had its pleasant aspects. Peterborough was a delightful Colonial New England town and a perfect summer resort.

Helen, whom I had married on July 3, 1945, and I had the pleasure of entertaining the artists in the old Peterborough Tavern, now restored. Albert Spalding, in addition to being an old friend, was a trustee of the Colony. Mary Davenport's father, Russell Davenport, had sung in my choir at Amherst. Mary has a great voice. She's a young Flagstad. Beveridge Webster was another friend of many years. When he came the first year to Peterborough, his mother was dying. I appreciated his gallantry in not letting us down, knowing how heavily her condition weighed on his mind. He made the concerts a distinguished success by his beautiful playing.

The latter part of August of 1949 Mary Davenport and Beveridge Webster returned to give two superb programs, and on August 26, which the program committee called Colonists' Day, the program was given by Dika Newlin, Thomas Matthews, and Irving Fine, three pianists who were in residence at the Colony. Their program had this novel quality, that the original compositions of the performers were presented.

Beveridge Webster performed under difficulties. It had been announced that he would play a Beethoven Sonata, four Chopin pieces, and ten MacDowell compositions. The skies were dark and lowering the Sunday of his concert. If it rained the recital was to be held in the Town Hall, a big pink Colonial brick building opposite the Tavern where we were staying.

Helen and I anxiously watched the heavy clouds all morning. The August atmosphere was hot and oppressive. Not a leaf stirred on the big elm trees which shaded Main Street. Occasionally we could hear a faraway rumble of thunder. But when Beveridge joined us at luncheon the sidewalks were still dry.

We relaxed. A concert in the beauty of the woodland setting of the MacDowell Colony amphitheater was one thing, music in the matter-of-fact Town Hall quite another.

We were getting up from the luncheon table when Mrs. Fillmore telephoned. The recital would be in the Town Hall. She had long-distanced the Weather Bureau at Boston. The storm would hit Peterborough around three o'clock that afternoon. We need not worry. She was notifying everyone. And the piano would be moved from the amphitheater to the Town Hall Auditorium.

Helen went across the street to take a look at the auditorium. My weak legs confined me to a rocking chair on the Tavern porch. As I sat there enormous drops of water began to splash on the streets. There was a sudden flash of lightning and a crash of thunder. Suddenly I saw Helen darting toward the Tavern. The chairman in charge of arrangements had just heard from Mrs. Fillmore. The piano at the amphitheater could not be moved in the rain and the one at Town Hall was out of tune!

We broke the news to Beveridge. "Never mind," he said. "I'll get through somehow. But I'd like to learn the piano's limitations before the concert begins."

Lightning zigzagged continuously across the dark sky. One peal of thunder followed another. The rain descended in a solid sheet of water. It was impossible to walk even to the Town Hall without being drenched.

A young man who had been sitting near us introduced himself. "I'm Raymond Morin, music critic of the *Worcester Telegram*. May I ferry you over in my car?"

We gratefully accepted his offer. It developed that he was a pianist himself and sympathized with Beveridge.

Like so many hazardous undertakings that final concert in

the Peterborough Town Hall was probably the most successful of the series. The audience appreciated all the difficulties.
They cheered as Beveridge rippled through one difficult piece
after another on that wretched piano, without a single slip.
Cries of "Bravo! Bravo!" filled the air when he pulled off the
final number in scintillating brilliancy.

If we hadn't been returning to New York directly after the
concert they probably would have kept him at the piano for
another hour.

At the end of that curious session in which he wrestled so
gallantly with the piano in the Peterborough Town Hall, he
rode with Mrs. Erskine and me to Boston, where we took the
airplane to New York. I reached home in not very good shape
with my nerves behaving rather badly.

Personally I think the programs were an outstanding success, since for the first time we had Colonists contribute, and
very creditably, from their own original work. That result, it
seems to me, thoroughly justifies the improvement of the amphitheater and the building of the platform, and so on. I hope
from now on the annual concerts can be developed as exhi-
bition occasions for the musicians who are using the Colony
and who can profit by the opportunity to be made known to
the public.

My own health was not good throughout the season. Helen
and I went to Peterborough not only to consult with Mrs.
Fillmore about the programs but again for an additional week
to oversee the performances and to help as far as we could.
I am afraid I exerted myself too much.

Following the advice of my doctor, I handed in my resignation as a member of the Colony Board of Trustees. I cannot
try to repeat the quite insignificant services I was able to
render the Colony. I shall always remember with great pleasure these two summer visits and what I believe has been the
good results of them. In particular I shall remember the devoted service to the Colony of Mrs. Fillmore.

In discussions after the performances I heard suggestions

that competent teachers or coaches should be provided to see that the composers choose programs not too long and of a quality not too monotonous. This suggestion may easily be carried out in future years. I hope there will be an increasing number of composers working at the Colony who will be glad of the opportunity to exhibit their work in the concerts at the end of the season. A committee could easily be formed consisting of such experienced musicians as Chalmers Clifton, Philip James, and Douglas Moore to advise the composers as to what to play and how much at any one time.

This is not to imply that the Colony should change its original purpose and become merely one more music school. It would be an advantage if it should assume some of the ideals of a first-rate school. At present altogether too few of the Colony buildings are fireproof. The beautiful Savidge Library and the Alexander Studio, and perhaps one or two other buildings, are notable exceptions, but the fire hazard at Peterborough is great, especially at the end of a dry summer.

Since the Colony was not imagined as a music school, Mrs. MacDowell never planned to equip the studios or the other buildings with musical instruments. The Colony has a small grand piano in the library. For the concerts which we have given now for two seasons in the Pageant Theatre, a concert grand has been rented from the Steinway agent in Worcester. This expense, with the other costs of these concerts, has been born by private subscription. The trustees of the Colony will no doubt decide eventually to what extent the concerts are to be developed and continued, and whether they should be paid for by subscription or otherwise.

II

No chapter on the MacDowell Colony would be complete without some mention of Mrs. MacDowell.

When Mr. MacDowell suffered his tragic nervous break-

down, I was leaving Columbia for my first post in Amherst.
I had never known Mrs. MacDowell, but she was not producing a pleasant impression upon the Columbia boys who
had been devoted to her husband but who also thought pretty
well of their alma mater. Mrs. MacDowell spread the legend
wherever she could that her husband had been overworked at
Columbia; in fact, had led something of a dog's life there. We
who had studied with him and had honored his cheerful,
manly nature were quite sure the poor woman must be misled
by her grief.

The cause of his breakdown we could not understand, in
spite of explanations offered by Hamlin Garland and others
of his intimate friends. The well-circulated report that my
university had not appreciated him and had no room for a
genius seemed to me more than a little outrageous. From my
first Amherst experience in teaching and from my observation
of the teaching schedule of Professor William P. Bigelow,
who managed the music department there singlehanded, I
concluded that MacDowell had not been overworked at Columbia. I had attended two of his courses. I was beginning
to be an experienced teacher, and I made up my mind that
MacDowell himself, being an honest man, had not com-
plained of overwork; also that Mrs. MacDowell, never having
been a teacher herself of any kind, anywhere, was not well informed of the duties and schedules of a teacher's life.

In the early Colony trustee meetings held at the end of each
summer, I soon made the acquaintance of a quite different
Mrs. MacDowell, no longer an embittered and grieving
widow, but an extremely efficient and happy person who had
discovered the career she had always been looking for. She was
a masterful character. The more she had to manage, the happier she was.

At the MacDowell Colony meetings she usually told us
with a bright, happy smile that several acres had come on the
market that year, bits of property adjoining what the Colony
already owned. She admitted that she had no authorization

to add to our holdings, and certainly she had no money to make additional purchases.

"But I might as well admit, gentlemen, that I bought the property in your name. Of course it must be paid for"—here she would laugh lightly—"but I suppose such business matters can be left to the trustees."

By her curious combination of devotion and recklessness she gradually increased the size of the MacDowell Colony, but gradually also she came to realize that the proceedings in which she played the leading part should become more regular and more businesslike.

As her age advanced she organized the ownership of her property rather definitely, but not entirely so. "Hillcrest," the home of Mr. MacDowell and herself, remains her property, and it may be a shrine to the memory of her husband and herself. She receives from the Colony an income, and members of the Colony have arranged that she should receive an income from her husband's music. The Colony itself is in the care of a remarkably able manager, appointed by the trustees and responsible to them. Various committees are in charge of the living conditions of the Colony and the proper use of the studios.

I have been fortunate to enjoy more of Mrs. MacDowell's confidence and friendship than I ever had any right to expect. Much of it has been in the form of a lively exchange of letters. A great deal of it, especially Mrs. MacDowell's replies, throws a new light on MacDowell himself.

III

In 1932 I wrote an article on MacDowell for the *Dictionary of American Biography*. Naturally I asked Mrs. MacDowell for information about MacDowell's family and about his background. She replied somewhat cryptically that she did not know his family, and she ignored all my questions, as though I were prying into something which did not concern me. She started me on some searching inquiries into her life as well as his. The inquiries are not entirely completed, and certainly I am not ready to publish them, but the spirited correspondence, altogether pleasant, which she and I have had ever since convinces me that she knows what I am up to and that I am not entirely on the wrong trail.

Writing that little piece and reading as intensively as I could what has already been written about MacDowell, I felt that there ought to be a much more complete and human biography of him than has yet been done. I think it is important that MacDowell's life should be seen more clearly related to his day than it appears in any of the brief sketches. His American and European background ought to be filled in.

I said as much to Mrs. MacDowell in a letter, adding that I could gather the material without much difficulty, and if she approved the general plan perhaps she would let me look over some of his unpublished letters, especially those which had a bearing on his general musical point of view.

My feeling was and is that MacDowell's personality and the ideals he stood for will count more and more in American music and it would be helpful to the cause as well as to his reputation if a strong life on him could be written just now. In studying the material for the biographical article, I was amazed to realize that his ideas for musical education at Columbia, to which the educators of his day were so pathetically unreceptive, are rapidly becoming the goal toward which American colleges are working. Many of the ideas which I have been putting out proudly as my own I see he advocated in his reports to the Columbia trustees. There wasn't the slightest chance for such ideas in any American university at that time, nor indeed in any university abroad, and I can understand the perplexity of the trustees, poor men, who in those days were gorgeously innocent of all the arts. But Mac-Dowell will be recognized as a sound educational prophet.

Mrs. MacDowell did not acknowledge my offer in writing, but the next time the trustees of the Colony met she told me rather quietly but firmly that she had already appointed her friend, Miss Nina Maude Richardson, as MacDowell's biographer, and she had put in her care a number of letters and other documents which might be useful.

In the course of a week or more I happened to meet Miss Richardson and Mrs. MacDowell at a concert in Carnegie Hall. Miss Richardson, with some embarrassment I thought, referred to my letter to Mrs. MacDowell and to her reply.

"I should be very happy, Mr. Erskine, if you would join me in this task. Why should we not collaborate on the biography?"

I declined the handsome offer with promptness.

A number of years later Mrs. MacDowell generously gave me the piano sketch of the Scherzo for the Second MacDowell Concerto. With the aid of others of the MacDowell Colony trustees this Scherzo was reproduced and sold for the benefit of the Colony.

When in 1947 I published *The Memory of Certain Persons* Mrs. MacDowell wrote me a charming letter about my memories of MacDowell which were included in this autobiographical volume. She said that I had given the best picture of him she had seen anywhere, and she wished that all members of the MacDowell Colony might enjoy it. Could not my publisher be induced to publish the chapter separately and make it available for members of the Colony and others who might appreciate it?

I replied as follows:

"It is sweet of you to want the MacDowell chapter reprinted separately. Perhaps it may be arranged, as you say, after the book has been a little bit longer in print. The publishers would probably object to reprinting so early.

"Perhaps you recall that a number of years ago when I asked your permission to write a full-length biography of MacDowell, I learned from you that you already had commissioned Miss Richardson to do that work. It occurs to me that if her book is ready it might be an advantage to put it out now with the benefit of your advice and supervision.

"It makes me very happy to know that you think my little chapter is helpful, but what we need is a full-length biography of MacDowell. His music makes its way steadily, I believe, but Americans in general know little about him. A full account of his life, of his friendships abroad and at home, of his work as composer, as pianist, as teacher, would, I believe, find a publisher at once and a welcome from all music lovers."

As I write this Miss Richardson's life of MacDowell has not been published.

In 1948 I found a brief note of Mrs. MacDowell in the *Musical Quarterly* which made the rather startling statement that a suggestion of MacDowell's had something to do with the organization of the American Academy in Rome. I wrote her the following letter:

"I have been reading with much interest your article on MacDowell's Peterborough idea which appeared in the *Musical Quarterly*.

"On page 33 you say that 'though Mr. MacDowell was the first representative of music on the Academy's Board of Directors, he did not live to see his ideas carried out. Indeed they were never even formally submitted to the Board, but among his papers still exists the outline made and dictated, embodying his hopes for the composer who went to Rome, and his further hope that his plans might affect the future of those working in other arts.'

"Have you ever published this outline? If you will let me have a copy of it, I think I can get it published, and its appearance at this time would, I think, benefit happily Mac-Dowell's reputation and the future not only of the Academy at Rome, but of the Colony at Peterborough."

I did not hear from Mrs. MacDowell for nearly a month. I was rewarded for the delay, since she gave me an entirely

different version of his fatal illness. She also mentioned Mac-
Dowell's mother and father in the only reference, so far as I
know, that she ever made to them. Her letter follows:

"You know how grateful I am for the unfailing interest in
MacDowell and his music and for the article you wrote about
him in your autobiography. Your letter was slow in reaching
me, owing to some blunder in Peterborough. Please pardon
the delay.

"You see where I am (California) and it would be a terrific
task for me to go through literally hundreds of papers regarding MacDowell, which I have accumulated through the last
forty years. As I remember the notes, they were so brief that
I doubt if I had understood them had he not talked so often
with me regarding the matter of the Academy at Rome. It was
a tragic thing that this position might not have been offered
to him two or three years earlier, and possibly that would have
changed his life.

"These little notes I speak of could not have been used
without incorporating them into an article by someone like
yourself. Briefly, he felt strongly the artistic influence of sur-
roundings, that is putting it very briefly. His idea was that a
man coming to Rome should be obliged for several months
to do a lot of traveling through Europe, seeing and absorbing
so much beauty that was to be found. Another point he made
was the great advantage to the students in the Academy at
Rome would be the close affiliations of those working in the
different arts, which idea, of course, we tried to carry out in
the MacDowell Colony. He referred I remember to a fellowship he had been able to give to a student when he was at
Columbia. A certain sum of money being given to that person to spend in Europe, not to study but to see and hear so
much that could not be found in this country. All of this with
the idea of stirring the imagination of the creative worker.
Those are the two points he made in his notes. He had a
very curious way, and for me a most wonderful way, of talk-

ing over with me everything he did and thought to the end because it helped to clarify in his own mind what he was thinking about. . . .

"I am very humble in my mind and very grateful for all your thoughts, and with all good wishes . . ."

I replied on November 22, a day or two after receiving her letter:

"Thanks for your letter of the 18th. I was hoping that the paper referred to in the *Musical Quarterly* article was still accessible, but I can understand how easily such things become overwhelmed in a mass of records.

"I have never forgotten the evening in the music room at Hillcrest when you brought down to us a number of Mac-Dowell's youthful notebooks, among them the book containing the Benedick and Beatrice sketches, and another which contained the pencil sketches of MacDowell's one symphony. I have never forgotten the delight on Albert Stoessel's face when he turned the page and came on the symphony. I do hope that those precious manuscripts of MacDowell's music will be accessible for future students of his music. Devoted though I am to the Colony and to the work there which you built up for the younger generation, I always persist in the loyalty of my youth to one of the few geniuses I have ever met. MacDowell's music, I am convinced, does not date. It will have a valid appeal always to temperaments sympathetic with his own, and they will recur constantly.

"Thank you for the interesting information. I have often wished I knew more about his father and mother than occasional biographical paragraphs convey. What became of his three brothers? There *were* three, were there not? Forgive me if I intrude upon your patience with such questions, but the answers ought to be known."

These questions were never answered.

It isn't easy to sift the chaff from the wheat and it will be more difficult as time goes on. Already the legends about MacDowell are contradictory.

Some years ago I was in Peterborough with Albert Spalding and Ernest Schelling. One of these gentlemen remarked to Mrs. MacDowell that MacDowell's music room in Hillcrest was as quiet a place as he had ever visited.

"How your husband must have enjoyed this retirement!"

"He did enjoy it," said Mrs. MacDowell. "He played the piano here entirely too much. That's why I gave him the log cabin in the woods quite a distance off. I couldn't stand the noise he was making."

This of course is not the story which usually graces the legend of the log cabin, but I dare say it's entirely true, and I tell it sympathetically. I've known more than one woman in the musical world who could not endure the noise of her husband's practicing. And though MacDowell, like anyone else, might on occasion compose without using a piano, he also was a concert pianist, and each year he was absent part of the time from his Columbia classes giving tours through the country.

The Peterborough Town Clerk, Algie Holt, described Mac-Dowell as he remembered him in his days at Peterborough.

"He was always walking," said Mr. Holt, "and I suppose he was thinking over his music. Every now and then he would stop by the roadside, usually at a convenient stone wall, and begin to write down some notes on the music paper he carried with him."

I am afraid that the people who live in Peterborough are in danger of forgetting MacDowell. Mr. Holt is the exception. Mrs. MacDowell they know well and speak of often. Perhaps they remember MacDowell only when they have occasion to pass the beautiful grave which Mrs. MacDowell built for him. But thinking of all that he represented to me in my youth when he was teaching at Columbia, I like to believe that his music and his true personality may be remembered in the Colony which has risen on the site of his old home.

❉❉❉

CHAPTER TWENTY-NINE

Present and Future

I

THE Juilliard Summer School had been going great guns in 1943. I was very, very glad for Ernest Hutcheson's sake. He had not been well. Finally, when the autumn session opened and we saw that he was not recovering as he should, we suggested that he lay aside for a while, in whole or in part, his work as president. This meant that I could not, as I had hoped, give all my time to writing and travel. I can see now that I wouldn't have had it otherwise. My heart has always been in the Juilliard.

The winter of 1942-1943 went smoothly at the School. Ernest was on hand much of the time. Oscar Wagner was a tremendous help and Albert Stoessel, with his incredible capacity for work, gave us a splendid season of opera. He was head of the Opera Department and concerned himself intimately with every detail of our opera productions. He gave the course in conducting, and he conducted the concerts of the Graduate School orchestra. As guest conductor he frequently visited other cities, or directed performances here in New York. With all these drains on his time and his energy, he kept up his technique as violin and viola player. He de-

voted hour upon hour to studying the scores of new compositions, and with the utmost generosity promoted the professional careers of young players and singers who had worked
with him here in the School, and of other young Americans
not of the School whose gifts seemed to him worthy. Remembering his prodigious labors, we wonder what premonition he
had that the time was short.

He enriched the life of the School not only by the happy
influence of his poised and friendly nature, not only by the
inspiration of his teaching and his directing, but by the confidence which the world of music had in him. Whenever he
could he took with him on his engagements afield some of the
young players and singers who in this hall had proved their
quality. He searched out and performed the works of young
composers, spending midnight oil and much eyesight on the
scores of the talented but inexperienced. To perform major
works, especially those of Bach demanding massive choruses,
he persuaded the members of the Oratorio Society and other
groups to join forces with us in an association which we remember with deep satisfaction. He helped the School to be
not only a proving ground for the young, but on distinguished
occasions a rallying point for the mature.

Present and future were bright for him when he ascended
the platform on the twelfth of May, 1943. He conducted a
symphony by his old friend, Walter Damrosch. At the final
chord in the last movement he fell to the floor as if struck
down by a bolt from Heaven. Before his wife, who happened
to be in the audience, could reach him, he was dead. Charac-
teristically, he had given a complete and splendid performance before leaving us.

It was a terrible shock to all, especially to Ernest Hutcheson—his friend for so many years. I was more than ever concerned about Ernest. We must find someone to succeed him.
That was not easy.

In considering anyone for the presidency, we had in mind:
1. His standing among other musicians as artist and man.

2. His ability as educator and administrator.

3. His sympathy with the aims of the School to date and the probability of his taking us further, let alone holding on to what we have.

The Board finally decided upon a very brilliant young American composer—William Schuman. His career had been a bit meteoric, and though I was a great admirer of his I rather expected, when I threw his name into a Board discussion, that he would be turned down at once because he was only thirty-five years old. To my delight and amazement, Mr. Drinker, Mr. Warburg, and Mr. McCollister knew him and his work through their children or through others who had studied and worked with him. For once we were all entirely unanimous. Bill Schuman is a dynamic person, in my opinion not a rash one, but certainly he is full of new ideas. He is one of the country's outstanding composers. He was born in New York, August 4, 1910, and was educated in the city schools, receiving bachelor's and master's degrees in music from Columbia University. He attended classes at the Mozarteum in Salzburg and studied privately in New York with Charles Haubiel, Max Persin, and Roy Harris. From 1935 to the spring of 1945 he taught music at Sarah Lawrence College, where he trained and developed a chorus that is widely known and admired. Since May 15, 1945, he has been director of publications of G. Schirmer, Inc. He continues to act as special consultant to that firm.

Mr. Schuman's works include five symphonies, a ballet, two cantatas, two overtures, a piano concerto, three string quartets, and many shorter compositions. Prizes he has won include the first Pulitzer Prize in Music.

I happen to know more about his work than most of the other members of the Board, some of whom felt at first that we were taking a risk to put the School in his charge. All that they knew about him was that his previous teaching had been done in a small school, he composed in the modern manner, and he was extremely youthful. I held out for Schuman on the ground that youth more than anything else was what the School needed. Most of the Board with whom the School had started were now growing old, many of our most brilliant colleagues had died, and I suspected that I began to resemble Methuselah too closely to be any longer a wise guide of the young. Fortunately, as I think, the Board approved Mr. Schuman. He has the confidence and support of Ernest Hutcheson, who still in my opinion and I believe in Bill's, is the strongest teacher in the School. When Bill was named president, the Board made Ernest president emeritus.

If we had no other reason for thinking highly of our young President, we should honor him in the very height of his inexperience for guiding the School safely through the difficult years immediately after the last war, when our halls were crowded with G.I.'s, when many of the faculty were temporarily scattered, and when the temper of the world was hardly favorable to the contemplation and study of an art. We have come through safely, and if in many respects we have now to begin again I am glad the School is so young and that it wears so few scars of time as it starts on its second chapter.

II

Just before we chose Mr. Schuman as our new president, the School Board considered a number of other candidates, or perhaps we should say, other possibilities. Bruno Walter, for example, never thought of himself as a candidate for the presidency of the School, but several of the Board wished that we could persuade him to take over the responsibility. He was not young, and he knew that with the end of the war his personal interests were once more in Europe. He wanted if possible to assist in the revival of the old Viennese world to which he had contributed much of its glory and which he would always love.

I persuaded him to meet the Board one evening in my home, and we talked over the prospects of the School and the possibility that he might be connected with it. At the end of the evening my colleagues on the Board went away convinced that they had met a great man—but convinced also that his heart was in Old Europe, and he was not for our School.

Though we were considering a successor to Ernest Hutcheson, Mr. Hutcheson was most helpful in arranging this meeting and in helping me to organize it. He was a warm friend and cordial admirer of Bruno Walter, and perhaps he foresaw that, if Bruno Walter would not come, I should ask the Board to consider a president younger and more contemporary. This of course was exactly what happened—altogether, as I think, to the advantage of the School. When I think now that if Bruno Walter, by some miracle, might have said yes instead of no, I shudder at the error we should have made. Bruno Walter is still a great conductor, delighting audiences in the Old World as well as the New—just now bringing his beautiful music to the Salzburg Festival as he did before World War II. But I doubt if he is bringing any *new* music to any audience. He is still living in the high moments of his youth when he was learning to admire, even to worship, the genius of Gustav Mahler.

Mahler once conducted opera in New York, and had charge of our Philharmonic. Musicians here know he was a great man, but he made no impression on the town. I do not believe that our students at the Juilliard School find any necessity to mention his name. It would be a great misfortune if Mahler were now held up to them as a model of the music young America should cultivate and love. All music lovers, whether the music be operatic or symphonic, are bound to the tastes of their youth, or at least of the years in which they were growing up.

The opera singer, or the conductor, or the pianist must spend hours or even years in mastering a fairly limited repertory, but this limited repertory will represent to them more and more as they grow older the ideal repertory for the younger generation. All musicians have one artistic life which is peculiarly their life. They may acquire mastery of a few more pieces, more or less, but as they grow older they find they have put their aspirations and can find their satisfactions in a limited repertory. Modern music, at whatever date, is not for them.

I was shocked when I learned that an excellent musician, one of my older friends, was far from sharing my love of the American operas of which I have spoken so frequently in this volume. The daughter of the elderly musician who disagreed with me suggested that the difference of opinion was inevitable.

"How could Father possibly admire this music?" she asked. "He knows only too poignantly the charm of it. In other words, he knows that it is not the music on which he was brought up. It is not the music that belongs to him. If he admits its superb quality he must admit that he and his day are finished. That is a good deal for an older man to admit."

The conclusion, which I am glad to believe is for the moment illustrated at the Juilliard School, is that each generation should step aside early and promptly, and leave the field for the youngsters. Having had myself a wonderful opportunity to do what I could for musical education in my time, I am glad that I stepped aside early indeed, and found a youthful spirit to take my place.

Kurt Wolff, the great publisher who long ago brought out my *Helen of Troy* in German and who now publishes Pantheon Books in New York, was dining in my home one evening, and I had asked William Schuman and his charming wife to meet him.

Afterwards Kurt said, "If I understood you correctly, you first tried to get Bruno Walter for your School head, and then you chose this boy. For me there is no sense in such a procedure."

I explained that I thought there was a good deal of sense. When we tried for Bruno Walter, we were trying to secure the best man possible. When we called Bill Schuman I believe we secured the best man possible.

"But he is so young!"exclaimed Mr. Wolff.

"Unfortunately," I replied, "that can remain true for only a day—a tragically brief day!"

❊❊❊❊❊❊❊❊❊❊❊❊❊❊❊❊❊❊❊❊❊❊❊❊❊❊❊❊❊❊❊❊❊❊❊❊❊❊❊

CHAPTER THIRTY

The Juilliard School After World War Two

THE Juilliard School was profoundly affected by two world wars. Had it not been for the first, the School would not have had the wealth of European talent to draw on. After the first conflict, as you might say, between America and the Old World, many great musicians, with whom in earlier days American talent would have gone abroad to study, crossed the ocean. The great teachers who were originally gathered at the Juilliard had not been displaced by the war in any sense which we should have understood in World War II, but they felt at least that an epoch had closed. Europe had been shattered by the war, and, so long as the world found it necessary to mend itself, those musicians who still had youth and energy were ready to look for another chapter in their careers in America.

The musical characteristics of that chapter deserve to be studied much further than we have had opportunity to do in these pages. New York was rich in famous artists who were busy giving concerts to delighted audiences. Many of the soloists were members of the Juilliard faculty, and we had a rare opportunity to study their art. The war was over; we

listened again to the beautiful violin playing of Kreisler, to
the superb artistry of Lhevinne, and many other pianists.
The first impression of returned peace was that the world
of music was happily restored.

In one field this was not true. The Metropolitan had sustained some serious losses. But on the other hand, in spite of
the deliberate slighting of German opera, our one touch of
war madness and fortunately brief for us, we discovered before
the end of the war a new American admiration for Wagner
which was soon greatly encouraged by the coming of Flagstad and her heroic voice.

Just why the war served to increase the interest in Wagner,
I cannot guess. Madame Flagstad was eventually a drawing
card at the Metropolitan, but not at first. She had no history
in Europe as a Wagnerian singer, and it was at the Metropolitan that she built up her reputation by singing Isolde
and the other roles for which she became famous.

Her success was supplemented and encouraged by that of
Mr. Melchior. They were a great team, and she at least was
a great singer.

I am persuaded, though many of my colleagues would not
agree with me, that both Flagstad and Melchior, for a reason
somewhat curious but to me convincing, owed much of their
immediate success to the loudness rather than to the beauty
of their voices. I say that with complete admiration of the
marvelous beauty of Madame Flagstad's voice. But she and
Mr. Melchior appeared together on the operatic stage just
when the opera audience had become a little spoiled by the
ease with which voices on the motion-picture screen were
setting a difficult standard for the natural singing voice on
the operatic stage. The Metropolitan Opera had once been
not too large a stage for Sembrich and other delicate artists
to fill adequately, but if Sembrich or Patti were to reappear
now their voices would seem small and inadequate. We
should wish for the reinforcement of a loud-speaker.

Just at the moment when the operatic world was learning

to appreciate the services of a loud-speaker, Madame Flagstad and Mr. Melchior burst upon us, each bringing his or her own loud-speaker.

If we got through World War I with less than the usual amount of war madness, we seem to be paying for our sanity now by the prolonged and perhaps senseless unwillingness in some quarters ever to listen to Madame Flagstad again. The members of the Opera Board saw the stages through which Madame Flagstad's relations with the Metropolitan deteriorated, and, so far as we have any reason to know, the trouble lay in no belated sympathy on her part for Mr. Hitler. She discovered unexpected merit in quite another gentleman, a young musician who had ambitions to become a conductor, and whose ambition Madame Flagstad wished to encourage. She served an ultimatum on the Metropolitan that either this young friend of hers should be installed at the Opera House to conduct whenever she sang, or she would not renew her contract.

Her favorite conductor was tried out, and the Metropolitan management did not feel justified in engaging him permanently. Madame Flagstad then walked out on us, snapping her fingers, as it were, at the Metropolitan which had given her the career that until then she had not found in Europe.

When recently we learned that she intended to tour in the United States, the question naturally came up whether the Metropolitan management should swallow the treatment it had received from her and should invite her back. I was one of those who spoke most vigorously against ever taking her back. Certainly her voice was practically as noble as ever, and we certainly needed her, but an opera company can have only one general manager. I felt that the Metropolitan might as well go out of business once and for all if any singer, even Madame Flagstad, should play fast and loose with her contracts whenever she met an agreeable young musician who in her opinion would be an improvement on the regular and trained conductors of the staff.

Our colleagues, with considerable experience with singers, offered an explanation of Madame Flagstad's sudden infatuation for a young conductor, which to me was illuminating and convincing. The great roles in which Madame Flagstad had excelled are a heavy task for a singer who with advancing years becomes slightly short-breathed. Some of the Isolde passages would be easier for Madame Flagstad if she took them a bit more slowly. This would be what she would do if she were singing with a piano accompaniment; the pianist would take his tempo from her, and only an expert musician would know the difference. But in a Wagner opera, unless the tempo is maintained at the pace which the composer requires, the opera can't be finished on time. At the Metropolitan and at other opera houses, each act, and even each long scene, is checked with a stop watch. The opera must be sung absolutely on time as well as in time, or the management will find itself at the end of the performance with a terrific bill for overtime wages for the orchestra.

This may seem a small matter which ought not to interfere with every prima donna's taking the tempo which is most comfortable, but it is not a small matter. The composer rather than the management establishes the tempo in terms of metronome beats. Tempo is not a matter of personal taste or choice. But in opera it is, unfortunately, closely related to the youthfulness of the singer. The breath supply begins to give out with the first touch of age. Otherwise the voice, let us say, of a Schumann-Heink would be unimpaired to the very end.

World War II put the Juilliard School under such a difficult strain that while it lasted we spent very little time on grand-opera problems. At the School itself the opera department, which had once been flourishing, faded away. If my memory serves me correctly, we were able to give one opera during the war by rewriting all the voice parts for sopranos and contraltos. The boys had all been taken by the Navy and the Army.

The moment the war was over, or nearing its end, we had too many students rather than too few. The government provided scholarships for study in any art in which the G.I.'s could prove themselves proficient. In plain words, we could reject any veteran who was not qualified to take a course at the Juilliard, but if we once decided that he was qualified to take the course we could not keep him out or any other of his buddies, no matter how numerous they proved to be. Those who were genuinely gifted in music and wished to study the subject were surprisingly numerous.

The building of the Juilliard School was originally designed to accommodate 1,000 pupils. For this number the classrooms, teachers' studios, and practice rooms were adequate. The attendance as of January 7, 1947, reached a total of 2,106. In consequence, the pianos were subjected to excessive usage. Many of the pupils were invading the teaching studios in order to get their hands on the best pianos and on those in fairly good tune. The piano industry was overtaxed, and there was a shortage of first-rate piano tuners.

Mr. Schuman and the piano teachers whom we considered our most experienced and ablest men—that is, Ernest Hutcheson, Beveridge Webster, and Sascha Gorodnitzki— were appointed a committee to examine the condition of the instruments, after the Army and Navy had got through with them. These three piano teachers examined every instrument in the School, and the chairman of the committee, Mr. Hutcheson, had some lengthy conferences with Steinway and Sons as to the best way to handle the problem. The cost of putting the School equipment in proper condition—that is, so far as pianos were concerned—would be very large, but it was decided that we could turn a difficult corner if we could spend $50,000 for repairs at once, leaving a second series of repairs, costing another $50,000, to be met the following season.

Without much difficulty I persuaded the members of the Juilliard Foundation, the bankers who took care of our endowment, to make these large expenditures at once. They saw the wisdom of celebrating the return of peace by putting the pianos and other musical instruments in perfect condition, and by buying new instruments where necessary.

President Schuman and Dean Schubart undertook to reduce the size of the School to the original proportions. I doubt if this part of the program has yet been completely accomplished, but we all agreed that a School of 1,000 is for us ideal, and we shall shortly reach that goal. One thousand pupils are no doubt necessary because a smaller number of students would not provide us, in all probability, with orchestral players or singers in desirable numbers. The quality of the talent which applies for admission to the School is amazingly high.

The trustees of the Juilliard Musical Foundation as of 1950 are: John Erskine, president; William L. Kleitz, treasurer; William A. Eldridge, William S. Gray, Jr., John M. Perry, A. Nye Van Vleck, Allen Wardwell.

The directors of the Juilliard School of Music as of 1950 are: John Erskine, chairman of the Board; Franklin B. Benkard, secretary; Henry S. Drinker, Edward Johnson, Parker McCollester, John M. Perry, William Schuman, James P. Warburg, Allen Wardwell.

CHAPTER THIRTY-ONE

~~~~~~

Realization of a Dream

MY RIGHT hand never recovered sufficiently for me to take up the piano again beyond a little elementary thumping. But I can't stay out of things. I went on with my life in music. Besides it wouldn't be a good life if I just sat back and looked over the good things that had happened. I must go forward. If I were to live I must be active.

I shuttled back and forth across the country on musical errands. I made myself a nuisance by speaking out of turn at Metropolitan Opera and Juilliard School Board meetings. As a trustee of the French Institute, I spoke many times for France during the war.

I think the French people, including the Parisians, are the most civilized folk I have met. A quibbler once pointed out to me that Paris has wretched slums and that the Paris mob when roused has at several points in history committed appalling violence. My country has its slums too. I know them in New York and Chicago and they exist in other large cities. In my country too I know the southern districts which are the basis for Erskine Caldwell's novels and the other social conditions which are the basis for "The Grapes of Wrath."

The French Revolution, like most French rioting, was for a great idea which has proved profitable to the rest of humanity. I can't think of any profit which has resulted from our American lynchings or Ku Klux outrages. We still indulge in race and color prejudice.

We excel the French in plumbing and in physical comfort. In matters of the mind and spirit, in culture, in scholarship, in general intelligence, and in manners I think we can still sit at their feet.

On a wall devoted to France, in our New York apartment, hangs a document which is precious to me—the diploma creating me an honorary citizen of Beaune, in Burgundy. It was bestowed upon me after the close of World War I. The AEF University at Beaune which I organized has been torn down many years. Nevertheless I have always dreamed of going back to Beaune. I love the town.

I had hoped that as soon as I could make Helen Worden my wife we would spend our honeymoon there. But at the time we were married the world was still at war and foreign travel impossible. Ever since, our lives have been a succession of plans and engagements which I have later had to change because a bad turn in my health made it impossible to keep on. Of course, first among these plans was the visit to Burgundy. Much happened, in addition to my poor health, to deter us.

In May, 1947, my son Graham married Hazel Peterson. Helen and I went to see them—in Reno, of all places, where Graham had permanently settled, practicing architecture with great success. He had made quite a record for himself, being the only architect in the state with a national license, enabling him to practice his profession in any state. He and his partner, Monk Ferris, were building a new high school for the city, and they had also just about forty other jobs. Graham had bought an acre south of town and was building himself a home. In spite of my one or two slight feeblenesses, high blood pressure, for example, we had a wonderful and happy time in Nevada.

Anna gave me a grandson early in 1947, Timothy Crouse, a complete paragon, as you can imagine. She and Russel had bought a house on our street, just beyond Lexington Avenue, and I was cultivating my grandson's acquaintance faithfully on Sunday afternoons.

In February, 1948, Hazel and Graham presented me with a grandson, John Peter Erskine, and Anna gave me a granddaughter, Lindsay Ann Crouse, the following May. I began to feel patriarchal. In the autumn of 1948 I planned to stop off in Reno on a lecture tour which would take me to the West Coast. I never made the tour.

In November, 1948, Dr. Walter Timme, discovering that my blood pressure threatened to be nearer 300 than 200, put his foot down and forbade more lecture tours for the rest of my days. He managed to reduce the blood pressure until it ceased to be threatening, so long as I didn't try to make speeches in public. The Doctor was kind enough not to condemn me to perpetual silence; a lecture now and then would not be fatal, he said, if it involved no travel and no unusual excitement. But unfortunately my lectures are exciting to me, even if not to others, and I find that anything which interests me warmly sends up my blood pressure. So I decided to spend the rest of my time at home varied with occasional inspections of the Juilliard and its work.

My despair over my health was lightened by a letter from France. The University of Dijon wished to confer an honorary degree upon me. Could I be present at the commencement exercises in 1949? Dijon was twenty minutes from Beaune! I said yes.

To my sorrow I felt obliged in February, 1949, to write Marcel Bouchard, the Recteur of Dijon University, on my doctor's advice, that my health was not mending as fast as it should and the difficulty I had in walking would prevent

my going through with the ceremony or any lectures at his
university. It broke my heart. The Recteur replied most
kindly that it would be agreeable to award the honorary degree in absentia. His letter was so sympathetic and so generous that it cheered me up.

Helen's mother was taken seriously ill, so we could not
have left even if my health had been better. Mrs. Worden
died in April, 1949. In June of that same year we went West
once again—this time to meet my son's boy, John Peter
Erskine. The country was lovelier than ever and the very interesting and—to people who like modern architecture—the
very attractive home that Graham had built for his family
made us sorry to come away.

When we returned to New York I began to feel that my
health would eventually improve so that soon we might look
forward with confidence to the trip to Burgundy. I wrote
the Recteur of Dijon University once more—this time that
I would arrive on or about the first of October since the
autumn term began at that time. But my health did not improve. Increasingly high blood pressure made it impossible
for me to leave in September as I had planned. However, by
rearranging my life and cutting down my work to half a day,
I could get by, or so I thought.

On November 16 the Board members of the Juilliard
Foundation held their monthly meeting in the Guaranty
Trust Company at 140 Broadway. Helen planned an early
luncheon so that I would not feel hurried. Having an errand
in lower New York, she rode downtown in the taxi with me.
The meeting was at half-past two. The business of the day
went smoothly. When we adjourned at half-past three Mr.
Perry congratulated me on the ease with which we had done
everything. Allen Wardwell and I strolled out into the main
section of the bank where Helen was waiting for me. He
asked if he might ride uptown with us. We were happy to
have his company. He dashed ahead to get a taxi as Helen
and I walked down the few steps leading to the street en-

trance of the bank. Before I reached the sidewalk, Broadway with its traffic and crowds began to recede. I heard Helen cry out as if from a great distance. I remember vaguely slipping to the sidewalk, of Helen tucking her fur scarf under my head, and of thinking that this was the end. For some odd reason a stanza from Robert Browning's "Youth and Art" flashed before me:

> "Each life's unfulfilled, you see;
> It hangs still, patchy and scrappy:
> We have not sighed deep, laughed free,
> Starved, feasted, despaired,—been happy."

I remember saying to Helen, "Don't forget me altogether." After that I remember nothing.

Helen and Allen Wardwell rode in an ambulance with me to the Beekman Downtown Hospital. The examining doctor said I had suffered a coronary thrombosis. This diagnosis was later changed to a cerebral hemorrhage. The impact of that two-ton Michigan state highway truck was still making itself felt.

My Mother used to say that I was born lucky. If being taken to any hospital could be called lucky, I was fortunate in landing at Beekman. Dr. Marsh McCall, the head of the hospital, proved to be a specialist in my particular brand of ailment. He and his staff were among the most kindly, human people we have had the good fortune to meet. They let Helen live at the hospital and they let her take me home, against their better judgment, at the end of ten days. I was still a very sick man, but I knew that if I was to get well my chances of doing it would be greater among my books and pictures and within sound of my piano. Fulton Oursler, dear friend that he was, saw me into the ambulance and followed us in a taxi. Helen and the nurse and a staff doctor rode beside me.

Smokey, our coon cat, Margaret Miller, my secretary, and Mary Rowland, our cook, were at the door to welcome us home. The last weeks of 1949 are shadowy. I remember hearing the voice of Graham, my son. I was not clear minded enough to know that he had flown from Reno to see me. It was enough that he was here. Often I heard beautiful music. I thought that was a dream. Later I learned Ernest Hutcheson had come to play Chopin for me. Other times Muriel Kerr and Beveridge and Frances Webster made lovely music. Muriel played César Franck. Beveridge played the piano and Frances sang—heavenly songs by Schubert, Brahms, and Bach. One afternoon Mary Davenport came to sing and Bertha Melnik to play. Music was healing me.

For eighteen days I lay on my back with my eyes closed. I could not speak, I was blind. Then one morning my nurse put on my dressing gown and lifted me into a wheel chair. I did not know why. I could hear people talking in the living room. I felt myself being wheeled to them. Some man greeted me in French. As he began to speak I understood. The degree had come from the University of Dijon! I recognized the voice of René de Messières, France's cultural ambassador. As he talked my sight returned. I saw that there were several people in the living room: Helen, my wife; my friend, Fulton Oursler; my daughter, Anna, and Russel Crouse, her husband; Miss Miller, my secretary; Dr. McCall, Pierre Bedard, director of the French Institute, and M. de Messières.

In de Messières' hand was a white, blue, and orange scarf handsomely trimmed in white ermine and ornamented by a big scarlet seal. As he made the speech of presentation in French, he placed the scarf over my shoulder. Without a second's hesitation I responded in French. It was the first coherent speech of any length which I had made since my collapse.

That was six months ago. On the mantel of our living room the old family clock still keeps time for me. From my desk in the study nearby, hearing the silvery strokes of its bell, I am startled out of these memories of my life in music to remember that the practice hour is up.

Or is it?

On my desk lie our passports—mine and Helen's. In her hands are eastbound passages on the *Ile de France*. Our destination?

Beaune!

The amount of playing I did as the Juilliard's president may at least be indicated by a brief list of the places where I played, the compositions, and the conductors who led the concerts.

February 1, 1928—Ann Arbor, with the New York Symphony Orchestra, Walter Damrosch conducting. Schumann's Concerto in A minor.

February 2, 1928—New York Symphony. Same program.

November 18, 1928—Baltimore Symphony Orchestra. MacDowell Concerto in D minor, Gustav Strube conducting.

December 1, 1928—Musical Art Quartet, at the John Golden Theatre. Brahms' Piano Quintet (Sascha Jacobsen, Marie Rosanoff, Paul Bernard, Louis Kaufman).

July 28, 1929—National High School Orchestra, Interlochen, Michigan. Schumann Concerto for piano and orchestra. A. A. Harding, guest conductor.

November 25, 1929—Plainfield Symphony Orchestra, New Jersey. Mozart Concerto in D major. Louis J. Bostelmann, conductor.

May 19, 1930—Recital at the Church of St. James the Less, Scarsdale, New York.
Variations in E Major, Handel
Five Tone Pictures, Grieg
Intermezzo in A Major, Brahms

July 23, 1930—Chautauqua Symphony Orchestra. Variations Symphoniques of César Franck, Albert Stoessel conducting.

November 23, 1930—Reading Symphony Orchestra. César Franck's Variations Symphoniques, Walter Pfeiffer conducting.

December 7, 1931—Plainfield Symphony Orchestra. Mac-Dowell Concerto in D minor, Louis Bostelmann conducting.

December 13, 1931—Milwaukee Philharmonic Orchestra at the Pabst Theatre. MacDowell Concerto in D minor, Frank Laird Waller conducting.

December 23, 1931—Three Sonatas with Paul Kochanski at the Juilliard School:
Bach Sonata in E major
Mozart Sonata in B-flat major
Beethoven Sonata in F major, Op. 24.

January 9, 1932—Syracuse Symphony Orchestra. Mac-Dowell Concerto in D minor, Vladimir Shavitch conducting.

January 15, and 16, 1932—Grand Rapids Symphony Orchestra. MacDowell Concerto in D minor, Karl Wecker conducting.

January 17, 1932—Kalamazoo Symphony Orchestra. Mac-Dowell Concerto in D minor, David Mattern conducting.

February 16, 1932—MacDowell Orchestra of New York, at George Washington High School. MacDowell Concerto in D minor. Philip James conducting.

March 5, 1932—The "Y" Symphony Orchestra (Y.M. and Y.W.H.A.) of Newark, N. J. César Franck's Variations Symphoniques. Philip Gordon conducting.

August 3, 1932—Chautauqua Symphony Orchestra, Mozart Concerto in D. Georges Barrère conducting.

August 6, 1932—Chautauqua Symphony Orchestra, Mac-Dowell Concerto in D minor, Georges Barrère conducting.

September 8, 1932—Westchester County Center Orchestra, White Plains. MacDowell Concerto in D minor, Jaffrey Harris conducting.

November 16, 1932—Guild of Musical Amateurs of New York. Schumann's Theme and Variations in B-flat major for two pianos, with Mrs. Charles E. Mitchell.

November 19, 1932—Philharmonic Symphony Orchestra, Young People's Concert. Bach Concerto in D minor for three pianos, with Ernest Schelling and Olin Downes.

December 5, 1932—Plainfield Symphony Orchestra. Schumann Concerto in A minor, Louis Bostelmann conducting.

April 17, 1933—Perole String Quartet at New York University. Brahms Piano Quintet in F minor for piano.

May 7, 1933—Brahms Chamber Music Series with Musical Art Quartet. Brahms' Quintet in F minor for piano and strings.

May 16, 1933—Denver Civic Symphony Orchestra. César Franck's Variations Symphoniques, Horace E. Tureman conducting.

May 31, 1933—Minneapolis Symphony Orchestra. Mac-Dowell Concerto in D minor, Eugene Ormandy conducting.

December 14, 1933—Brooklyn Bureau of Charities, at Brooklyn Academy of Music. Brahms-Haydn Variations for two pianos, with Ernest Hutcheson.

January 17, 1934—at Juilliard. Four-piano Concerto transcribed from Vivaldi's Concerto for four violins, with Ernest Hutcheson, Rosina Lhevinne, and Oscar Wagner.

March 23, 1934—Gerhart String Orchestra, Altoona, Pa. Mozart's Concerto in D major. Russell Gerhart conducting.

Index

275